This book explores the role of written communication in Greece and is the first systematic and sustained treatment at this level. The subject of literacy is hard to think about objectively, and extensive oral communication is commonly regarded merely as a feature of the primitive. Ancient Greece challenges many of our assumptions about both and is receiving increased attention from scholars. Rosalind Thomas examines the recent theoretical debates about literacy and orality and explores the uses of writing and oral communication, and their interaction, in ancient Greece. She is concerned to set the significance of written and oral communication as much as possible in their social and historical context, and to stress the specifically Greek characteristics in their use, arguing that the functions of literacy and orality are often fluid and culturally determined. Her book draws together the results of recent studies and suggests further avenues of enquiry. Individual chapters deal with (among other things) the role of writing in archaic Greece, oral poetry, the visual and monumental impact of writing, the performance and oral transmission even of written texts, and the use of writing by the city-states; there is an epilogue on Rome.

All ancient evidence is translated and there are illustrations. Students of ancient history and classics and anyone interested in literacy and orality will find this book of importance to them.

KEY THEMES IN ANCIENT HISTORY

Literacy and orality in ancient Greece

KEY THEMES IN ANCIENT HISTORY

EDITORS

Dr P. A. Cartledge
Clare College, Cambridge
Dr P. D. A. Garnsey
Jesus College, Cambridge

Key Themes in Ancient History aims to provide readable, informed and original studies of various basic topics, designed in the first instance for students and teachers of classics and ancient history, but also for those engaged in related disciplines. Each volume will be devoted to a general theme in Greek, Roman, or where appropriate, Graeco-Roman history, or to some salient aspect or aspects of it. Besides indicating the state of current research in the relevant area, authors will seek to show how the theme is significant for our own as well as ancient culture and society. By providing books for courses that are oriented around themes it is hoped to encourage and stimulate promising new developments in teaching and research in ancient history.

Other books in the series:

Death-ritual and social structure in classical antiquity, by Ian Morris
0 521 37465 0 (hardback), 0 521 37611 4 (paperback)

Slavery and society at Rome, by Keith Bradley
0 521 37287 9 (hardback), 0 521 37887 7 (paperback)

Law, violence, and community in classical Athens, by David Cohen
0 521 38167 3 (hardback), 0 521 38837 6 (paperback)

Public order in ancient Rome, by Wilfried Nippel
0 521 38327 7 (hardback), 0 521 38749 3 (paperback)

Friendship in the classical world, by David Konstan
0 521 45402 6 (hardback), 0 521 45998 2 (paperback)

Sport and society in ancient Greece, by Mark Golden
0 521 49698 5 (hardback), 0 521 49790 6 (paperback)

LITERACY AND ORALITY
IN ANCIENT GREECE

ROSALIND THOMAS

*Lecturer in Ancient History, Royal Holloway and Bedford New College,
University of London*

CAMBRIDGE
UNIVERSITY PRESS

Published by the Press Syndicate of the University of Cambridge
The Pitt Building, Trumpington Street, Cambridge CB2 1RP
40 West 20th Street, New York, NY 10011-4211 USA
10 Stamford Road, Oakleigh, Melbourne 3166, Australia

First published 1992
Reprinted 1995, 1999

Printed in Great Britain by Athenæum Press Ltd, Gateshead, Tyne & Wear

A catalogue record for this book is available from the British Library

Library of Congress cataloguing in publication data
Thomas, Rosalind
Literacy and orality in ancient Greece / Rosalind Thomas.
p.   cm. – (Key themes in ancient history)
Includes bibliographical references and index.
ISBN 0 521 37346 8 – ISBN 0 521 37742 0 (pbk.)
1. Greek language – Social aspects – Greece.   2. Written
communication – Greece – History.   3. Oral communication – Greece –
History.   4. Oral tradition – Greece – History.   5. Language and
culture – Greece.   6. Literacy – Greece – History.   7. Writing – Greece –
History.   8. Greece – Civilization.   I. Title.   II. Series.
PA227.T46   1992
302.2′ 0938 – dc20   91–37416   CIP

ISBN 0 521 37346 8 hardback
ISBN 0 521 37742 0 paperback

Contents

Figures

Acknowledgements

This book has benefited greatly from the advice of the editors of the series, Peter Garnsey and Paul Cartledge, who saved me from many errors and infelicities of style. Many other friends and colleagues have offered valuable suggestions or encouragement, particularly Riet van Bremen, John Carter, Walter Cockle, Tim Cornell, Michael Silk, Tony Spawforth, Martin West, and the members of the informal seminar on literacy in University College London organized by Michael Clanchy and David Olson in Spring 1991. Tim Cornell and Keith Hopkins kindly showed me in advance their contributions to *Literacy in the Roman World* (by Mary Beard *et al.*, 1991), which unfortunately appeared when this book was already in press. I would also like to thank Pauline Hire and Glennis Foote at Cambridge University Press and the History and Classics departments in Royal Holloway and Bedford New College which allowed me a sabbatical in which I could finish the manuscript. I remain responsible, of course, for whatever errors remain in the text.

Abbreviations

AJA	*American Journal of Archaeology*
AJP	*American Journal of Philology*
Anc. Soc.	*Ancient Society*
Ath. Mitt.	*Mitteilungen des deutschen archäologischen Instituts: Athenische Abteilung*
BCH	*Bulletin de correspondance hellénique*
CAH	*Cambridge Ancient History*
CJ	*Classical Journal*
CPh	*Classical Philology*
CQ	*Classical Quarterly*
CR	*Classical Review*
CRAI	*Comptes rendus de l'Academie des Inscriptions et Belles-Letters* (Paris)
GR	*Greece and Rome*
GRBS	*Greek, Roman and Byzantine Studies*
HSCP	*Harvard Studies in Classical Philology*
IG	*Inscriptiones Graecae* (Berlin 1873–)
JHS	*Journal of Hellenic Studies*
JRS	*Journal of Roman Studies*
LCM	*Liverpool Classical Monthly*
L–P	E. Lobel and D. Page, *Poetarum Lesbiorum Fragmenta* (Oxford 1955)
LSAG	L. H. Jeffery, *The Local Scripts of Archaic Greece* (Oxford 1961); with Supplement by A. Johnston, 1990
ML	R. Meiggs and D. M. Lewis, *A Selection of Historical Inscriptions to the End of the Fifth century BC* (Oxford 1969); new edition with Addenda, 1988
Mnemos.	*Mnemosyne*

xi

OGIS	*Orientis Graecae Inscriptiones Selectae* I–II (ed. W. Dittenberger, Leipzig 1903–5)
Par. Pass.	*La Parola del Passato*
PBSR	*Papers of the British School at Rome* (London)
PCPS	*Proceedings of the Cambridge Philological Society*
PMG	D. L. Page, *Poetae Melici Graeci* (Oxford 1962)
REG	*Revue des Etudes grecques*
SGDI	*Sammlung der griechischen Dialekt-Inschriften* I–IV (ed. H. Collitz, Göttingen 1884–1915)
SEG	*Supplementum Epigraphicum Graecum*
Syll.³	*Sylloge Inscriptionum Graecarum* I–IV, 3rd edn (ed. W. Dittenberger *et al.*, Leipzig 1915–24)
TAPA	*Transactions of the American Philological Association*
Tod	M. N. Tod, *A Selection of Greek Historical Inscriptions* II (Oxford 1948)
YCS	*Yale Classical Studies*
ZPE	*Zeitschrift für Papyrologie und Epigraphik*

CHAPTER I

Introduction

Impossible men: idle, illiterate,
Self-pitying, dirty, sly,
For whose appearance even in city parks
Excuses must be made to casual passers-by.

Robert Graves

'Make and send me copies of Books 6 and 7 of Hypsicrates'
Komodoumenoi (Men Made Fun of in Comedy). For Harpocration
says that they are among Polion's books. But it is likely that
others, too, have got them. He also has his prose epitomes of
Thersagoras' works *On the Myths of Tragedy...*'
    Note added in another hand: 'According to Harpocration,
Demetrius the bookseller has got them. I have instructed Apol-
lonides to send me certain of my own books which you will
hear of in good time from Seleucus himself. Should you find
any, apart from those which I possess, make copies and send
them to me. Diodorus and his friends also have some which I
haven't got.'

Letter found at Oxyrhynchus, second century AD[1]

'Oh, he's illiterate', someone may say, and they mean, not that the
object of their scorn is unable to read and write, but that he is
uncivilized – or simply boorish (as above), or that he has not read
the great works of literature, that he is not educated to a high
standard. In other words, we use the descriptions 'literate' and
'illiterate' today to denote a whole range of meanings, for both the
ability to read and write, and the degree of refinement or culture.
The confusion is a significant one, which may tell us more about
our own culture than others. What about societies other than our
own, where books are hard to come by, or where artistic achievements were largely transmitted orally, entirely without writing, or

---

[1] Quoted, Turner 1968: 87.

where poetry was performed and sung rather than read silently in written texts? What about ancient Greece? The close and comforting identity of literacy with civilization that is so strong in twentieth-century culture begins to seem peripheral and at worst irrelevant to the understanding of a society like that of classical Greece – and to some extent the whole of the ancient world. For the lines between culture and lack of culture, education and backwardness, were drawn differently; the relation of written and oral communication, and of both these to higher education, took on rather different forms. The second passage above is interesting partly because it is an exchange between learned men in the more rarefied and scholarly atmosphere of Graeco-Roman Egypt under the Roman Empire. Even here, it is clear that the very acquisition of books is complicated and involves delicate search amongst booksellers, private individuals, friends. Most important, when you have tracked something down, you should secure it by making your own private copy.

It is exceedingly hard for us to think objectively about literacy or its opposite, oral communication by word of mouth only, 'orality'. In modern, western society, illiteracy is indeed a severe handicap. The modern world is inconceivable without the written word, the illiterate is excluded. Illiteracy, in a culture so dependent on the accumulated wisdom of books, is tantamount to backwardness and barbarism. For most people who read with complete ease, the application and uses of writing seem obvious and inevitable (so inevitable that it is difficult to imagine a world where they are not central). It is taken for granted that we should all be alarmed at recent surveys in Britain which reveal many people unable to fill in a simple form, or in America, where there is talk of a 'literacy crisis'. We probably *should* be concerned, but so much is assumed about the centrality of 'literacy' itself, that there is surprisingly little discussion of why such low literacy rates should be disturbing, and even less of what 'literacy', which is a very complex phenomenon, really means. Are we talking here about a specific modern brand of western literacy, for instance, or about literacy in general? The value of literacy in modern society is more likely to be defended by contrasting it vaguely with illiteracy, but this evades the most interesting issues. Our current modern identification of literacy with civilization as such was crystallized during the eighteenth-century Enlightenment.

The ancient world makes many of these ideas seem simplistic and naive. Three centuries after the arrival of alphabetic writing in Greece, classical Greeks (fifth to fourth centuries BC) were able to leave a substantial body of literature in writing, and the city-states used documents, inscriptions, even archives, in varying degrees, for government. So at first glance, ancient Greece seems self-evidently a society which relied extensively on the written word, which included a very large number of literates among its population, and which, in short, could be considered 'a literate society'. After all, it is these literary achievements of Greek civilization which Western society has inherited. Yet ancient Greece was in many ways an oral society in which the written word took second place to the spoken. Far more was heard or spoken, rather than written and read, than we can easily envisage.

That the spoken word continued to have value is a platitude for any society – even the modern obsession with paper-work leaves some room for it, after all. But it is a question of balance. The extent of oral communication needs particular emphasis for classical students who are so familiar with the ancient world through reading written texts that an effort of imagination is required to appreciate the sheer extent to which written texts were simply not created or used. Certainly there was an extraordinarily sophisticated range of literary and intellectual activity in the classical centuries. Yet most Greek literature was meant to be heard or even sung – thus transmitted orally – and there was a strong current of distaste for the written word even among the highly literate: written documents were not considered adequate proof by themselves in legal contexts till the second half of the fourth century BC. Politics was conducted orally. The citizens of democratic Athens listened in person to the debates in the Assembly and voted on them there and then. Very little was written down and the nearest Greek word for 'politician' was 'orator' (*rhetor*). Tragedy was watched in the theatre, and rhetoric or the art of speaking was a major part of Greek education. A civilized man in Greece (and indeed Rome) had to be able, above all, to speak well in public. Socrates pursued his philosophical enquiries in conversation and debate and wrote nothing down. His pupil Plato attacked the written word as an inadequate means of true education and philosophy: he may have published his own work in dialogue form in order to recreate the atmosphere of oral discourse and debate, and towards the end of his life he may have decided against committing any of his most important views to written form at all (*Seventh Letter*, attributed to Plato).

Even where a written text existed, it was read aloud. The historian Herodotus was said to have given public readings.[2] In the second century AD the Sophist and philosopher Lucian could take it for granted, even in that learned age, that of course Herodotus had recited his *Histories* to the huge audiences at Olympia – rather than separately in different places – simply because that was the most rapid and economical way of propagating his work (Lucian, *Herodotus or Aëtion* 1–2). Public oral transmission was still commonplace in the second century AD and its prevalence in earlier times taken as obvious. In other words, whether or not a written text existed, oral transmission, performance, and discourse were predominant. The divisions were drawn along very different lines from ours.

Scholars have indeed tended to see Greece as a literate or an oral society according to their predominant interests and tastes. And Greece lies at the centre of the general debate about the value of literacy. Havelock, for instance, a famous cultural historian, stressed that it was largely an oral society until Plato's time; scholars more concerned with the study of literature itself tend to see it as literate. But a lot depends on where you look, and it is not in any case clear what these terms really mean. The tendency to see a society (or individual) as either literate or oral is over-simple and misleading. The habits of relying on oral communication (or orality) and literacy are not mutually exclusive (even though literacy and illiteracy are). As we have seen, the evidence for Greece shows *both* a sophisticated and extensive use of writing in some spheres *and* what is to us an amazing dominance of the spoken word. Fifth-century Athens was not a 'literate society', but nor was it quite an 'oral society' either. Clearly oral communication and writing are far from incompatible here (nor are they now, of course, in the modern world, though people often speak as if they were). We can see that the presence of writing does not necessarily destroy all oral elements of a society, and orality does not preclude complex intellectual activity. Not only did philosophers discuss extremely difficult problems without using writing to help, but dense and complex literature was regularly heard rather than read by its public. The written word was more often used in the service of the spoken.[3]

---

[2] See Momigliano 1978: esp. 64–6 for Hdt.; see also Flory 1980.
[3] As Andersen 1987; R. Thomas 1989.

From the start, then, literacy and orality must be examined together in ancient Greece, as indeed in the whole of the ancient world. Rather than separating the literate areas in one period from the oral, or still worse, the earlier centuries, supposedly oral, from the later, supposedly 'literate' ones, we should examine the interaction of oral and written communication techniques. This approach can be very profitable in anthropological studies, for it is now extremely hard to find societies totally unaffected by the written word in any way.[4] As the example of Socrates makes so clear, the totality of Greek life cannot be understood unless the oral side of Greek society is appreciated as well as the written and, if possible, the relation between the two. The study of literacy and orality thus embraces the whole of ancient civilization.

Another fundamental point is that the degree, extent, and significance of literacy will change over the centuries (as will orality), and from society to society, even within the multifarious communities of Greece. This perhaps sounds obvious but there is a strong tendency among scholars to treat literacy, particularly ancient literacy, as if it were a constant. This is partly encouraged by the nature of the evidence which is anecdotal and partial: indications crop up here and there that someone was literate, or that writing was necessary in a certain sphere, but we do not have the evidence for a coherent picture, let alone a statistical one, even for the heavily documented fourth century BC. So it is tempting to take evidence from later or earlier centuries as if it were equally relevant. Our instinctive perceptions of literacy also reinforce this static image: it is easily assumed that once writing became known in Greece in the eighth century BC, it rapidly gained all the obvious functions it had later. Modern interest in Greek literacy has tended to focus on the developments of the period of alphabetic origins and on the general question of the extent of literacy. This is now changing somewhat, but the implications of change for the meaning of literacy itself are still not fully appreciated.

If the use of the written word changes considerably over the period, so does its relation to the spoken word. This fluidity must be accommodated by any wider theories of the implications of literacy or orality and we shall return to these in more depth in chapter 2.

---

[4] Finnegan 1988: ch. 8 for theoretical points, the rest for their application; also 1977.

First, however, we should define the terms 'orality' or 'oral' and 'literacy' more precisely. It should be emphasized that each has a straightforward descriptive use – either something is written or spoken (oral) or it is not. But these terms also tend to be used with what I would call a prescriptive meaning, where 'oral' or 'literate' or 'written' are meant to imply a certain mentality or a range of characteristics in addition to the simple descriptive meaning. This may serve as a preliminary to the wider controversies discussed in the next chapter.

'Orality' is especially prone to vagueness. 'Oral' essentially means 'by word of mouth', without writing. Thus 'orality' should strictly mean the habit of relying entirely on oral communication rather than written. It was coined deliberately on the analogy of 'literacy' in order to denote this quality in a positive sense: avoiding the implications of failure in 'illiteracy'. Oral communication means communication by word of mouth alone. When ancient historians used living witnesses as sources for events they had lived through, they were employing oral communication and oral tradition. When ancient literature was read aloud or recited to listeners, it was, in a sense, being communicated and spread around orally (the written texts could also spread it through writing). An 'oral poet', like Homer, composes in his head without writing, as well as singing his poetry aloud to an audience.

But as is clear even in this brief summary there are various degrees of 'orality' and they are not always separated or even discerned. For instance an influential school of thought believes that poetry can only be classified as 'oral poetry' if it is actually improvised on the spur of the moment (see chapter 3). This involves going beyond the basic meaning of 'oral' to a complex classification which would exclude much poetry that was indeed composed and propagated completely without writing. Moreover, oral communication in one sphere does not necessarily entail oral communication in another. We should therefore be careful to distinguish (at least) three components of orality: oral communication, oral composition, and oral transmission, as the anthropologist Ruth Finnegan has stressed.[5] Each of these components has a different relation to writing.

Moreover orality is often idealized, invested with the romantic

---

[5] Finnegan 1977: 16–24; also Gentili 1988: 4–5.

and nostalgic ideas connected with folklore, folk culture, and folk tradition, or the 'noble savage'. 'Oral culture' is often used interchangeably with folklore, folklore is seen as 'oral tradition', and with little critical examination, but much idealism, orality and 'oral societies' take on the romantic and exaggerated attributes of folk culture. In other words they become more than merely descriptive tools and start to imply a whole mentality or world view which is partly born of a reaction to the modern world. Oral culture is innocent, pure, and natural, uncorrupted by the written word, or perhaps, depending on one's standpoint, the pure manifestation of a people's character. In the study of Greece, this romanticism is most clearly visible in modern discussions of Homer and oral poetry.

Part of the problem here seems to lie in the fact that for cultures with no writing at all, there is little evidence for the past other than memories and oral tradition – and these themselves become altered by time. This by itself will produce a highly distorted picture in which variations and changes in the past have been levelled out. It has sometimes been thought, for instance, that primitive cultures (which would lack writing) do not change. But this image of oral culture as totally static, often undermined by archaeological excavations, has surely been fostered by the fact that no written evidence has survived from the past to contrast with the present. The slow, subtle changes in customs and habits are the last things such societies would try to remember in their oral traditions. A shallow, unchanging past can be the effect of the oral tradition, not a fundamental characteristic of oral societies.[6]

Similarly, some studies of orality emphasize that oral societies are 'warm' personal societies, since all communication of any kind has to be done face-to-face, and the alienating individualism of the reader is absent.[7] Yet the remote and old-fashioned village communities in modern Greece, for instance, where every family is pitted against the rest, hardly conform to this ideal.[8] Nor, of course, are all societies without writing the same: this is self-evident as soon as we think, for instance, of Greece in the ninth century B C before the alphabet arrived, and the Somali in the early twentieth century before literacy had much influence. Yet most work on

---

[6] Vansina 1985.
[7] Ong 1982, and 1986.
[8] See e.g. du Boulay 1974; Campbell 1964; now Winkler 1990 for ancient Greece.

orality has been looking for the crucial common features of such societies: deliberately or not, it is all too easy to give the impression that they are identical. Studies which stress the general characteristics of orality, and which believe that the method of communication is decisive in determining a society's character, inevitably tend to see oral culture as homogeneous rather than varied.

There are even more pitfalls in defining literacy, but literacy – or its products – can at least be more easily isolated and imagined. It is important to draw out the possibilities because they must lie behind any plausible attempt to study literacy. Some of the modifications suggested in our approach to literacy should have important implications for the concept of orality.

Firstly, there are obviously many different levels of literacy. No single definition is adequate and any attempt to take a single one will over-simplify and distort. We might define literacy as the ability to read and write, but read and write *what*? Different levels are involved today, for example, in reading simple signs and notices, a popular newspaper, or a lengthy book; many people can manage the first two but not the last. A definition of literacy as the simple ability to read short passages of written texts or to fill in a simple form (common tests of literacy) tells us nothing about the impact of books. In the Greek context, reading a passage scratched on a potsherd and reading a poetic papyrus are quite different activities. In the fifth century BC there were hardly any books, and the tragedian Euripides was thought most eccentric for owning a 'library' of several books (papyrus rolls). So even in classical Athens at the height of its power hardly any of its citizens would have had the opportunity, let alone the need, to read a book, and we should assume they would have found it hard. Persevering through a whole papyrus roll, which might be as much as twenty-two feet long, had no word-divisions, and required a special posture,[9] needed a vastly different skill from the keeping of simple accounts which we hear of in comedy, or reading the list of public debtors, or even the proposals for new laws posted up in the agora. Well-documented examples can be multiplied from more recent periods of history where 'literacy' is a totally inadequate term to cover the many degrees of reading ability and reading contexts: in early modern England, for instance, there were a large number of differ-

---

[9] Reynolds and Wilson 1991: 2; Parassoglou 1979.

ent scripts in use, and it was quite common for someone to be able to read printed texts, but not handwriting.[10] There has been little attempt to pursue the possibility of clearly defined types of reading skills in the ancient world, but it is surely very likely. When a prosperous freedman, Hermeros, in Petronius' *Satyricon* says he knows only 'lapidary writing' (*lapidariae litterae, Sat.* 58.7.), by which he must mean the capitals of inscriptions,[11] we gain a rare glimpse of differentiated reading skills in the ancient world which may have been quite regular.

The tendency to treat literacy as if it were a monolithic skill may be a modern fallacy. It is characteristic of twentieth-century definitions of literacy to lay weight on the ability to read a totally unfamiliar text, even a nonsense text. But this is a recent development, and one which tends to regard literacy merely as a technique or skill that can be measured in isolation from the kind of texts likely to be read. In the Middle Ages, tests of literacy gave the individual a text he would be familiar with, the Bible, and a great deal of reading would be devoted not to new texts but to the familiar Biblical ones. This brings us back to the importance of *what* is being read. The ancient reader was not constantly inundated with totally new texts (novels, newspapers): much available reading matter would be partially familiar or even memorized (e.g. Homer), or else reinforced by having been read aloud first (e.g. proposals of decrees). It may well be more appropriate to think in terms of 'phonetic literacy' and 'comprehension literacy', concepts used by P. Saenger to denote two common degrees of reading ability in the later Middle Ages. 'Comprehension literacy' was 'the ability to decode a text silently, word by word' and understand it fully; 'phonetic literacy' was the ability to 'decode texts syllable by syllable and to pronounce them orally', close to oral rote memorization.[12] 'Phonetic literacy' seems particularly relevant to the ancient context where reading was not done silently, and where literary texts would often be read in order to be memorized (see chapter 5).

The degree of skill will also partly reflect the need for writing in daily life. Much evidence suggests that the ability to read and write is forgotten if there is no use for it (this has happened in some

---

[10] K. Thomas 1986: 100: see 99–103 for a devastating critique of monolithic definitions of literacy.
[11] W. V. Harris 1989: 252 takes them to be simply capitals; see also Daniel 1980: 158–9.
[12] Saenger 1989: esp. 142.

modern literacy campaigns). From fairly early on, Athenian potters wrote in the names of the figures they painted, and the incentives to write may have made them some of the more literate in archaic Athens.[13] Women had no part in public life, and were probably almost all illiterate unless they kept domestic accounts, but their male counterparts in Athens were surrounded by the written records of democratic business. The subsistence farmers in remote parts of Greece could probably manage without writing entirely. News was spread by word of mouth (even after the invention of printing, newspapers were not a regular part of life till the eighteenth century in England[14]). Most legal transactions actually required witnesses and oaths in preference to written documents which were distrusted as valid proof.[15]

A further dimension is easily missed and should be reinserted into the debate: reading and writing are quite distinct processes which are not necessarily mastered by the same individual. Throughout history many more people have been able to read than write. In the Middle Ages it was mainly scribes and monks who wrote; in sixteenth-century England many quite educated people could only read, not write, and it was common to go to a specialist writer, a scrivener or secretary, if you needed something written.[16] Sweden's extraordinarily high rate of 'literacy' achieved by the eighteenth century was actually in reading alone, for the main aim had been to read the Bible (incidentally, it was achieved without school provision, though it is generally assumed today that only formal schooling can procure high literacy rates).[17] In ancient Greece, then, we should probably assume that many more people could read to some degree than could write – at least in cities like Athens, where there existed material and incentives to read. But the evidence is always skewed towards those who could write, for only they leave clear evidence of their skills.

I should say something here about calculating the extent of literacy from the evidence of ability to sign one's name. This method has been widespread in historical surveys.[18] It raises more

---

[13] Street 1984; Stoddart and Whitley 1988.
[14] K. Thomas 1986; 113.
[15] Todd 1990; Humphreys 1985; Pringsheim 1955.
[16] K. Thomas 1986.
[17] Swedish literacy: Graff 1986, and 1987; cf. Harris' stress on schooling, 1989.
[18] Cressy 1980; Schofield 1968; Houston 1985, and 1988; contrast K. Thomas 1986.

interesting questions than immediately meet the eye, anticipating some of the themes of chapter 2. The method is useful because so many surviving documents needed a person's mark or signature. But how much does this really indicate about literacy (let alone anything more complex)? In any period where more people can read than write, leaving your 'mark' may yet allow reading skills and therefore participation in written culture. Alternatively, signing your name could be the only grain of literacy acquired. Clearly this is likely if signing your name brings advantages or privileges (compare the incentive to learn Latin in the Middle Ages to obtain clerics' privileges). In Graeco-Roman Egypt the proof that someone was literate was his ability to sign his name. We actually know of one 'scribe' (whose profession brought privileges) who was clearly illiterate except for this one skill: the papyrus on which he had to keep practising his signature has been found, and he could not even copy his own signature correctly for very long.[19] In classical Greece on the other hand, the signature was unknown and seals and witnesses were used for proof and authentication. What emerges here is that the ability to sign one's name is not a neutral measurement of literacy (though it may in fact correlate with wider literacy in modern England). It can only be a function of the social or cultural context.

It is therefore highly misleading to produce some statistical calculation of 'literacy rates' for ancient Greece, based inevitably upon some single definition of literacy. Various studies have produced some kind of estimate, but the likelihood of vastly differing degrees of literate skills has been ignored except perhaps by the most sensitive.[20] Given the complexity of literacy and the paucity of detailed ancient evidence, all we can say with any plausibility is that probably more people could read than write; the ability to read or write very simple messages, often in capitals, was probably not rare; and in cities like Athens where there was a profusion of democratic documents, most citizens had some basic ability and perhaps 'phonetic literacy' was pretty widespread; but that the written texts of poetry and literary prose had a reading audience confined to the highly educated and wealthy elite, and their secretaries.

[19] See Youtie 1971b; see ch. 7. pp. 151–5 for Egyptian context.
[20] Cf. Turner 1952; Kenyon 1951; Greene 1951; Harvey 1966; Woodbury 1976; Burns 1981; Cartledge 1978; most comprehensive is W. V. Harris 1989.

This all sounds pitifully vague. But the complexity of 'literacy' is fundamental. What we should be turning our attention to is not calculating literacy rates, but examining what literacy is used for: the calculation of literacy rates assumes we understand the significance of such rates. This may be true for the modern world, but is manifestly not for the ancient (or intervening periods). Close examination reveals a bewildering range of ways of using the written word, which seem very largely to reflect the society in question and its beliefs. Wider theories about the significance or implications of literacy (in general) must also be modified by such variation.

In the next chapter we turn to this wider debate about the significance of writing. Before doing so, however, it will help to survey the main lines of development in the use of writing and the place of orality. Such chronological change in the use and significance of literacy (and so of orality) underlies the structure of this book.

Mycenaean culture (*c.* 1500–1100 BC) had a syllabic script we call Linear B, which seems to have been used only for palace records. It apparently died out with the palace culture that had supported it. The alphabet was adapted from the Phoenician alphabet probably in the first half of the eighth century, but its use spread only gradually. It was apparently not used for public functions till the middle of the seventh century – to judge from the surviving stone inscriptions – but the flood of documents on stone mainly dates from the 460s in Athens, the time of the radical democracy. The Greek city-states seem to have used writing very sparingly till the fifth and fourth centuries.

The earliest Greek literature we possess, Homer's *Iliad* and *Odyssey*, seem, however, to belong to a society which had little or no use of writing. Usually dated to the eighth century, they seem to be the product of entirely oral composition as well as oral performance. This thesis, proposed by Milman Parry in the 1930s, has had enormous influence: it drew the attention of classicists to the extent of oral communication in Greece, raised the alarming possibility that fine literature might not always issue from a highly literate culture, and focused attention on oral poetry all over the world. Though there is still disagreement about how Homer's poetry eventually got written down, it clearly does belong to an early period at which writing was barely known, if at all, and had not affected a primarily oral culture.

In the archaic period (*c.* 700–500 BC), writing was used for private inscriptions, the first written laws and many religious purposes. The poets of this period are assumed to have made their own written copies of their poems, though these were performed and heard, not read. Presumably most of life was conducted without the written word. Classical politicians cultivated the arts of oratory, but without written texts. The Athenian general and politician Pericles was said to be the first man to have a written text with him when he spoke (440s–430s).[21] But he left no published speeches, and the controversy about written speeches carried on into the fourth century (see Alcidamas, *On Those Who Compose Written Speeches*). Published written literature was becoming fairly common from the beginning of the fifth century, but books were very rare until about the end of the century. Jokes about *biblia*, 'books' or rather papyrus rolls, appear in Athenian comedy in the last three or four decades. There is even some evidence now of a book-quarter, or at least 'book shops'.[22] Our earliest evidence for the book trade is Xenophon's reference to a shipwreck with a cargo of *biblia* (*Anabasis* 7.5.14). By the middle of the fourth century they were much more common, though they still cannot have been numerous.[23] The first reference to a solitary reader of literature as opposed to communal reading is in the *Frogs* (405 BC), where the god Dionysus says he has been reading Euripides' *Andromeda* to himself (Aristophanes, *Frogs* 52). But solitary and silent reading was almost unknown. In both Greece and Rome written texts, particularly literary ones, were usually read aloud.[24]

Even where public documents were made, they were not yet kept with any sophistication or even necessarily used again (see chapter 5 below). Athens itself had a central archive only from the end of the fifth century and had to revise the laws at the same time, probably because their proliferation on inscriptions and in archives

[21] Turner 1952: 18 (from the Suda Lexicon). For imagery involving writing, Aeschylus, *Supplices* 944–51; Pindar, *Olympian* 10.1 ff; and Pfeiffer 1968: 25–6, Easterling *JHS* 105 (1985): 4, for further refs. which show that writing is familiar in the fifth century.

[22] See Davison 1962: 108 for 'book-sellers' (*bibliopolai*); Turner 1952: 20–2. But note that Aristophanes, *Birds* 1288ff, evidence for the 'book-sellers' quarter', is hopelessly full of punning (*biblia* puns on books/rinds of papyrus) and *biblia* does not only denote 'books'.

[23] See Turner 1952; Easterling 1985; Flory 1980; Kenyon 1951.

[24] See Knox 1968, arguing, however, that silent reading was not so rare as to be astonishing: he cites esp Euripides, *Hippolytus* 856ff, Aristophanes, *Knights* 115–28 (add [Aristotle], *Problems* 18.1 and 7 on reading in bed?); see Immerwahr 1964 for books on vases; Svenbro 1987, and 1988a more generally; Knox 1985; cf. Saenger 1989 for later Middle Ages.

left it quite unclear what was legal. But in the fourth century a new spirit of professionalism creeps in and the written word seems to be accorded greater respect. Plato's strictures against writing as a medium of education are to be understood against a proliferation of books and written manuals. The written document becomes more common in other spheres, and is now being used for the first time by Greek historians as evidence in a manner we would recognize as adequate. Athens by the end of the fourth century has become what I have called 'document-minded' (borrowing a phrase from the medievalist Michael Clanchy). This looks forward to the methods of the Hellenistic period and Rome. Yet still, it should be remembered, literature went on being read aloud. Rhetoric was important in Roman higher education as well as Greek. And even the most learned and antiquarian writers of the Greek world under the Roman Empire exerted enormous effort and energy in giving declamations, or displays of rhetorical and verbal skill, to packed audiences.

Greek civilization has lain at the centre of the controversies which have raged – and still rage – over the general or universal meaning of literacy and the nature of oral society. The subject has suffered from a great deal of such schematization. This book will argue that a rather different and richer approach to ancient orality and literacy is called for. Neither literacy nor orality are constants, and their roles can be extraordinarily diverse, often reflecting much more of the society using writing or oral communication than any expectations of general characteristics. Moreover, the patterns of literacy and orality in the ancient world have in part governed what has been written down and therefore preserved for us today. This means that far more is involved than a calculation of the number of literates. The study of ancient literacy and orality may encompass a large part of Greek culture or else reflect upon it.

CHAPTER 2

Literacy and orality

'Literacy' has a multiplicity of levels and meanings. It also has a history, as does its interaction with oral communication. But how important is literacy to a society? What effects does writing have? How does the coming of writing change a society which has previously relied entirely on oral communication and tradition?

The wider significance of writing is much debated. Influential theories have seen it as a fundamental agent of change – change either to the workings of society or to the mentality of individuals. Is it, or is it not, such a powerful agent? The debate could be said to have been focused – if not actually triggered off – by the example of ancient Greece. But it encompasses anthropological and more modern or more ancient historical data, as well as psychological research. It is difficult to characterize the broad state of play at the moment. The extreme picture of literacy as a catalyst for certain changes has been much criticized. Most historians and anthropologists seem happier with a more relativist concept of literacy, which allows for diverse implications in diverse societies and periods; psychologists tend towards the fundamentalist view. The controversy is certainly showing no signs of dying down.[1] From our point of view, I would single out two main trends in recent studies. Put crudely, the first seeks broad psychological and cultural implications (or effects) of literacy. The second pursues detailed, culturally specific studies of the manifestations of literacy in a given society, often eschewing entirely any of the wider claims made for the effects of literacy. Some of the most exciting recent work is in the latter group, some concerning the ancient world, much of it the medieval.

---

[1] Journals devoted specifically to literacy and orality include: *Visible Language; Scrittura e Civiltà; Word and Image*; and to start in 1993, *Literacy*, edited by Clanchy and Olson.

How far is literacy an agent of change? Today, literacy is equated with high culture and literacy rates are assumed to correlate with cultural activity: in other words, literacy is consciously or unconsciously equated with civilization. It is not always clear whether the number of 'illiterates' is lamented because literacy helps people fill in forms, or get jobs, or read books and enlarge their cultural experience. But at any rate, the range of possibilities underlines how much literacy has come to be identified with modern civilization and modern values. Literacy now bears a heavy burden of expectation. The UNESCO literacy campaigns aim to eliminate illiteracy totally, in the hope that literacy will promote economic development, rational thought and scientific endeavour in the Third World.[2] No one would deny that the written word is of fundamental importance to the modern world, and that someone without literacy faces extreme difficulties. The problem is whether – or how far – literacy can be the main agent of change in the transformation. Or does it rather reflect and strengthen tendencies already there? (The failures of literacy campaigns in the Third World and elsewhere suggest that literacy is very much more complex.)

The case of ancient Greece has played a large part in this idealization of literacy. It has been broadly claimed that the rational thought of the Greeks was a product of literacy: Greece was a test case for the consequences of literacy since the alphabet came to a totally oral society. Literacy in Greece, it is argued, and therefore elsewhere, is a powerful agent which changes mentality. It would be hard to exaggerate the influence this view of literacy has had. Increasingly it is being questioned and attention is turning to other issues. But the controversy rumbles on. It raises fundamental questions about the role, importance, and character of literacy, and about the difficulty of analysing literacy in another society than our own, when our understanding of literacy tends to be instinctive. It deserves to be examined in some detail.

The controversy began as one about alphabetic literacy. In an immensely thought-provoking article first published in 1963, Jack Goody and Ian Watt, social anthropologist and scholar of English literature respectively, used ancient Greece as a test case for 'the consequences of literacy'. Against a general analysis of oral societies, they argued that it was writing which in Greece had produced

[2] Street 1984.

democracy, rational thought, philosophy and historiography. Since the alphabet was so much easier to learn than any other script, Greece avoided the specialized 'scribal literacy' of the Near East: her alphabetic literacy fostered a democratic base. In the realm of intellectual thought, writing enabled thought to be separated from social context, and thus scepticism and analysis became possible. The cultures of the ancient Near East, with three millennia of writing, were held back by their 'restricted literacy' and non-alphabetic writing. Thus Greece was a blueprint for the liberating, democratizing, and intellectual effects of literacy in the Western world – and by extension anywhere which cared to introduce the alphabet.

Goody and Watt warned against seeing literacy as the *sole* cause, but any original reservations were forgotten by their followers. Eric Havelock's work on the classical Greeks also stressed that the alphabet changed people's mode of thought.[3] The alphabet, he argued, has the peculiar quality of representing each sound by one letter. This breaks up language into its constituent parts and therefore encourages an analytic frame of mind. It was the Greeks who, taking over the Semitic letters from the Phoenicians, had the brilliant idea of adding vowels (but see chapter 4). They thus produced the most perfect means ever for representing any language (linguists point out, however, that the needs of some languages are not met well by the alphabet). Havelock was, at the same time, most influential in propounding a view of Greece as a primarily oral society down to the time of Plato[4]: he astounded the scholarly world by arguing that Plato was reacting to and seeking to eliminate what were essentially features of an oral society. Yet the extent of oral communication in the fourth century actually undermines his argument about the effects of the alphabet. For the obvious question is, why had it taken four centuries to work?

Goody and Watt's article was reprinted in the volume *Literacy in Traditional Societies* (1968) alongside comparative studies of present-day societies by others (some of which actually contradicted the theory). Goody now conceded that they were investigating the implications of literacy, rather than the consequences. But the argument has shifted to the implications of writing in general.

[3] Havelock 1963; 1982; 1986; also Havelock and Hershbell (eds.) 1978.
[4] Havelock 1963.

Goody has developed and refined the theory, mainly in *The Domestication of the Savage Mind* (1977), and *The Logic of Writing and the Organization of Society* (1986) (note also *The Interface between the Written and the Oral*, 1987). In the first, he replaces the various divisions suggested by anthropologists between 'scientific' and 'non-scientific' thought, 'primitive' and 'advanced' societies, with the single one of literate and non-literate: the presence of literacy is, he argues, the single most important determining factor in these observed differences. But in some respects he modifies his previous views of the effects of literacy. Sensitive studies of specific examples show how writing may encourage certain kinds of activity which are very difficult, if not unknown, in oral societies. For instance, the list and other 'non-grammatical' written texts are totally divorced from normal speech, and, he would argue, were an early product of writing. The theory now includes non-alphabetic writing. More allowance is also made for differing uses of literacy in different societies.

But the essential argument remains, as indicated in his later work. He returns again to the absolute image of the consequences of literacy in *The Logic of Writing and the Organization of Society* (1986). Writing and literacy are a force for logical and scientific thought, bureaucracy and the modern state, and law. In effect, he shows how fundamental literacy is now and seems to take it that this tells us about literacy as such rather than the societies using it. The 'consequences of literacy' in classical Greece are not far behind.

Closely linked is the wider school of thought which takes the medium of communication by itself (writing, speech, television) to be a vital determining factor in mentality. In the 1960s McLuhan and the Toronto school were famous for the theory that 'the medium is the message'. Walter Ong takes writing to be 'a technology that restructures thought',[5] and has done much to develop study of the differences (as he perceives them) between orality and the mentality it engenders, and literacy and the 'literate mentality'. Psychologists have added research that seems to confirm that the ability to read and write is indeed associated with different mental processes.[6]

The intellectual effects of literacy have been sought in periods of

---

[5] The title of his 1986 paper; see also Ong 1982.
[6] E.g. Luria 1976; Olson, Torrence, Hildyard (eds.) 1985; cf. works in n. 31.

later history. A study of early modern England, for instance, has suggested that, despite vastly differing levels and functions of literacy, writing did make possible the scientific revolution and probably does structure thought.[7] Rather amusingly, a monumental study of the effects of printing by Eisenstein (1979) has attributed to printing many of the consequences Goody attached to writing in ancient Greece – though in the case of printing one is dealing with mass dissemination. Literacy seems to crop up increasingly as a suggested factor in historical change. The economic function of literacy appears as part of historical analysis.[8] The present American concern with literacy rates seems to be related to ideas of national identity.[9] Literacy is the universal catalyst: the economist links it with economic advancement, the historian of ideas with intellectual preeminence, the anthropologist with the transition from primitive to advanced society, the historian of nationalism with the development of the nation state. At some time or other almost every feature of the modern Western world has been linked closely to literacy. The theory is occasionally modified to one which sees literacy as an 'enabling factor', a necessary, but not sufficient, cause of these developments – but the modification is seldom worked out in detail.[10] One begins to wonder how often these effects can occur, and to what extent these analyses are based simply on an easy – but incorrect – correlation between Western values, modernity, economic development, and literacy.

Surely something more than literacy is at stake, and this is strongly suggested by comparative evidence. One need not search long to find counter-examples where writing produces anything but rationality and analytic thought. When literacy was taken over by Buddhist monks in Tibet they used it for what to them was its obvious and necessary function, to print prayers on the water.[11] Writing is often used for magical purposes and this is not confined to the semi-literate or (vicariously) to the illiterate who might be expected to treat writing with awe. In the Old Testament a woman who has committed adultery is made to swallow water into which a

---

[7] K. Thomas 1986; cf. Stone 1969; Houston 1985, and 1988; McKitterick 1989 on the Carolingians; Furet and Ouzouf 1982 on France.

[8] E.g. Cressy 1983; see also Cressy 1980.

[9] E.g. Gellner 1983; cf. Herzfeld 1987 on modern Greece.

[10] A notable exception is Lloyd 1979, 1987.

[11] Goody 1968; 16.

curse written out 'in a book' has been diluted. She is literally drinking the curse (Numbers 5.23–4). Diluted writing is also widely used for medical remedy: in Somali for instance, powerful passages from the Koran are written out, then washed into the cup of water and the water is then drunk.[12] Are we confusing 'literacy' with Western literacy?

There are obvious problems with the theory even as it is applied to the ancient world.[13] How could literacy have such momentous consequences in classical Greece and not elsewhere? In Rome, for instance, which knew of the alphabet, after all, as early as the seventh century? Or in the rest of Greece? Philosophical development occurred mainly among the Athenians and Ionians (on the west coast of what is now modern Turkey). Many cities had acquired writing but not experienced an intellectual revolution. Sparta deliberately turned her back on philosophy, and undervalued both written literature and writing generally.[14] Nor was democracy all that common in Greece before the fourth century, and if one must calculate rationality strictly in the philosophical sense, the effects of literacy seem to be even more confined to a tiny educated elite.[15] How can the consequences of literacy act so broadly in one sphere, that of politics, and so narrowly in another? In any case, we tend to have evidence only for what got written down: how can we know, for instance, that there was no logical thought before writing? Even the most sympathetic view must wonder why the effects of writing took so long to emerge. Much more must have been involved in the Greek intellectual revolution. As Lloyd has pointed out, much of the Greek philosophical achievement may be related to the habit of discussion and questioning in Greek society, the intense atmosphere of competition and the very political structure of the *polis* itself.[16]

It perhaps needs pointing out, now widespread literacy of some sort has been achieved over so much of the world, that dramatic cultural and intellectual differences still remain. But the 'failures'

---

[12] Old Testament case cited by Goody 1986: 40; Egyptian parallels, Baines 1983: 588–9; Somali, I. Lewis 1986: 138.
[13] Cf. Larsen 1989, also 1988, for the ancient Near East.
[14] Cartledge 1978.
[15] Who would be most likely to be literate anyway (see W. V. Harris 1989); Goody would explain these other instances as the product of 'restricted literacy'.
[16] Lloyd 1979; and 1987: 70–8; Pattison 1982 emphasizes the Greek use of language; see also R. Thomas 1989: ch. 1; Andersen 1989; Stoddart and Whitley 1988.

are equally suggestive: literacy campaigns have sometimes failed because the people in question had no use for this new literacy, or have perhaps fallen short of their grand aims because much more than literacy was necessary for industrialization.[17] It is increasingly clear that literacy by itself is not having the effects that were expected.

There have been counter-attacks against the 'optimistic' view of literacy. If literacy is essential for social and economic advancement, why is it that evidence for nineteenth-century industrial cities shows, if anything, a decreased literacy rate and poorer schooling in just those areas so advanced economically?[18] Others argue that literacy, far from liberating a culture, actually forms a means of control. So here the often malign power of writing is stressed. Lévi-Strauss suggested this long ago in *Tristes Tropiques*, surveying the course of world history and empire building:

the primary function of writing, as a means of communication, is to facilitate the enslavement of human beings. The use of writing for disinterested purposes, and as a source of intellectual and aesthetic pleasure, is a secondary result, and more often than not it may even be turned into a means of strengthening, justifying or concealing the other.[19]

French scholarship has continued to approach literacy with a certain scepticism. The fact that modern totalitarian societies have stressed mass literacy just as much as democratic ones certainly suggests that literacy can help the state keep watch over its subjects.[20]

The pursuit of literacy often has a religious function totally unadorned by ideals of economic or cultural advancement. This suggests that its applications and uses can be as varied as human culture. The astonishingly high proportion of Swedes who could read by 1740 (over 90 per cent) was the result of reading tests in many parishes and a rule that you could not marry in church unless able to read. The principle behind this was the Lutheran ideal that everyone had to be able to read the word of God for themselves. It

---

[17] See Street 1984: esp. sect. 3; Pattison 1982; Heath 1986; see also Winterowd 1989; Resnick (ed.) 1983; Wagner (ed.) 1987, from a vast literature relating to the modern 'literacy crisis'.

[18] Graff 1979; also 1987.

[19] First published in 1955; Engl. transl. 1976: 393; cf. Larsen 1988.

[20] See Graff 1986, and at more length 1987; Pattison 1982.

might have had other side effects, but the aims and immediate consequences were religious (and Protestant).[21] Compare also the intriguing example of early 'literacy campaigns' in Melanesia, brilliantly dissected by Brian Street. Here, from the 1830s, the teachers were Christian missionaries who had the avowed and limited aim of enabling the Melanesians to read the Bible. So of course they taught only reading. Street shows how the Melanesians' reactions were trivialized as primitive and amusingly ignorant by the Europeans, yet could in fact be seen, in the circumstances, as intelligent interpretations of this limited and specifically religious literacy.[22]

But where do we go from here? The grand theory concerning the effects of literacy does not hold true universally. Counter-examples can be produced suggesting that literacy can be 'exploitative' rather than intellectually improving. What does this tell us about literacy? Should we adopt a completely relativist interpretation of the meaning of literacy, or are there still discernible characteristics of writing which retain a fundamental importance in every culture? Should we re-examine the nature of literacy itself?

A number of recent studies have begun to do precisely this. A forceful case is being built up for regarding the effects or implications of literacy as heavily dependent on whatever society is using it. The variety in the possible uses of literacy is now abundantly clear (and was indeed suggested by some contributors to *Literacy in Traditional Societies* (1968)). They seem very largely determined by the customs and beliefs, not to mention the political and social system, already present. We have already encountered examples where literacy is seen essentially as a religious adjunct, the motivation to read a totally religious one. The uses and 'consequences' of literacy in Hindu India are extremely closely related to the pre-eminent position of the Brahmin caste and their control of the sacred written texts.[23] The Japanese have a fundamentally different approach to the written word from the Western one, for whereas we would tend to think writing makes the spoken word permanent, the Japanese think knowledge resides in writing – Chinese characters – rather than the mere spoken word; knowledge can *only* be expressed by writing and the spoken word is inad-

---

[21] See Houston 1985 on the role of Calvinism in writing; Pattison 1982; K. Thomas 1986; Strauss and Gawthrop 1984.
[22] Street 1987; see also Harbsmeier 1988.
[23] See J. P. Parry 1989; Gough 1968.

equate.[24] In the ancient world, the Athenians prided themselves on having written law and regarded that as fundamental to their democracy, whereas Sparta was proud of not needing it.[25]

Particularly interesting work has been done on the Middle Ages. Clanchy's fascinating study *From Memory to Written Record* (1979) shows, among other things, how the use of writing for certain kinds of proof and documents was not by any means obvious or immediate. It was the predominant attitudes to the written word that did much to determine the place of writing in medieval England. These attitudes changed, but in a culture which still relied very largely on the spoken word and material objects as proof or memorial, writing had first to be *accepted* as better proof. Saenger's recent work on silent reading in the later Middle Ages also confounds our every expectation.[26] Silent reading became increasingly common with the advent of word-separation. It would be easy to think up armchair interpretations of its significance. But these would be twentieth-century ideas. What the men and women of the later Middle Ages were concerned about was the transition now made possible from the customary oral recitation of prayers to their silent contemplation. There was much impassioned discussion on the implications – but the implications they were worried about were peculiarly religious and medieval in character. The silent and therefore internal recitation of prayers from books in the vernacular was now possible – hence more individualized prayers – and the production of these books could not be controlled by the Papal authorities. Private reading during Mass might be forbidden because it violated communal participation. Erotic illuminations began to accompany Books of Hours as they became objects of contemplation. There seems to be a variety of responses available: the ones chosen tell us a great deal about the anxieties of the late Middle Ages. On a rather different theme Carruthers' recent study, *The Book of Memory* (1990), stresses the immense importance of memorization and the trained memory to the learned and literate in the Middle Ages; memorization was not made redundant by the presence of books, but on the contrary, books were regarded as only one way to remember and therefore to attain knowledge.

[24] Bloch 1989, esp. 29–34.
[25] Plutarch, *Life of Lycurgus* 13.3.
[26] Saenger 1989; also 1982.

Such detailed analyses, often strongly buttressed by the views of contemporaries themselves, make a persuasive case for the complexity of writing and of the responses to it in different periods from our own. We must clearly link the uses of literacy with these bewilderingly varied beliefs about writing. They suggest that we should abandon the idea that literacy is a single, definable skill with definite uses and predictable effects. Its manifestations seem, rather, to depend on the society and customs already there. Perhaps writing can exaggerate or strengthen tendencies already present, rather than transform them, but what is fundamental are the pre-existing features. Writing does not descend onto a blank slate.

This more complex approach to literacy has been analysed and explained most persuasively by Brian Street (*Literacy in Theory and Practice*, 1984). He divides studies of literacy into two camps according to their general conception of literacy. They tend to fall into one of these whatever field they concern. Once the distinction has been pointed out, it is hard to disregard it, and it dispels enormous confusion. One approach looks for *general* effects of literacy as such (e.g. Goody (1968, 1977, 1986)). Street calls this approach the 'autonomous' model of literacy: this claims or assumes that literacy is a simple skill or technology which has certain standard, predictable effects on a society (e.g. rationality). Here literacy is rather like a catalyst in a chemical experiment – add it to a society and, without being changed itself, it will cause that society to change. The 'autonomous' model can be traced back intellectually to Marshall McLuhan. In this tradition, methods of communication *are* matters of technology only, and in the age of early television, technology (which was conceived as totally 'autonomous') was to change everything. Exponents of this approach can be accused, with considerable justification, of a kind of 'technological determinism'.

This approach contrasts with the other, 'ideological' model, which tends to be found in detailed studies of writing, oral communication or literacy, particularly those concerned with past societies. This sees literacy as much more fluid: its uses, implications and effects are largely determined by the habits and beliefs (i.e. 'ideology' or mentality) of the society already there. Literacy does not itself change society, but is, as it were, changed by it. It thus has different manifestations in different periods and areas – for example in medieval England and in Japan, as we have seen. These

gulfs had been explained, rather unsatisfactorily, by some idea of a
line of evolutionary development from 'craft literacy' to 'scribal
literacy', along which every society must be placed on its way to a
full, rational, modern literacy.[27] The examples already discussed
do indeed suggest that the 'ideological' model is a more sophisticated and historically convincing interpretation of literacy.
Clanchy's study of medieval England could almost form a case
study for it. Finnegan's work on orality and its relation to the use of
writing is also important here. More recent work involving literacy
tends to confirm it. Of those I have not yet mentioned, I would
draw attention to the studies of Brian Stock, Detienne, my own
book on classical Athens, and the striking recent collection of
papers entitled *Literacy and Society* edited by Schousboe and Larsen.[28] This last volume argues for precisely this social and 'ideological' construction of literacy over a wide range of literacy types
and societies. It is in effect an answer to Goody and Watt's 'Consequences of literacy' and the accompanying volume of case studies.[29]

One final point: many psychological tests seem to find a correlation between literacy and a more rational and analytical way of
thinking, which would confirm the basic theory of the rationalizing
effects of literacy. But what is the precise correlation involved here?
If manifestations of literacy are usually conditioned by culture,
they must also be inseparable from the education that accompanies
that culture. Literacy is intimately linked to the educational
system. When children go to school they learn to read and write
alongside many other skills. They are also imbibing a certain mentality or certain ways of thought which are part of the culture in
question. The psychological tests may thus be measuring the effects
of literacy within a *Western* educational system: the rational way of
thinking is just as likely to be the result of general education as of
literacy. Thus when people talk of the intellectual effects of literacy
in, say, Third World countries, they are probably really seeing the
effects of Western education and Western-style literacy. Goody has

---

[27] See Pattison 1982, and Graff 1986, 1987, for fulminations against the evolutionary idea;
see also Finnegan 1988: ch. 8.
[28] Stock 1983; Detienne (ed.) 1988; R. Thomas 1989; Schousboe and Larsen (eds.) 1989;
also Chartier (ed.) 1989.
[29] So is Pattison's extremely readable book, 1982; for printing, Graff 1987 has recently
shown for modern England how writing and printing are not themselves agents of change
but depend on how they are used.

held up the example of writing developed among the Vai in West Africa as proof of the intellectual effects of literacy,[30] but what is revealing is that the two men most responsible for developing the new Vai script had in fact worked in the British colonial service – so their use of writing must have been deeply influenced by the colonial administration. If literacy reflects culture at all, then it is extremely hard to isolate any effects of literacy from those of the culture in general – or, for that matter, from the culture promoting or introducing that literacy from outside.[31]

We tend to focus on literacy, but similar objections may be made to attempts to invest orality with general qualities and give it an overriding explanatory force – particularly in Greek society and literature. Here is the same general principle that the technology of communication is *by itself* an explanatory and active force in the character of a society. Though the effects of 'orality' are more often discussed in very general terms, we can distinguish three main strands: the propositions that (a) orality determines style; (b) orality determines content; (c) orality determines mentality. Homeric composition has been thought to prove (a). (b) is best seen in the character of oral traditions about the past, though it is more generally implied that orality will affect anything in an oral society. (c) is best seen in theories such as Ong's in which orality, being the reverse of literacy, engenders a warm communal, uncritical, non-rational society which lacks a sense of the individual or of individual thought, highly traditional, prone to the levelling effect of *homeostasis*. Thus Greek history and culture can be seen partly in terms of the progressive weakening of the oral mentality, increasing individualism, rationality, and discovery of the self, as literacy undermines it.[32]

But if literacy has widely varying implications, then it is likely that orality has too. The controversial example of oral poetry may be used to show that not all 'oral poetry' shares certain features simply by virtue of its being orally transmitted and composed.[33] The oral nature of composition does not totally determine its con-

---

[30] Goody 1987: ch. 9 (with Cole and Scribner) and ch. 10.
[31] See esp. Cole and Scribner 1981; Street 1984; S. de Castell *et al.* (eds.), 1986: esp. Heath's essay.
[32] Ong 1982 for the clearest exposition; Goody 1968; Havelock 1963 and 1986; critique, in Finnegan 1977: 126–8; Andersen 1987.
[33] See Finnegan 1977; 1970a; and my ch. 3 below.

tent or form. When one also distinguishes the main elements of orality, oral transmission, oral composition, and oral communication,[34] it becomes clearer that each element differs in its implications, its relevance to a given society, and its relation to writing. Writing is not necessarily the mirror-image and destroyer of orality, but reacts or interacts with oral communication in a variety of ways. Sometimes the line between written and oral even in a single activity cannot actually be drawn very clearly, as in the characteristic Athenian contract which involved witnesses and an often rather slight written document,[35] or the relation between the performance of a play and the written and published text. It is doubtful that orality in itself can have analytic value in *explaining* Greek civilization. But its various components can illuminate much of Greek society.

These points are now beginning to be taken up elsewhere. Some modern historians have noted how written culture was usually accessible even to those who could not read and there seems generally more readiness to break down the strict barriers between literate and oral.[36] Clanchy's work (1979) on medieval memory and written record has become a landmark in the study of the interaction between memory and oral communication and the written document. Carruthers' study of memory and its relation to written texts in the Middle Ages should join it (1990).

This throws any study of literacy back onto the characteristics of the society in question, to its use of writing, and above all to the attitudes it has to the written word. The mere presence of writing in the ancient world tells us comparatively little: what is most interesting is how it comes to function, and what particular use is made of its potentials. Similarly with orality, where we can go beyond general observations about 'oral culture' to examine the specific manifestations of oral communication or poetry in ancient Greece.

For the general problem of the nature of literacy or oral communication, many questions may still remain. Why does writing seem to take over? Does it in fact have some intrinsic features that distinguish it from oral communication? One would think so: everyday experience suggests that something written down has a

---

[34] Finnegan 1977: 16–24 (the most thorough discussion of all the ramifications); see also Gentili 1988: 4–5.
[35] See R. Thomas 1989: 41–2, 55–58.
[36] K. Thomas 1986; Houston 1985, and 1988; Stock 1983; Goody 1987; Scribner 1984.

far better chance of survival and accurate transmission than something reliant on memory and oral communication (especially if
there is no special reason for remembering it). Writing does have a
useful ability to preserve information and makes communication
over long distance much easier. It obviously facilitates the transmission of a complex literary tradition. Studies of oral tradition
emphasize how changeable such traditions are unless there are
deliberate and effective mechanisms to secure accurate transmission: memory is very selective. But whether even these fairly
simple features of writing are acted upon is quite another matter,
and we should not ignore other possibilities of writing which are
not pursued. When the new technology of printing was invented, it
was at first used to produce books as near to medieval manuscripts
in appearance as possible[37] – in other words to perform what
people were doing already but more quickly. There still seems to be
an endless capacity for variation and manipulation in the use of
writing – written texts can be made and interpreted in such a way
that they are just as selective as memory. There is thus a difficult
balance between the features of writing and oral communication
which may make certain developments easier, and the question of
whether they are taken advantage of, or the way they interact with
cultural expectations. In the end it is hard to overestimate the
extent to which their 'implications' are culturally determined.

   This should encourage a student of ancient literacy and orality to
pay more attention to ancient society itself. Much of the most
recent work on the ancient world is breaking away from attempts to
measure Greek intellectual progress in terms of the increase of
literacy, or to measure the extent of literacy without going further.
Harris' recent book on *Ancient Literacy* (1989) devotes much space to
the uses of writing (though he is ultimately interested in arguing for
very restricted literacy). The work by Detienne and Svenbro,[38]
and in particular the interesting collection of papers in *Les Savoirs de
l'écriture. En Grèce ancienne* (1988), edited by Detienne, approach the
use of writing in a much more fluid, less deterministic manner.
There is slightly more readiness to countenance both literacy and
orality together.[39] In a sense, there has been a shift of attention
from literacy to the use of writing.

[37] Clanchy 1983.
[38] Detienne 1988a, 1988b, and 1986; Svenbro 1988a.
[39] R. Thomas 1989; Andersen 1987, and 1989; W. V. Harris 1989.

CHAPTER 3

Oral poetry

I INTRODUCTION: ORAL POETRY AND ORALITY

Modern study of Greek orality – perhaps even of orality itself – is founded on Homeric epic poetry. In a brilliant series of articles between 1928 and his untimely death in 1935, Milman Parry argued that Homer's *Iliad* and *Odyssey* were traditional oral poetry, the product of a long tradition rather than the creation of one poetic genius. Parry and his pupil Albert Lord turned to the contemporary illiterate bards of southern Yugoslavia in the 1930s and 1950s. Here they could see how an oral poet actually composed in performance and, in particular, how he used a traditional stock of set pieces, formulae and set themes to help him compose as he sang. Parry's detailed analysis of Homer seemed to reveal a similar system of traditional formulae: thus the Homeric epics were oral poetry.

This theory had precedents in earlier work but it proved to be revolutionary.[1] Homer is now widely known at an oral poet. Oral poetry was put on the map. The 'oral theory' or 'Parry–Lord theory', as it is sometimes known, has been applied to other poetic traditions of epic or archaic nature – Old Norse, Anglo-Saxon, African epic, Karakirghiz poetry, to name only a few. For the Greek world, Parry's theory focused attention on the oral side of Greek life more generally: Havelock's theory that Greece was an 'oral society' even down to the fourth century BC was a direct offshoot. The scholarly image of a highly literate ancient Greece was shattered irrevocably.

The theory also still lies at the heart of our image of orality, both

---

[1] See Parry's collected works in M. Parry 1971; best discussion and critique (from a vast choice) is by A. Parry (his son) in the Introduction to this (1971; repr. in A. Parry 1990: 195–264).

in Greece and in general. This is partly because studies of orality
have clustered overwhelmingly around the Homeric epics, the
Yugoslav bards and other epic poetry. It is ultimately because of
Parry's theory that we must now recognize the importance of
audience and the context of performance in oral and traditional
societies; similarly the character of improvisation. The extraordinarily influential idea that oral poetry is essentially different from
'literate poetry', and therefore that it is killed by literacy, can also
be traced back to Parry's and Lord's original formulation. So can
the idea that an oral society has specific predictable characteristics
which distinguish it sharply from a literate one.[2] The oral poet –
and oral society – become mechanical tools of tradition.

The 'Homeric question' thus deserves our attention for the sheer
influence it has had. Moreover, I have been suggesting so far that
literacy and orality are flexible and highly variable in their manifestations, indeed that we should blur the line usually drawn between
'literate' and 'oral' and examine their interpenetration. Surely the
Homeric poems disprove this idea at once? Certainly the 'oralists'
in the Parry–Lord tradition would think so. But many of the
assumptions about orality based on the Homeric oral theory may
be mistaken, as I hope to show. If oral poetry is very much more
varied and creative than the Parry–Lord theory held,[3] this should
enable us to go on to a more subtle and sympathetic appreciation of
the variety and complexity of oral cultures. Discussion of orality is
still often too generalized, uncritical, and woolly, the alleged
character of 'orality' surprisingly often a matter of faith rather than
evidence. Scholars have tended, as I have said, to look for the
similarities between oral poetry of different cultures (and therefore
the features of 'oral society') rather than the differences. This is
surely patronizing and fails to recognize the diversity and achievements of societies without writing. Little comparative evidence is
known except the Yugoslav, especially amongst classicists (and the
Yugoslav evidence has still not been studied in the depth it
deserves). Yet orality turns out to be as complex and variable in its
manifestations as literacy.

It is now generally accepted, then, that the Homeric poems are

---

[2] See, for example, Lord 1960; Havelock 1963 and Ong 1982; Foley's survey, 1988.
[3] Here I am much indebted to Finnegan 1977; Jensen's discussion of comparative evidence
(1980) is also extremely refreshing. Note publication of Yugoslav songs and interviews in
M. Parry and Lord 1954 and 1974.

essentially the product of an oral tradition of poetry and of more than one poet (called 'Homer' for convenience), written down probably in the eighth century BC when the alphabet came to the Greek world. But classical scholars are increasingly inclined to resist this conclusion. The debate, which may be followed in a vast number of books and articles, is not simply of esoteric interest, for it bears directly on some of the most fundamental questions about the nature of oral poetry and the society which produces it. Let us start with the Parry–Lord thesis itself.

2 THE PARRY – LORD THESIS

Milman Parry's original studies concentrated on painstaking analysis of one of the most curious features of the epics, the Homeric 'stock epithet'. Each Homeric character has a recurrent descriptive but 'ornamental' epithet: 'grey-eyed Athena', 'noble Odysseus', 'swift-footed Achilles'. Parry argued that there was an extremely complex system behind their use and distribution: each noun-epithet unit was suited to one particular section of the hexameter line. If the same character was mentioned in another part of the verse, he would have another epithet which suited the metre there. Epithets changed not according to the immediate needs of the narrative, but simply for metrical reasons. That is, the poet would use the 'formula' that fitted his metrical needs. There were also whole-line formulae: a conventional verse for Achilles answering someone would run, 'Then in answer again spoke swift-footed Achilles', and the verse could be endlessly varied for other heroes. The sense usually ended with the end of the verse. There were also whole passages which could be repeated *en bloc* for certain recurrent descriptions.

Parry argued that there was strictly one phrase or 'formula' per section of the hexameter, with little unnecessary duplication. The system was both so economical and so complex that it could not be the work of one poet, but was the result of a long series of bards working within the same tradition, who each composed out of these ready-made formulae and passed the tradition on to the next generation. By a Darwinian survival of the fittest, presumably, the formulaic system had been exquisitely refined until it was an instrument of complexity and yet perfect economy. Parry made the principle of 'economy and extension' central to oral poetry. He believed that the whole of the *Iliad* and *Odyssey* would turn out to consist of formulae, given careful enough analysis.

Parry's researches in Yugoslavia helped shift the emphasis from traditional to *oral*: the Homeric poems were now traditional *oral* poetry. The poets could have composed without writing because they could call up the formulaic phrases as they needed from the vast oral store. The Yugoslav poetry was heavily formulaic epic, often lengthy, and clearly composed and transmitted entirely without writing. Sometimes these poets or *guslari* 'repeated' songs they had sung already in similar form, but they could also improvise on the spot from their traditional store of formulae and themes. An analogy with modern jazz may be helpful here.[4] Poets would 'learn' songs from other singers, but far from repeating them word for word, they re-created them in their own manner. Even when a singer insisted he was singing the 'same song' as before, there would often be quite serious differences between the two songs, and the tape recorder would reveal numerous tiny changes. The audience and the context of the performance affected the poet quite markedly. Thus the formulaic style of oral poetry was illustrated in practice, and most important, this living poetry revealed what was impossible to deduce from a stable written text, the importance of performance and audience to the poetic creation, and the fluidity and changeable nature of oral poetry.

The Yugoslav poetry certainly helps us understand how the *Iliad* and *Odyssey* could be at the end of a long tradition of poetry stretching across the Dark Ages, the culmination of a fine tradition rather than the work of a poet of genius *in isolation*. The so-called monumental poet (or poets) must lie pretty close to the purely oral tradition simply because the alphabet arrived in Greece only in the early eighth century. Moreover, we must at least revise our demands for originality for a type of poetry in which the very building bricks are highly traditional. Extreme proponents of the oral theory claim that the canons of traditional literary criticism are appropriate only to written poetry, but this presupposes a complete gulf between oral and written poetry. However, if the poet composed partly or entirely from a stock of formulae, set themes and traditional language, then his songs would indeed consist of older elements as well as newer ones: any bard in this tradition would be

---

[4] Suggested by Silk 1987: 26.

partly creating a new song, partly repeating or re-creating an older tradition.

Moreover in any performance he would be improvising as he went along, unable to go back and change bits if he had a good idea later on in the performance. So there would be inconsistencies, a few indications of later invention and composition on top of the older layers. This explains some of the long-noted inconsistencies in Homer: for instance the famous embassy to Achilles in the *Iliad* starts with three men (9.168ff.), then seems to have two, then returns to three.[5] As Horace said, 'Homer nods' (*Ars Poetica* 359). This can allow both the tradition and the master poet(s) at the end. For if each oral poet composes afresh from a traditional stock of language, themes, and formulae, then he is simultaneously creating a unified song – unified at least by his own personality and story-telling – and being the repository and reproducer of traditional, even ancient, formulae and tales. The old themes and formulae have been swept up by successive generations of bards, reproduced, and transmitted – and no doubt discarded (discussion has neg-lected this process), so that each bard is at once a creative poet and a traditional one. Certainly this upsets our conception of poetic originality and creativity. The extreme version of this structured system seems to leave no room for any innovation.

The performance, stressed so much by the Parry–Lord theory, has further implications for oral poetry. The oral poet is influenced by the audience in a way a writer is (supposedly) not, prompted to expand or alter his song according to audience reaction and the circumstances of performance. This variation is widely attested in oral poetry all over the world. No two performances would be identical. That means that the Homeric bard too would have sung different songs in different performances, altered, expanded, and probably improved his repertoire. He could not have sung the *Iliad* as we have it every time, or even sections of it, and in any case, it was far too long (almost 15,700 lines) for a single performance. Given that the poet is also supposed to have composed completely in performance, we should have to envisage an extremely fluid type of poetry in the Homeric tradition, consisting of the whole body of epic tales from the Trojan Wars – not just those of the *Iliad* and *Odyssey* – composed in performance and lacking any stable text. On

[5] Well explained by Nagler 1974: 95–6 and n. 35.

this view, our texts of the *Iliad* and *Odyssey* record just one of very many performances of those epics.

There has been much criticism of the Yugoslav analogy. Firstly, it is merely an analogy, not proof. The poetry is very inferior in quality to Homer's, as Parry and Lord admitted, so many doubt that the Homeric epics can be at all comparable.[6] This inferiority implies, unfortunately, that oral poetry really cannot achieve excellence (and Homer must have been a literate poet after all) – many scholars assume that any sign of care or finesse must indicate the use of writing. Another result, perhaps, is that the tools of oral analysis developed expressly for the Yugoslav context have not given enough attention to individual poetic quality and subtlety. I should emphasize, contrary to what is often thought, that oral poetry and poets vary in quality just like literate poetry and poets. Fine oral poetry, even of epic scale, *has* been found elsewhere in the world, especially in the Karakirghiz tradition and in Africa.[7] It should be possible to understand how an oral poet can produce fine poetry without the help of writing. Much still needs explanation. It is not clear that the Parry–Lord idea of oral composition is enough to account for our texts of Homer, or that it covers all oral poetry.

In the field of Homeric research we can now discern two main trends. On the one hand, the formulaic theory of Parry and Lord is being refined and extended to other oral poetry (based mainly in America, this trend in scholarship amounts to a school of thought adhering to 'the oral theory of composition');[8] formulae and themes are the focus, poetic individuality denied. On the other hand, after a period in which the Parry thesis was absorbed and generally accepted, there has been what might be called an aesthetic reaction, and scholars have returned again to the literary qualities of Homer. Oral theorists tend to deny any poetic intentions on the part of the individual poet, stressing mechanisms and tradition over innovation and creativity. Yet it is hard to believe that the *Iliad* with its twenty-four books, over-arching structure binding the whole together, and ability to transcend the basic tale of Achilles' wrath, could really have been the result of on-the-spot

---

[6] E.g. Kirk 1976: ch. 5; Dirlmeier 1971; Hainsworth 1968: ch. 1.

[7] See Jensen 1980: esp. chs. 2–4.

[8] For a survey (rather uncritical) of the development of 'the oral theory', see Foley 1988; Lord 1986.

improvisation alone. The overall coherence must surely indicate that, however traditional the language and basic story, the *Iliad* bears the mark of a master poet at the end of a long line, a so-called 'monumental poet'. And *this* reintroduces the possibility of individual creativity and innovation within the tradition, not to mention the strong possibility that the poet worked extensively on the poem. Recent studies have examined how the Homeric poet may have transcended the limits of the tradition, using and improving upon the traditional formulae.[9]

The manifest literary qualities of Homer should surely affect our appreciation of oral poetry and its mechanisms. Yet there is a wide gulf between the literary study of Homer and the oral-formulaic school. The literary study of Homer tends merely to chip away at the oral-formulaic theory or neglect it altogether.[10] Assertions, for instance, that the epics are of such high quality that writing must have been involved assume that care indicates a literate poet, but simply shift the responsibility onto equally variable methods of communication.[11] On the other hand, even though Parry and Lord acknowledged the superior quality of Homer's poetry, their followers have not attended to the subtleties of language and thought pointed out by other Homeric studies, let alone tried to explain them in oral terms. The result is deadlock and mutual disregard. Yet surely if modern understanding of oral poetry and its mechanisms is to have any validity at all, we should be able to explain how a poet of genius *might* work within an oral tradition and produce a work of art (perhaps like the *Iliad*). The American oral-formulaic school has so far failed to do this. But nor can we dismiss the oral theory entirely, since the *Iliad* and *Odyssey* so obviously do share some features of other oral poetry and they were composed when writing was barely known, if at all. For a balanced, rounded view, one needs to appreciate not simply oral poetry and 'orality', or writing and literacy, but both. It should be possible to find some accommodation between the two very different positions. This can best be done by focusing on three main areas where the traditional

---

[9] E.g. Fenik (ed.) 1978; Bremer, de Jong, Kalff (eds.) 1987; A. Parry 1971.

[10] As A. Parry points out, 1971: 57, and still true. But see now Nagy 1990b.

[11] Heubeck 1978; Lohmann 1970, from analysis of the speeches; Lesky 1966; Wade-Gery 1952; also A. Parry 1966 but not on grounds of quality alone.

oral-formulaic theory seems to need modification: (i) method of composition, (ii) the formula, (iii) the role of writing.[12]

3 METHOD OF COMPOSITION: MEMORY, IMPROVISATION, REFLECTION

As we have seen, Parry, Lord, and the 'oral formulaic' school stress above all that the oral poet does not memorize but actually composes in performance, responding to audience and situation. Contrary to the folklorists' belief in exact memorization over generations, verbatim accuracy among the Yugoslav bards was almost unknown and no song was sung in exactly the same way again. Composition in performance was absolutely essential to explain not only the Yugoslav evidence but the Greek epic poems which were in any case too long to memorize exactly.

To a large extent we must accept this of Homer and indeed most, if not all, oral poetry. Absolute verbatim accuracy would have been impossible to achieve for the Homeric bard. Perhaps more important, it would be impossible to check without a written text and tape-recorder, and one wonders whether it would even have seemed desirable to a society not obsessed (as we are) with verbatim accuracy. But does composition-in-performance (postponing the issue of writing for the moment) really account for the production of the *Iliad* and *Odyssey* as we have them?

It no longer seems possible to leave out memory and memorization entirely.[13] On the simplest level the poet knew some 'set pieces' by heart, for example the lengthy descriptions of preparing a meal. He must also have remembered the formulae. Of course memorization is involved.

For more complex aspects of the poems, composition entirely in performance becomes even more problematic. Take, for instance, one of the most powerful scenes of the *Iliad*, the speech of Achilles in

---

[12] On what follows there is no good general guide: Lord 1960 is fundamental, and Kirk 1962, 1976 – a collection of important articles; Finnegan, 1977: esp. ch. 3, an important general work. Silk 1987 and Mueller 1984 are helpful; Heubeck 1978 surveys Homeric studies and their future. For critical discussion of the comparative material, Jensen 1980 (earlier chapters) presents new material and analysis of oral poetry, though her views on the later (Peisistratid) recording of Homer are less plausible; Young 1967, Bowra 1966, and Hatto 1980 are stimulating.

[13] Jensen 1980: 22–7; Lord 1981 would admit only 'unconscious' memorization.

book 9.308ff., in which he refuses to return to the fighting and rejects the embassy's offer and the main elements of the heroic code of behaviour along with it[14] – a scene which, incidentally, could well have been performed on its own.[15] Its language is forced and highly unusual. Moreover, the language of all Achilles' speeches is consistently richer and more unusual than that of other characters (as is the language of Homeric speeches in general compared to that of the narrative).[16] So the poet has at least two levels of composition and is capable of highly wrought and unusual language for the central figure of the epic. This would hardly be surprising on dramatic and literary grounds but it is not well accommodated by the oral-formulaic theory. It is hard to see how such finely crafted speeches could be produced by fresh improvisation each time. Some think such subtleties actually disprove the oral theory. Or perhaps the problem can be resolved by recognizing that improvisation or composition-in-performance has simply been exaggerated.[17]

There was surely nothing to prevent a bard, particularly a gifted one, from working on the traditional tales, developing certain characters, and working up certain scenes *between* performances. If any elements at all were worked on outside the performance itself, then more than improvisation is involved. The only obstacle to this, as we shall see, is our conception of oral poetry drawn from the Yugoslav bards. It tends to be thought that oral poetry, by its very nature, is improvised in the heat of the moment, fluent, traditional, unreflective, and the opposite of written poetry which involves often long reflection, rewriting, and compressed and intense language.[18] In Greece the transition from the leisurely style of epic to the briefer style of lyric has sometimes been taken to reflect a transition from orality to literacy.[19] But the Yugoslav evidence itself does not entirely uphold these ideas, and beyond Yugoslavia,

---

[14] A. Parry 1956; *contra*, Reeve, *CQ* 23 (1973): 193–5.

[15] Silk 1987: 39.

[16] Griffin 1986: esp. 50–56. See also Lohmann 1970.

[17] Jensen 1980, 22–7 and refs. in n. 20 below; cf. Lord's description of the process as 'recreating' (e.g. 1960: 120, cf. 13–29, 102–20) which is vague and ambiguous. Jensen's defence of Lord therefore seems to go too far (and as she admits, he exaggerated the extent of creativity).

[18] Fluent and unreflective oral poetry: e.g. Havelock 1963, 1982; Lord 1960; modified by Kirk 1976: ch. 4.

[19] E.g. Gentili 1988: esp. chs. 1 and 3.

much oral poetry is far closer in style to this ideal 'literate' poetry than to the Yugoslavian brand.

For fairly exact repetition does sometimes occur. Lord understandably stressed the extent of change from song to song in order to counteract the more usual (and unfounded) faith in exact repetition. But as Jensen and Kirk have pointed out, there are striking examples in the Yugoslavian material of very close if not verbatim repetition of a song even after a period of several years. Examples of apparent memorization and fairly close reproduction in other oral poems are hard to explain away.[20] Accuracy is probably higher if an oral composition has ritual importance, for a ritual function may introduce distinct reasons and even mechanisms for comparative accuracy.[21]

The possibility of private reflection, as well as of memorization, should also be reinserted into our concept of the oral poet (and therefore the oral society). The idealization of the oral poet as spontaneous and unreflective and, being illiterate, only able to function in front of an audience is inaccurate as well as unduly minimalist. In several societies oral poetry is composed by the poet in complete isolation from other people, to be performed only later, from memory. As Finnegan points out, the Eskimo poet seeks complete solitude when he is inspired; one such poet called his songs his 'companions in solitude'. In the Gilbert Islands the inspired poet leaves the village to compose. When he is ready, he returns to try out his creation before his friends, and he may alter it further after their criticism.[22] Jensen points out that Lord's Yugoslav singers *did* usually practise in private first, and cites a Romanian epic singer who regularly kept his wife awake by practising to himself on the night before he was to perform at a wedding.[23]

As for style, one need only glance at examples of oral poetry from

[20] Jensen 1980: 23–5, 40–5 esp. 40 with refs., citing Kiparsky 1976. See also Kirk 1976: esp. 118–25 (but arguing that the Greek tradition would be more accurate than the Yugoslavian); in 1976: ch. 6, he believes memory has been underrated. See also Finnegan 1977: 73–86; Young 1967; Hainsworth 1968, 1ff. accepts an element of recitation.

[21] For the (supposedly) oral transmission of the Vedic hymns over centuries: see J. P. Parry 1989: 53–5 and Smith 1977, who stress the liturgical role; Finnegan 1977: 134–69, and Goody 1985, for scepticism of such accuracy by oral transmission alone; contrast, e.g., for extreme fluidity, *The Hindu Oral Epic of Canaini*, by Shyam M. Pandey (Allahabad 1982) (I owe this ref. to Martin West).

[22] Finnegan 1977: 80–86.

[23] Jensen 1980: 42, referring to Lord 1960: 114; M. Parry and Lord 1954: 266. Premeditation, practice, and perfecting in private by Serbo-Croatian boy, Lord 1960: 21.

all over the world to see the huge variety of genres, styles, lengths of poems, and types of composition.[24] For those coming to oral poetry from the epic Homeric context, the occurrence of short oral songs deserves particular emphasis (compare, in fact, the so-called Homeric Hymns of the archaic period). In other words, the sheer orality of a poet does not by itself tend to produce a certain style.

Some would argue that examples of memorization and private composition apply only to shorter poems and are irrelevant to Homer; would composition in performance not still be necessary for the longer genres of poetry?[25] There may be some truth in this. But on one level the argument is couched in terms of what an oral poet can and cannot do as an oral poet – whether he is driven by illiteracy to certain methods and styles rather than others. The debate often slides quietly from Homer or Yugoslavian poetry back to what we would suppose is possible without writing. The Yugoslav bards have also dominated our idea of what *all* oral poetry must be like. But if we cast our net wider, it would indeed seem that oral poets do occasionally indulge in careful silent composition and memorization. The techniques available to the oral poet are far more varied than the Yugoslav analogy implies.

If we accept that oral poets are capable of premeditation and reflection, of developing an idea without the aid of writing, then I see no reason to doubt that the final Homeric poet of the *Iliad* could have worked on the grand structure over a period of many years. Certainly he would have inherited much, but a truly gifted singer would innovate on his own (and, after all, someone had to invent even the most basic formulae at some point, let alone the main themes). So a large-scale poem like the *Iliad* could have been developed very gradually – and not necessarily with writing.[26] The greatest scenes might have been carefully crafted in private and refined continually, reproduced in at least roughly the same form in successive performances.

There is remarkably little modern study of how a singer may repeat or develop a particular song over several years – how far he may correct or refine, or in other words, work *consciously* on a

---

[24] See above all Finnegan 1977, and 1982 – though note that her definition of oral poetry is extremely broad.

[25] Lord's defence e.g. 1981.

[26] Kirk on gradual development: 1976: 137 (but he prefers the possibility of composition without writing); Hainsworth 1968: 1–2 accepts the possibility of rehearsal.

song.[27] The emphasis has been on fluidity and formulaic composition. But it is probable that a song may reach a state of relative stability if the poet achieves a form that pleases him.[28] We should at least admit that, if a poet does give many performances of the same song, he has the chance for successive change, alteration, refinement, even 'rehearsal' – and unlike the literate author, he can continue this process for his whole life (this is a striking thought for literate authors, bound unavoidably by their previously published work). Improvisation could still occur in performances, and scenes be expanded or left out. Some scenes would be remembered carefully, others not. Presumably the monumental poet worked on Achilles' speech in *Iliad* 9 particularly carefully, then committed it to memory, before slotting it into the more fluid embassy scene. Composition without writing would not in fact be as incredible as we might expect from the Parry–Lord theory. Nor is there reason to think that memorization (of any degree) hampered improvisation and creativity:[29] it can merely supplement improvisation and preserve the finest scenes.

The oral poet begins to emerge more plausibly. Care is not the monopoly of the literate. The accommodation of careful composition in private as well as a certain degree of memorization will go far towards explaining the composition of the *Iliad* and *Odyssey* by an oral poet in a long tradition of oral poetry – and in any case much other oral poetry. Moreover it allows for literary and poetic appreciation.

4 THE FORMULA: THE FORMULAIC POET?

Formulae lie at the heart of the discovery that the Homeric poems were composed orally, and the idea that the composition of oral poetry is mechanically traditional. It is the formulaic system that helps an oral poet improvise in performance. It is still commonly thought – but incorrectly – that the presence of formulae shows that a poem has been composed orally. Accordingly, work on oral

[27] Jensen 1980: 42–3.
[28] Jensen 1980: 42. Lord 1960: 100 thinks that a *short* song will tend to become more stable the more it is sung.
[29] As Lord assumed, perhaps seeing memorization as analogous to having a fixed text, which he *did* think destroyed oral poetry.

poetry has concentrated on the formula.[30] But the centrality of the formula in oral poetry has been much exaggerated.

Many problems remain unresolved – and perhaps unresolvable. Parry thought *all* Homer would turn out to consist of formulae, but that was rapidly shown to be untrue.[31] Indeed Homer's language contains many words which the poet uses only once (often, incidentally, for particularly highly charged descriptions). A recent calculation suggests that 35 per cent of the vocabulary used in the *Iliad* is used there only once, 33 per cent for the *Odyssey*: that is, out of about 6000 words used in the *Iliad*, about 2000 are unique. The parallel figure for Shakespeare, well known for his breadth of vocabulary, is 45 per cent.[32] This is a high proportion of words occurring only once: at the very least, these rare words can hardly be formulaic.

But in any case students of oral poetry disagree about what constitutes a formula (thus statistical analyses of formulaic content can be very misleading). Since exactly repeated phrases are less frequent than originally imagined, oral theorists have turned to phrases which, though not exact repetitions, seem 'formulaic'. There is corresponding disagreement about what will count as 'formulaic':[33] for example, verses which partially repeat a formula but add other words are clear variations on a basic formula. But other phrases occur with the same grammatical pattern as each other but totally different vocabulary. Some scholars argue that these are 'structural formulae', that is, formulaic in pattern. Yet if you allow anything to be formulaic which merely repeats a structural or grammatical pattern found elsewhere, you are in danger of ending up in tautology. With a wide enough definition, any utterance that fits the hexameter will be formulaic. This would fit the oral theory rather well, but it would allow similar analysis of

---

[30] E.g. (from a vast list): Hainsworth 1968: esp. chs. 1–3, extremely technical but one of the clearest discussions; also Hoekstra 1964; A. Parry 1971: xxxii–iii, and 1966: 194–6; Russo 1966; A. T. Edwards 1988; Shive 1987.

[31] Further critique in: Hainsworth 1968: 23–32, 72–3 (*analogy* from the noun-epithets is inadequate); also Lord 1953: 127 and elsewhere, who stresses the creation of formulaic expressions. See also Rosenmeyer 1965; Russo 1968 and 1966; Hoekstra 1964; Finkelberg 1986.

[32] Pope 1985: counting *Iliad* and *Odyssey* separately. See also Richardson 1987 on similes and rare words; Griffin 1986 on speeches; Russo 1968 on Homer 'against his tradition'. M. Parry 1971: 313 attempted to deal with the problem.

[33] See esp. Finnegan 1977: 58–72 and Hainsworth 1968: esp. chs. 2–3 on definitions of the formula.

written poetry. As Silk has pointed out, for instance, all poets, even Shakespeare, compose in metrical patterns.[34] 'Formulaic expressions' would therefore cease to be a feature special to oral poetry.

The naive formula-theory is undermined still further by a recent book by David Shive (1987) which tackles Parry's original analysis of the Homeric noun-epithet phrases. Whether modified or marginalized, Parry's original analysis seems to be generally accepted. Shive is the first to re-examine in quite the same detail as Parry the original building blocks of the theory. He shows exhaustively that the analysis was crucially flawed because it did not look at *all* the ways in which the poet referred to a Homeric hero (here, Achilles), only the noun-epithets. The wider range of data transforms the picture: the choice of a particular phrase is not dictated solely, or even very frequently, by the metre alone, but often by literary considerations. There is less 'economy' and a lot more 'extension' than Parry and others have thought. Thus Homer was using traditional diction, certainly, but often meditating so carefully on the most apt phrase, rather than using a ready-made expression, that he begins to look very like Milton or Virgil. Shive implies that this care and thought could only be achieved with the aid of writing as a mnemonic aid.

The Homeric poems certainly contain a combination of clear 'formulae' (epithets, set-piece scenes, for example), language which is formulaic to some degree, and language which is unusual. It is perhaps better to accommodate this variation, instead of defining it away, and think in terms of a spectrum of levels, from the extreme, fixed and repeated elements (formulae) to clear-cut parallel and analogous stylistic elements, to 'free' composition.[35] Students of the oral-formulaic theory have so far been reluctant to pursue the implications of the 'free' passages for the nature of oral composition.

We should also question the equation of formulaic style with oral composition much more rigorously. For not all formulaic poetry is oral. Formulaic expressions have been found in Anglo-Saxon, Old French and Old German poetry, some of which was certainly composed by literate poets. So the formulaic theory has had to be adapted; much attention has shifted to the now rather urgent

[34] Silk 1987: 21; see also Shive 1987: esp. ch. 8.
[35] Silk 1987: 22.

question of precisely how formulaic a poem needs to be for it to be (certainly) orally composed (other criteria are sometimes used, particularly that of 'economy', stressed by Kirk). This quest of course presupposes that an oral poem must be formulaic. A closer look at the evidence suggests a more blurred line between oral and written literature.

Albert Lord, for instance, believes that the poetry of the Yugoslav bards is 100 per cent formulaic, of Homer 90 per cent.[36] The Homeric figure is quite unrealistic, especially when the whole corpus has not yet been analysed. But stranger results emerge. For instance much Anglo-Saxon poetry which is formulaic was actually composed by literate monks, and sometimes even translated from Latin.[37] Lord himself quotes some poetry written in the oral epic style by a Franciscan monk in 1759 – clearly not orally composed in the manner of the Yugoslav *guslari*. Yet this poetry consists of '58 per cent formula and formulaic with 27 per cent straight formula'. Lord takes this proportion to be an obvious correlate of the fact that it was not 'real' oral poetry. But 27 per cent straight formulae is a rather high proportion for a non-oral poem, and once we allow that this is possible, we are admitting that formulae, even in large quantities, are by no means confined to true oral poetry. Lord concludes confidently that 'a pattern of 50 to 60 per cent formula or formulaic, with 10 to perhaps 25 per cent straight formula, indicates clearly literary or written composition'.[38] Yet again, 60 per cent formulaic expressions is very high for written composition. Surely the formula and formulaic style cannot be so clear and absolute a sign of oral poetry.[39] The choice of clear dividing lines for formulaic content on either side of which poetry must be either oral or literate begins to appear arbitrary, and the search for oral formulaic proportions seems ultimately to rely on faith rather than statistics.

Furthermore, not only does some written poetry have a heavily formulaic style, but some orally composed poetry lacks formulae. Eskimo poetry, for example, and some other oral lyric poetry are not formulaic.[40] The Yugoslav and Homeric epics have so domi-

[36] Lord 1960: 142–4; 1967: 18.
[37] Benson 1966; Finnegan 1977: 69–72.
[38] Lord 1967: 24.
[39] As Hainsworth 1981: esp. 8ff.; and Kirk (1966, repr. 1976: ch. 8): who therefore tried to define a non-oral formulaic style. See also Kirk 1976: ch. 4; defence by Foley 1981.
[40] Finnegan 1977: 69–72, 80–6.

nated the study of oral poetry that, even when it is conceded that
the oral-formulaic theory is mainly applicable to oral epic,[41] it is
still widely believed of oral poetry that its oral character *alone* will
make it formulaic – and that all oral poetry is roughly similar in
style.[42] There are wider implications. Mechanical formulaic style
and lack of individual creativity have been widely attributed to the
literature of oral societies. But the formula and its implications
have been stretched too far and it is surely time to reassess the
whole debate. The formulaic system certainly shows how illiterate
bards could improvise in performance. But improvisation was not
their only option. If we concede that a degree of memorization and
private composition (followed by successive elaboration in performances) would usually occur in the composition of oral poetry,
then oral-formulaic improvisation becomes a less central feature of
oral poetry, both for fine epic like the *Iliad* and *Odyssey* and for
small-scale poems composed without writing.

As for the poetry composed by highly literate writers in an oral
formulaic style, it may not simply be a half-hearted and failing relic
of true oral composition, but is perhaps better explained by the
force of tradition in poetic style. Tradition is hardly exclusive to
oral society,[43] and in some sense all literature works within some
kind of tradition. Virgil's *Aeneid* has a compressed, largely unfor-
mulaic style, not because it is written epic – this would be to reduce
poetic creation to one very crude criterion – but partly because
Virgil is heir to the whole poetic tradition of Graeco-Roman culture. On the other hand a seventh-century poet like Archilochus
went on composing partly in Homeric language and Homeric expressions adapted to the new metre, not so much because he was
still an oral poet,[44] or still belonged to a 'partly oral' culture (a
description which would stand for the whole of the ancient world),
but rather because the poetic tradition was dominated by the
Homeric cycle.

5 WRITING AND ORAL POETRY

One of the most widely held beliefs about oral poetry is that it is
killed by writing. Parry and Lord found that, when the Yugoslav

[41] Lord 1981, and in his response to Finnegan's conference paper, Finnegan 1985.
[42] Largely refuted by Finnegan 1977; also see Kirk 1966.
[43] Shils 1981, e.g., examines its modern role from a sociological perspective.
[44] As argued by Page 1963.

bards learned to read and write, their poetic composition deterior-
ated and they ceased to use the old and picturesque formulaic style.
Lines like this appeared: 'In the bloody year of 1914, on the sixth
day of the month of August, Austria and Germany were greatly
worried'.[45] The change was thought to be induced by writing,
though how was left unclear. At first Lord assumed that writing,
being the antithesis of orality, would undermine the old oral traditions. Then he conceded that it was not writing itself so much as a
respect for the fixed text that writing brought with it which undermined the oral tradition of poetry.[46] That is, writing engendered a
respect for a fixed (written) text that destroyed the flexibility of oral
poetry and the tradition and necessity of improvisation, so that the
living tradition died (similarly he denied any element of memorization).

That Yugoslav picture has had immense influence on general
perceptions of the effects of writing, and it plays a part in another
strand of the Homeric problem: how and in what circumstances the
great epics were committed to writing. The main possibilities are
(a) the monumental poet himself dictates to a scribe; (b) the poet
writes it down himself; (c) the poems, transmitted orally, are only
written down much later. The debate is fraught and complex.
Ultimately we will probably never know whether Homer 'used
writing' at all, but the controversy deserves closer scrutiny for it
draws attention to problems important for our approach to orality
and literacy in general. I would argue that the debate has been
inconclusive partly because it draws too strict a division between
oral and written poetry, and between oral and written communication, and partly because it is based on a misunderstanding of the
nature of writing and literacy.

One common solution can be summed up crudely as follows.
Oral epic in the living (Yugoslavian) tradition seems to recognize
no set canonical version: composed solely in performance, it therefore changes rapidly. Only writing it down will preserve one
version for ever. At some point the *Iliad* (one version at least) was
written down and therefore preserved. Since it bears the mark of a
final master poet (it is not a concoction of miscellaneous songs), it

---

[45] Lord 1953: 129.
[46] First in 1953; modified in 1960: 149, where he admits that oral poets do write down poems
but in his experience they are inferior in all ways to oral dictated texts; and in 1967 in
answer to A. Parry 1966.

must have been written down at much the same time as 'Homer' was composing it – indeed only Homer could have performed it in the form we have in our texts – for in the hands of other oral bards the poems would change drastically and, as Adam Parry argued, would cease to be the work of the master poet.[47] But Homer cannot have written the poems down himself, for – it is usually assumed – once literate he would stop being an oral poet. So he must have dictated his great work to someone who could write. The alphabet reached Greece just in time to preserve the two main epics. Homer thus came at the very end of the tradition of oral poetry, which was captured in writing and then killed by that act.[48] For once a written text existed, it would have had such prestige that it would have superseded the master poet's own continued oral composition and all other versions. It is thus essential on the usual view that Homer is part of the pure oral tradition but is just touched enough by the new writing for his masterpiece to be preserved; alternatively, that the master poem was either preserved until, or actually composed in, the later sixth century.[49]

But the premise that when oral poets learn to write they lose their capacity to improvise, drawn from the Yugoslav experience, is most probably false. The Yugoslav bards were inhabitants of fairly backward Christian and Muslim communities in the 1930s to 1950s. When they learnt to read and write, they were not just acquiring a simple skill (see chapters 1 and 2). As Adam Parry pointed out, they went to state-run schools, they began to read newspapers, and through their education they were now exposed to the whole paraphernalia of modern Western culture.[50] It was this they were acquiring, not simply literacy. Western culture places a high value on the written word, books, newspapers and written

---

[47] The main thrust of his important article, argued with great care, 'Have we Homer's *Iliad?*', 1966. Kirk's idea of lengthy and accurate transmission by *oral* bards for several generations after Homer (1962) will therefore not work; he has to postulate a respect for the 'fixed text' of the master poet by these 'reproductive bards'. We have no evidence for such a stage.

[48] Thus Lord 1953 thought Homer dictated his work; A. Parry 1966, using similar points, that Homer himself could have been literate so as to write it down himself. But the act of dictation can be very productive for a poet: see below.

[49] Kirk 1962, 1976 and Jensen 1980, respectively: but we just do not know whether eighth-century writers were incapable of lengthy recording (some of the earliest graffiti are in verse). If Homer really lived in the sixth century, the Greeks would surely have known more about him.

[50] Pointed out by A. Parry 1966: esp. 212–15.

proof, unlike the high culture of the Ottoman Empire, which laid greater stress on oral communication. Now literacy carried a greater weight and social status. Along with their literacy they also learnt a new respect for the written and published text.[51]

In fact more was involved than respect for the written text. Lord says that once the Yugoslav songs were written down, the singers had great respect for the texts: one singer believed the songbooks were somehow 'true' because they were reviewed by a committee.[52] But that suggests, on the contrary, that the singers were in awe not simply of the fixed, written text of their own poems, but of what they saw as the superior culture and scholars who recorded and published them. The record of an interview with Hivzo Džafić suggests that his assurances that Avdo was singing the poem 'just the same' as it was in the songbook were the result of leading questions and an anxiety to give the 'right' answer.[53] The new written texts were accorded great status by the poets because they belonged to what they saw as a more authoritative body of culture. Similarly when anthropologists write down oral traditions, the published material often gets reincorporated into the oral traditions. This phenomenon, known as 'feedback', is usually attributed to the power of writing. But it is more plausibly related to the perceived superiority of the Western scholars and their culture. The power and 'effect' of writing, then, can be closely linked to its social or political associations,[54] and this was surely the case in Yugoslavia.

That disposes of the analogy of Yugoslavian oral poetry, but what of ancient Greece itself? When the alphabet was first used in eighth-century Greece, it was not being imposed by a centralized state, nor as part of an educational system which brought with it many other new ideas and conventions. Given that the effects and significance of writing may largely be determined by the customs and attitudes already there, we have to think hard about the contexts in which writing appeared. We cannot assume an immediate

---

[51] Pointed out briefly by A. Parry 1966: 213, suggesting the prosaic influence of newspapers and text books; general point missed by Lord's reply, 1967 (NB he admits influence of songbooks, p. 2).

[52] Lord 1967: 2–3.

[53] See M. Parry and Lord 1974: 10 (where Avdo and other singers are quite aware they elaborate on songs they have heard), 74, 77 (leading questions?).

[54] Note also the possible influence of the scribe and the circumstances of dictation (below); also the way oral poetry may be presented on the written page.

(and modern) reverence for the written word, when that is elusive
even as late as the fourth century.

Our evidence for the earliest Greek writing suggests that it was
first used at least to mark objects or to make a memorial, even to
write down verse. But it is not clear in this context that writing
would yet be intended to *fix* a text for ever. Even as late as the fifth
and fourth centuries, the concept of fixed, absolutely verbatim
accuracy is surprisingly hard to find. It is notorious how variable
the supposed copies of Athenian fifth-century (written) decrees can
be. Authoritative texts of the great fifth-century tragedians were
only produced in the second half of the fourth century under the
auspices of Lycurgus, a clear attempt to fix the tragic texts in a
period when a greater respect for the written word – and fifth-
century literature – is visible in several areas.[55] It is therefore hard
to imagine that the presence of a written text of any poetry in the
eighth century could have stifled the tradition of oral composition.
How could a written text have such authority in a society which
still relied almost overwhelmingly on oral communication and was
to continue to do so for at least another three centuries?

Indeed comparative evidence tends to suggest that the impetus
for writing down poetry almost always comes from outside, not
from the oral poet himself;[56] thus the written text would impinge
even less on the poet. For the poet, the dictated performance might
be only one performance among many and, since he was doing only
what he had always done, it is probably anachronistic to think that
he would regard the written text as superseding all his own performances: after all, it recorded only one out of hundreds.[57] The
performance being written down could be profoundly influenced by
the occasion, the presence or absence of an audience, the sympathy
and role of the scribe, but in that respect it would be simply like any
other performance. An oral poet spared the pressures of twentieth-
century Yugoslavia would be comparatively unaffected by a
written text.

Continuity in style and methods even after the coming of writing
is much more likely in early Greece; writing in the eighth and

---

[55] R. Thomas 1989: 47–9.
[56] Jensen 1980: ch. 6, esp. 92. M. L. West 1990 points out that even the Greeks thought
Homer recited, while *others* wrote his poetry down.
[57] Jensen 1980: 87; M. L. West 1990, following Jensen, also suggests that, even once the *Iliad*
was written down, new songs and variations would still be possible.

seventh centuries probably merely duplicated orally composed poetry rather than cutting it dead. Improvisation of songs continued in later Greece, in symposia and funerals, for example, and there is no sign that the improvisatory nature of drinking songs was altered by the fact that some were written down. Mozart, Beethoven, and their contemporaries were brought up to improvise as a matter of course. If we may again follow the analogy between oral improvisatory composition and modern jazz,[58] there, too, jazz musicians are able to play written music without destroying their ability to improvise. Even amongst the Yugoslav bards, there was closer continuity between their oral improvisations and their initial use of writing than is usually remembered. The first thing they used their writing skills for was to write down their own poetry in its fully formulaic style; only later did they change to a more prosaic one.[59] Oral poets in Africa who learn to write seem to write down their poetry with just as many formulae as when they composed it orally.[60] (This brings us back to the earlier point that the traditional formulaic style may be found in written poetry.)

It is also possible, however, that the very process of dictating an oral poem can enable the poet to elaborate his song and sing at far greater length than was usually remotely possible. The effects of dictation are understudied. The recording by dictation of the African Mwindo epic was the occasion for the poet to create his masterpiece, and he had a rapturous audience for several days.[61] The dictation of 'The Wedding of Smailagić Meho', the masterpiece of 12,000 lines by the Yugoslav singer Avdo, was actually a very laboured and long-drawn out affair, for Advo had to rest his voice every half hour.[62] Cited as an achievement analogous in length to the *Iliad*, this dictation may not be typical either in quality or effort. Other oral poets seem to have found it very much easier to perform continuously for a considerable period of time.

In short the severe division so often drawn between the oral poet and the literate one does not hold universally, even if it holds true

---

[58] Offered by Silk 1987: 26.

[59] Lord 1953: 129; A. Parry 1966: 213.

[60] Finnegan 1977: 70 for Xhosa and Zulu oral poetry in S. Africa; Jensen 1980: 89–90; cf. evidence in Lord 1953: 129 (formulaic patterns eventually break down when poets write down their songs) and 1960: 149.

[61] On dictation, see Jensen 1980: 37–40, ch. 6, citing Biebuyck. Dictation would also be better for the poet because he is simultaneously playing an instrument (M. L. West 1990).

[62] Bowra 1966: 351; Young 1967: 299.

in some areas. The use of writing in early Greece, when seen in the wider context, more probably duplicated the activity of the oral bards rather than suppressing it. It is even conceivable that the poet of the *Iliad* could have used writing to record his poetry, or more likely, part of it. Memorization was also possible. It would not necessarily destroy his ability to improvise. Whether or not Homer knew the art of writing, he would have remained an 'oral' poet in any meaningful sense of the word.

6 CONCLUSIONS

The oral poet, then, could have had various techniques at his disposal, and we should avoid the idea that oral poets can only function before an audience and through totally formulaic and traditional language. The epic poet is still faced with formidable problems of scale and structure, but they may not be insurmountable to a poet who lacks writing. The outstanding quality of the Homeric epics which students of the oral theory have been reluctant to explain (or indeed admit) still remains the crux. It perhaps becomes more explicable as part of an oral tradition once we have widened the possibilities open to the oral poet. If Homer's poetry is generally 'oral', then the oral theory should be able to accommodate it. Is exquisite care in language impossible for an oral poet if we allow memorization and meditation? Or perhaps the challenging process of dictation itself could be an opportunity for the poet to perform his masterpiece.

These possibilities narrow the gulf so often perceived between 'oral' and 'literate' poetry. The transition from oral to written, moreover, is not a single event, or an irreversible one: the oral poet goes on singing a song even after he has dictated it (e.g. the Yugoslavian Avdo), and the written text can itself be tampered with (ironically, modern critics of written literature are now prepared to talk of 'open' texts). It is exceedingly hard to identify a clear-cut 'oral style'. Oral poetry may be formulaic (and formulae help the poet improvise), but not all formulaic poetry is oral – and indeed not all oral poetry is formulaic. We should perhaps think more in terms of poetic or literary tradition than of orality *alone*. The presence of writing alone does not necessarily transform the oral tradition, let alone kill it. Both writing and oral communication are infinitely complex and variable and the case of the Homeric epics, the basis for many general ideas about literacy and orality, may therefore help set the scene for a reappraisal.

It is not only the oral poet who emerges as a more rounded and individual figure. A society with little or no writing is not necessarily the homogeneous and totally traditional one that one might infer from some literature on oral poetry. Creativity, individuality, and innovation did exist; the real difficulty was for later generations to remember that they had existed, since memory is so fallible. Unless there was a powerful reason to remember over several generations, these individuals would drop out of the communal memory. The problem was not so much performing, composing, and creating in a society without reliable means of recording, but preserving and transmitting what was created for more than the short span of living memory – oral transmission, that is, rather than oral composition. Poetry holds a central place in archaic Greece precisely because it was memorable and structured enough to be one of the few effective forms of preservation.

CHAPTER 4

The coming of the alphabet: literacy and oral communication in archaic Greece

In early Greece from the eighth century BC we may observe the gradual development and extension of the written word in a society which, as everyone agrees, still performed almost entirely without writing. Much attention has been devoted to the very earliest uses of this alphabet, less to its later application. It has also been tempting to concentrate on the more intelligible examples of early writing, especially those which foreshadow later usage, and ignore the less straightforward – or even quite incomprehensible – pieces. Yet the many obscure graffiti are just as important a part of the impact of the alphabet, and I shall stress them in this chapter precisely because no picture of archaic writing can be complete without them. Nor can we discern the impact of writing at all adequately without assessing the nature of the non-written background. Very few discussions really attempt this (and since our evidence is slanted overwhelmingly towards what was written, it is very hard).[1] The debate is often dominated by the controversy over whether the alphabet was invented to record poetry, which disregards much of the evidence.[2] But we would also like to ask more generally whether – or how far – early Greek writing simply represented speech. Did writing make any difference to the lives of the average Greek citizens? Did it fit into (or overturn) the oral methods of conducting business? How did it affect the development of the early and emerging city-states? Or the performance and composition of poetry? Various important problems connected

---

[1] Best discussions: *LSAG*: Part II, still the most comprehensive discussion of the archaic uses of writing, with Supplement 1990; Johnston 1983; Heubeck 1979; Guarducci 1967. More generally on archaic period, Andersen 1989; Stoddart and Whitley 1988; Powell 1989; cf. Bremmer 1982.
[2] E.g. Robb 1978; Powell 1989 (but see Powell 1991).

with the study of the impact of literacy are raised here in an extreme form.

I THE ALPHABET

Alphabetic writing arrived in the Greek world during the first half of the eighth century BC. The script and the very principles of the alphabet were adopted from the Phoenicians of the Levantine coast, with whom Greeks were now increasingly in contact. Certain signs were adapted to denote vowels which were not marked in Semitic languages, other letters were eventually added. For the modern world, its arrival is heavily charged, for it rescued Greece from the oblivion of the Dark Ages. Most effort has therefore been devoted to determining its date and place of origin.

Much depends on the letter-forms, which varied according to area and period. The region which has letter-forms closest to the Phoenician script and for which early writing is attested has the most plausible claim to be the place of origin: good candidates are Crete, Cyprus, Al Mina in Syria or other areas where Euboians traded, all regions where Greeks and Phoenicians mixed. Conditions here would be suitable for some Greek merchant familiar with Phoenician writing, perhaps bilingual, to take the basic system over, but also make the crucial invention of vowels which was to render the 'cumbersome' Phoenician script so adaptable.[3] On the grounds of letter-forms, Near Eastern scholars have been trying to push back the date to the ninth or tenth century.[4] But actual finds of written material which can be archaeologically dated still cling obstinately to the eighth century, and this period remains the most probable on historical grounds, for it was a time of intense and increased contact between Greeks and Phoenicians.

The controversy will continue. Informal writings or graffiti from the eighth century are still so scarce that new archaeological discoveries may yet radically change the picture. But occasionally the debate degenerates into a quest for 'the first inventor' which seems akin to straightforward cultural chauvinism. This problem is part

---

[3] See *LSAG*, and Suppl. 1990; travelling Phoenicians in Greek parts are also possible, and may explain much of Greek orientalizing (Burkert 1984: 29–35).

[4] Naveh 1973: 1–3; Isserlin 1982; cf. Bernal 1987 (arguing that the alphabet existed far earlier and could have travelled to Greece then); see also *LSAG* Suppl. 1990: 426–7.

of the larger claims made for the superiority of the alphabet. Eleva-
tion of the Greek 'invention' of the alphabet obscures the Phoenician contribution and possible Phoenician influence on the Greeks'
use of the medium. Yet if the use of writing is partly determined by
context, then Phoenician predecessors of the Greek alphabetic
system need more serious study.[5] The question of origin also has a
tendency to obscure other important issues, such as the actual role
or effect of this new writing. The Greek alphabet did not transform
Greek life overnight: some areas probably did not acquire it for
some decades and in any case it was probably used at first for very
limited purposes.

The alphabet has, as we have seen, been claimed as revolutionary both as a writing system and as a tool in intellectual development. It seems to be far simpler than all other writing systems
(syllabaries, pictograms, for example), and it is often asserted that
because it achieves an 'exact fit' between sound and letters, it is the
single most convenient writing method ever devised: this means
that many more people can learn to write and that writing is
'democratized'. With the addition of the vowels, its economy
perhaps makes it superior as a means of reducing speech to writing.
But its 'revolutionary' principle of one letter per sound has also
been linked with the development of Greek abstract and analytical
thought, since it apparently indicates abstract identification of
letters corresponding to sounds.[6] We have already discussed the
pitfalls of the general argument about the effects of alphabetic
writing. The other problems are equally important. In general the
whole theory, with its stress on vowels, is concerned to give primacy to the Greeks against all others.

Some of these claims are born of ignorance of anything but
alphabetic written culture. Specialists of non-alphabetic societies
have begun to hit back. In the ancient Near East, there did exist
intellectual and scholarly development despite the apparent intrac-
tability of the scripts.[7] Present-day Chinese who learn what is
perhaps the most difficult script in the world hardly lack rational

[5] For ignorance of Phoenician use of writing, see Powell 1989; for Phoenician use of writing,
which is obscure, Isserlin 1982; cf. Robb 1978.
[6] Originally argued by Goody 1968 and Havelock 1982, corrected in Goody 1977, but still
going strong elsewhere: e.g. Powell 1989: 322, 'In the Greek alphabet was discovered the
principle of close phonetic approximation between written sounds and speech.'
[7] Larsen 1989.

thought.[8] Different habits of thought can be better explained by wider cultural and educational traditions.

On a more fundamental level, it has even been suggested that our very idea of writing is often conditioned by the alphabet itself and our experience of how the alphabet works: 'proper' writing is unconsciously defined as alphabetic writing – and sometimes an erroneous idea of alphabetic writing – and other writing systems judged accordingly.[9] For, in fact, even the alphabet clearly represents only an approximation to pronunciation – as English spelling and regional pronunciation make so clear. There is *not* an exact fit between sound and sign: much is purely conventional. Secondly, the conceptual significance of the addition of vowels has probably been exaggerated. The Phoenician alphabet also has letters corresponding to sounds (so do syllabic systems, including the Cypriot Greek syllabary). The phonetic principle is hardly a Greek discovery. So why are the Phoenicians never credited with a revolution in abstract thought? Certainly Phoenician in its written form, like other Semitic languages, did not have vowels, but then it did not need to do so for comprehension. Greek, on the other hand, did need vowel signs because (a) it has clusters of vowels in the middle of words (i.e. the stem), and (b) the inflected case-endings often consist of vowels or end with vowels, so that vowels may be absolutely essential to sense and grammatical construction.[10] (Vowels were thus not necessary for the Greeks simply to write down poetry, as has been claimed.[11]) In any case, when the Greeks adapted certain signs as vowel-letters, it is very likely that they *thought* they were hearing a vowel sound approximating to their vowels. It is notorious how sounds characteristic of one language may be heard very differently by speakers of another, and perhaps what the Greeks heard as vowels were the Phoenicians' guttural stops.[12] Modification of Semitic pronunciation can be seen most clearly in the way the Greeks took over the Phoenician names of the letters, alpha, beta, etc., which meant something in Phoenician and corresponded to earlier forms of the letters, and adapted them to Greek

---

[8] See Gough 1968; Bloch 1989.
[9] See for the most readable and spirited attack, R. Harris 1986; also Sampson 1985 (dealing with several non-alphabetic systems); Larsen 1989.
[10] See Sampson 1985: ch. 6, esp. 101–2.
[11] As argued, e.g. by Robb 1978 (with interesting remarks about Phoenician practice); Powell 1991.
[12] Sampson 1985.

pronunciation. Herodotus thought that the Phoenicians taught the Greeks writing (5.53). What we are seeing in this whole debate is the result of an extreme Hellenocentrism and an unjustified diminution of the Phoenician contribution to Greek culture of exactly the kind that Bernal (for instance) has drawn attention to.[13]

The famous definition of writing once given by Diringer as 'the graphic counterpart of speech' is thus a definition at least partly conditioned by knowledge of the alphabet and implicitly approximating all true writing to the alphabet. For it suggests that letters correspond to sounds, therefore that writing represents speech. But several writing systems which we should certainly class as 'writing' include signs that symbolize objects but which do not represent the pronunciation of that object (so-called pictographic systems). Chinese script, peculiarly, can be read by people all over China though they speak different dialects: the signs have the same meaning to all but are pronounced quite differently. Supposedly so cumbersome, it actually helps communication over the whole country. (Again, why not argue that this system could actually facilitate abstract thought?) Nor is it true (as often supposed) that all writing systems are striving to represent speech and will change towards that goal. The philologist Anna Morpurgo Davies, for instance, has shown how some ancient non-alphabetic systems actually changed their spelling quite deliberately in such a way that the new spelling was less close to speech (e.g. Hittite). The Cypriot syllabic system was actually refined at a time when the alphabet was already known.[14] This reminds us that the modern alphabetic system may be spreading for political and cultural just as much as linguistic reasons. It is notorious that a writing system can be taken over from a country whose language it suits, and used for a language it does not suit, for primarily non-linguistic motives.

It is useful to recollect that writing is not necessarily equivalent to speech, when we consider the relation of orality to literacy.

2 THE EARLIEST USES OF WRITING

We can probably never know whether the Greek alphabet was initially developed for commercial use (imitating the Phoenicians perhaps), or in the more romantic and popular theory, to write

[13] Bernal 1987; cf. Burkert 1984.
[14] Morpurgo Davies 1986.

down poetry. For the question as it is usually framed involves the private and therefore unknowable inspiration of a single 'inventor'. But if the Greek alphabet really was adapted in an area of Greek and Phoenician interaction and the invention of the vowels perhaps a misunderstanding of the Phoenician guttural stops, its adaptation could well have been gradual and deeply influenced by the Phoenician tradition.

What we can trace are the uses of writing as it spread rapidly amongst the Greek communities. Writing engraved on pottery and on stone provides the bulk of our evidence, other materials have largely perished. Leather and wooden tablets would have been used, perhaps even papyrus in the eighth and seventh centuries. Waxed tablets were certainly used by the Phoenicians, and the Etruscans in the seventh century,[15] and were surely used early on by the Greeks too: the very word *deltos* (writing-tablet) is of Semitic origin. The early laws of Solon in Athens were preserved on wood not stone. So the first evidence we have for a certain kind of writing does not necessarily represent the very earliest use. But this large gap in our picture can be an excuse not to look at what is preserved. Recent finds underline the use of bronze and gold plaques, and lead, particularly for letters.[16] Perhaps most important, potsherds were probably the nearest equivalent to our paper – hence their use in ostracism at Athens – for papyrus was very expensive. So at least the graffiti (the technical term for informal writing not engraved on stone) may represent the more casual and more common uses of writing (and in fact these graffiti offer a window onto the more commonplace uses of writing for all periods).[17]

Certainly early Greek writing was not 'esoteric': the range of its uses, from public inscriptions to graffiti, dedications and *dipinti* (writing added to painted pottery along with the design before firing), does not give the impression that it was confined to scribes. In Athens, at least 154 graffiti have been found dating from the seventh century alone, though this seems to be exceptional.[18] But nor was its use quite so straightforward as usually thought. A rounded picture of the impact of writing is hard to find, as I have

[15] cf. Phrygian use of wax; a tablet with some wax still clinging to it was found in the fourteenth-century Ulu Burun wreck *AJA* 93 (1989): 10–11.
[16] *LSAG* Suppl. 1990: 429–30; see further, ch. 5.
[17] For later graffiti also, see esp. Lang 1982: 75–87; 1976.
[18] See analysis by Stoddart and Whitley 1988.

said. Illuminating work has been done on early Greek writing as the counterpart of speech: as we shall see, it is often both more and less than speech. Our evidence indicates that alongside the recording of poetic tags, the marking or guarding of property was one of the earliest uses of writing.[19]

Two of the earliest and most famous pieces of graffiti are in verse, like many of the longer graffiti of the archaic period. The famous 'Nestor's cup' found in the Euboian settlement at Pithecusae in southern Italy reads, according to one interpretation: 'I am the delicious cup of Nestor. Whoever drinks from this cup the desire of beautifully crowned Aphrodite shall seize.' The pot itself can probably be dated to c. 730–720,[20] the poetic message apparently alludes in humour to the Homeric 'cup of Nestor'. Another very early piece of writing from Athens, on the 'Dipylon vase', also starts in verse: 'He who of all the dancers now performs most daintily'. With its long spidery writing, this is certainly the earliest graffito of any length (but not the earliest writing), since the jar itself dates probably to c. 740–730.[21] So already we see the world of drinking parties, dancing and poetry reflected in the use of writing. Here writing is replicating or preserving the kind of poetic creativity which evidently preceded the arrival of the alphabet. Yet we should not be too idealistic. The Dipylon graffito tails off into incoherence and a bit of the alphabet, a reminder that the writer was diffident and inexperienced;[22] the Nestor cup verses do not seem to be entirely metrical, and the verses also seem, already, to make fun of a well-known form of curse which begins, 'Whoever takes/does this . . .'.[23]

The other recurrent use of this early writing is to mark or protect ownership. The earliest writing found so far, from Pithecusae (c. 740), is a fragment of pottery proclaiming that it belongs to someone: 'I am of. . . (and a name in the genitive)'.[24] Another very early inscription painted on a krater, also from Pithecusae (c. 700), reads '[Name] . . . made me', the first potter's signature.[25] Many early fragments appear to consist simply of an owner's name or else of isolated letters whose meaning one can only guess: indeed most

---

[19] Stressed by Johnston 1983.
[20] *LSAG*: 233, no. 1.
[21] *LSAG*: 76, no. 1, and p. 68.
[22] *LSAG*: 68; Powell 1988, arguing for two writers here.
[23] P. A. Hansen 1976: 25–43, following a suggestion of Russo.
[24] Johnston 1983: fig. 1; *LSAG* Suppl: 453, A.
[25] Johnston 1983: fig. 4.

early graffiti consist simply of proper names, or are unpoetic, even unintelligible. From the same tomb as the 'Nestor cup' came another, painted, inscription, reading merely ΘΕΟ – perhaps some form of the word for god, an indication of divine property or an abbreviation? We do not know. But one gets a strong impression that the new writing was seized on widely as a way for individuals to mark their possessions and keep interlopers off (the debate on whether they used writing for accounts therefore misses the point). In this respect they were only following the Phoenicians, who seem frequently to have marked property.[26] In the expanding world of trade in the eighth-century Mediterranean, such labelling, especially for goods being transported, would facilitate exchange. There is also surely an element of that self-advertisement and competition which are so characteristic of later Greek society.

The two aspects most familiar from later inscriptions, the labelling of an offering to the gods and marked tombstones, appear next. Offerings, which are usually in the form 'X dedicated this to Y (god)', are attested from 700 and surprisingly not earlier (unless the ΘΕΟ graffito above is a dedication).[27] Marked tombstones also do not appear till the first half of the seventh century and then only sparsely: this may be related to the fact that inscriptions on stone only start appearing in earnest in the middle of the seventh century.[28]

Less innocuous, vituperative cursing is attested in some of the very earliest graffiti. The Nestor cup seems to parody the curse form, and a small Corinthian perfume flask from Kyme, datable to *c.*675, declares 'I am the *lekythos* of Tataie; may whoever steals me be blind' (*LSAG* p. 238 no. 3). A curse aimed specifically at a named individual appears at the sanctuary of Zeus on Mt Hymettos in Attica in the seventh century: it abusively declares someone to be *katapugōn*. The word recurs in later graffiti in contexts where the aim was to curse or harm the individual, for sometimes the name itself has even been scratched out.[29] Though the lead curse tablets or *defixiones* do not occur till rather later,[30] it is hard to

---

[26] Johnston 1983: 67.

[27] Powell 1989: 331–2; Johnston 1983.

[28] cf. the very early graffito on stone from Athens, *LSAG*: 76, no. 2 (= *IG* 1²: 484).

[29] Langdon 1976: 42, third quarter of seventh century (perhaps another example fifty years earlier); see Milne and von Bothmer, *Hesperia* 22 (1953): 215–24 on vituperative graffiti with *katapugōn* ('bugger'), esp. pl. 66b and fig. 2, p. 215; Dover 1978: 113, 141–3.

[30] W. V. Harris 1989: 82–3 (now from sixth century); also Jordan 1980 and 1985.

1. One of many abecedaria scratched on sherds found in the Athenian agora.
Note the extra loop in the beta. (After M. Lang, 1976, pl. 1.)

escape the conclusion that writing down someone's name rapidly
acquired a magical force.

The rest of the seventh-century finds at the Mt Hymettos sanctuary throw another curious sidelight on early attitudes to writing. A
mass of graffiti was found here many of which were clearly
inscribed on what was already a broken sherd rather than a whole
pot. Several consist merely of a personal name and the word
'ἔγραφσε', i.e. 'so-and-so wrote this', and abecedaria were dedicated later in the sixth century. It seems that the very dedication of
bits of writing was thought appropriate for this shrine. The sanctuary was dedicated to Zeus Semios, that is, Zeus of the weather
signs, and 'signs' must therefore have been interpreted to include
written signs. Hence one dedication reads, 'I am the property of
Zeus. So-and-so wrote me'.[31] It is even possible that people
brought along to the sanctuary any piece of writing they could
find.[32]

---

[31] Langdon 1976, no. 29, seventh century; see also ch. 2, no. 2.
[32] Suggested by Jeffery in her review of Langdon, *JHS* 98 (1978): 202f; cf. boastful graffiti by
Greek mercenaries in Egypt, ML 7a (= Austin and Vidal-Naquet 1977, no. 35).

Many more early pieces of writing (not to mention later graffiti), easily ignored because they seem brief and incomprehensible, may be closer to the Hymettos approach to writing than usually recognized. We do not really know whether single names denote owners' names or something more. No one really understands, for example, why so many graffiti at sanctuaries have single letters on them: perhaps the first letter of the deity (e.g. A for 'Athena'), perhaps closely 'touching on the world of the magic symbol' as has been suggested of the sixth-century graffiti from the sanctuary at Samothrace.[33] And why write only the first letter of the deity, if that is what it is? These examples underline the piecemeal and (to us) often unintelligible use of writing in its earliest stages.

Much more work needs to be done in this area (and not merely for archaic Greece). What is certain is that these curt or abbreviated graffiti are hardly the counterpart of speech, nor do many of them reflect the sophisticated world of oral poetry. The written form was perhaps thought to intensify a curse in some cases.[34] But why was there such a preponderance of proper names? Even the earliest Greek writing was perhaps being used in the competitive spirit familiar from later Greece, in order to leave one's memorial and eternalize one's own name against all others. Much archaic writing was also highly experimental and imaginative – or simply faltering. In the graffiti we catch a glimpse of a world of writing which seems barely to touch on its refined use for literature and memorial more usually associated with the ancient world.

3 EARLY WRITING AND THE SPOKEN WORD

It is time we explored rather more fully quite what the relationship was between early writing and the spoken (or sung) word. It has recently been argued extremely plausibly by Andersen that early writing in Greece was primarily used in the service of the spoken word. This was partly an attempt, long overdue, to stress the extent to which the new writing drew its meaning from earlier oral habits, rather than undermining them. However, as we have seen already,

[33] Lehmann 1960: esp. 29; see also Langdon 1976: no. 158 with comments. At Sparta, 'A' seems to be used for 'Athena'.
[34] As suggested, with interesting elaboration, by Gordon (forthcoming): see further, ch. 5 below.

early writing seems to bear almost bewilderingly varied relationships to the spoken word or to the context or object to which it is added.[35] Some of the most stimulating studies are now moving away from the somewhat one-dimensional vision of writing and its relation to orality: in so short a space here we can only get a taste of some of the more interesting possibilities.

The written word could be thought to ensure immortality through its permanence. The marked tombstones and votive offerings (not to mention other objects) which became so common from the late seventh century presumably hoped to perpetuate the name of the individual through the permanence of writing. The written message was immutable, whether it be a curse or a memorial, and the message could get across without the author's presence. As one archaic epitaph puts it so succinctly, 'To all men who ask, I answer alike, that Andron son of Antiphanes dedicated me here as a tithe'.[36] Much if not all of the early writing put on stone was meant to represent statements which were to be uttered aloud, usually in verse: so here writing is the servant of the spoken word, a means of communicating what would usually be sung or said. This seems to be confirmed by the fact that, while poets began to write their poetry down in this period, the performance remained the main vehicle of transmission. Indeed poets continue to think of poetry itself, and thus song, not the written word, as conveying immortality. The late sixth-century poet Simonides implied with scorn that his poetry would last far longer than a mere inscription (*PMG* fr. 581) (see also chapter 6). Writing here could only be thought of as a mnemonic aid for what was to be communicated orally.

Writing also seems to reinforce previous customs. Memorials to the dead, for instance, had existed before the use of writing.[37] The use of objects as mnemonic aids (without any written message) is well known, from medieval swords to boundary stones and perhaps even markers of debt in Greece.[38] At a funeral there would also have been some form of poetic commemoration, a dirge or lament.

[35] Andersen 1987, and 1989; see also Svenbro 1988a, for extended discussion of relation of writing to speech; and Pucci 1988.

[36] Late sixth-century Athens, *IG* i²: 410 = Friedländer *Epigrammata* no. 131; Svenbro 1987: 38–9 takes it as a sign that silent reading was now in existence, the 'earliest example using the metaphor of the voice'.

[37] *Iliad* 7.86–91; 23.331–2; *Odyssey* 4.584; 11.76; cf. the primitive stone markers which bear the name alone from Thera, pre-650 BC, *LSAG*: 61–2, pl. 61, no. 3.

[38] Clanchy 1979: 21–28; R. Thomas 1989: 55–59.

So when writing was added to the visual memorial in the form of an inscription, it was surely being grafted onto the older customs: after all, tomb markers did not cease when writing appeared and funerary customs in particular would tend to be conservative. Writing increased the representative power of a statue, as Pucci suggests (1988). The inscription is usually isolated in modern collections from the surrounding material, thus the total impact of the memorial is lost. But the importance of the whole memorial, visual impact, imagery as well as writing, also cannot be ignored. One good (if extreme) example has recently been analysed to reveal a subtle and complex combination of visual imagery and written inscription, which even includes the sound of the words as they would have been heard.[39] Thus when we consider the impact of writing here, the written message, added onto the memorial, does not bear the whole weight of communication. It is only one part of the memorial, albeit one which allows the poetic element of commemoration to be preserved. It may also itself have visual importance quite independent of its written context. Its very presence has been influenced by pre-literate (visual) methods of commemorating and remembering the past. Writing might preserve and perhaps exaggerate earlier customs.

This is probably why so many archaic grave inscriptions are in verse.[40] In an oral society the best hope of preservation had lain in poetic form. It was therefore obvious that when you started to add writing to the memorials, you recorded verse. It was not a simple matter of recording speech but rather of poetic utterance.

These inscriptions often seem to seek to give the inanimate object a voice. Many of the early graffiti and inscriptions on statues speak in the first person, giving the object they are written on the appearance of speaking: 'I am the cup of Nestor', 'I am the *lekythos* of Tataie', or on numerous dedications 'So-and-so dedicated me'. For grammatical reasons, these first-person inscriptions may be even more common than usually thought,[41] and they are common on archaic objects from elsewhere. But why this form? One suggestion is that the objects are conceived to have souls, to be living, and that statues used to have a 'halo of magic' – a symptom of primitive

---

[39] Svenbro 1988a: esp. ch. 1 (also 1989).
[40] See Friedländer *Epigrammata* 1948 (all translated); G. Pfohl 1967; Peek 1955; P. A. Hansen 1975, with Addenda and Corrigenda, 1985.
[41] Svenbro 1988b.

mentality.[42] Or is the written message rather a way of giving a voice to an object in a world where fame was customarily conveyed only by oral or sung poetry? Given the Greek habit of reading aloud,[43] any passer-by who read the inscription would give his voice, as it were, to the object. One epitaph actually salutes the traveller in thanks for lending his voice to the name of the deceased.[44] It is probably over-literal to object that the reader would then be forced to say aloud 'I am...' when he was not the 'I' in question,[45] for surely the readers could make the imaginative jump of attributing their own spoken 'I' to the object.

Svenbro has put forward the interesting thesis that from *c.* 550–540 we begin to find non-'ego-centric' inscriptions: the inscription may read 'This is the tomb of...', or more sophisticated, 'Here lies Aristylla: you are pretty, O daughter', where there is no conflict between the inscription as read aloud and the meaning[46] (but for 'daughter'). What this may suggest is that writing was at first used as a straightforward counterpart to speaking – writing gave statues the oral communication that human beings took for granted – as well as to allow them to explain what would otherwise be forgotten, but that by the late sixth century writing could be used in a more impersonal manner, as a third-person notice of information.

If so, this might represent a change in the relation of writing to speech and song; perhaps from the late sixth century writing was becoming more 'autonomous', more easily envisaged as an independent conveyor of information separate from oral communication. It was after all in the middle of the sixth century that prose literature began to be produced, which was at least freeing itself from the more usual archaic assumption that anything worth preserving had to be in verse.[47] But there are problems here and I doubt that the theory can be pressed too far. It cannot be a later development for writing – at least in Greece – to represent statements that would not be spoken (for instance labels, lists), precisely because the casual graffiti do this from rather early on. (Goody has

---

[42] Burzachechi 1962; *contra,* Svenbro 1988b, esp. 476–9.

[43] For non-silent reading: Knox 1968; Turner 1952: 14 n. 4; cf. Svenbro 1988a: ch. 2 (rather differently).

[44] Friedländer *Epigrammata* no. 5 = *IG* VII 2852 from Haliartos. See Rasch 1910 for the genre of conversation with the passer-by.

[45] As Svenbro suggests, 1988b; repr. in 1988a: ch. 2.

[46] Analysis by Svenbro 1988b: 470.

[47] See Andersen 1987.

examined the facility that writing provides for recording words that are ungrammatical and unrelated to oral conversation.[48]) This needs much further investigation. The change Svenbro analyses may be a phenomenon confined to the memorial alone. It is probably unwise to expect any clear-cut linear development and in any case the written word long continues to reproduce the spoken. Even the sophisticated public inscriptions of classical Athens recorded the decrees of the Assembly as they were passed with amendments added after: their form is that of the spoken decree as it was read out in the Assembly.

So to a large extent archaic Greek writing does seem to be at the service of speech, repeating verse, enabling the objects to 'speak' as if they were animate, preserving and reinforcing the pre-literate habits of the society, extending and deepening the customs of poetic and visual memorials. Yet many of the casual graffiti seem to bear a rather different relation to speech with their dedicatory abecedaria, single letters, personal names, and the writers of these seem set on exploring a quite different range of possibilities offered by the written word.

4 PUBLIC WRITING AND THE ARCHAIC *POLIS*

When we come to the impact of writing on the city-state, our evidence suggests that it was concentrated in two main areas: lists of officials and written law. We should certainly be careful not to exaggerate the extent to which the archaic *polis* used written records. In both these spheres, which I propose to focus on, we may see how the role of writing was affected considerably by social and political context and by the oral background. Both illuminate the reality of life in a primarily oral society where writing is beginning to be more important.

Our evidence suggests that writing only began to be used publicly by the city-states from the middle of the seventh century, the period in which they were beginning to develop laws and offices, and about a century after the initial private use of the alphabet. It is just possible that many of the *polis'* first written records were on perishable wood and bronze, but literary evidence actually converges with epigraphic to suggest that the first and most important

---

[48] Goody 1977.

2. (a) The earliest written law surviving on stone, from Dreros on Crete, *c.* 650–600 BC. Written on a temple wall in *boustrophedon*, it limits tenure of political office. (*LSAG* pl. 59, 1a.)
(b) Compare the later style of a law from Gortyn, Crete, *c.* 600–525 BC; in *boustrophedon*, on a wall-block. (*LSAG* pl. 59, 2.)

public writing recorded laws and that this began some time in the second half of the seventh century.[49] Zaleucus – if not entirely mythical – was the lawgiver for Locri in South Italy perhaps as early as the middle of the seventh century, Drakon established laws for Athens in the late seventh century, Solon, the best known of all, left an extensive written code for Athens *c.* 600. The first attested law on stone is one from Dreros in Crete which can only be dated roughly to 650–600 BC (ML 2). This is the beginning of that phenomenon so central to the Graeco-Roman world, the public inscription.

Sacred laws also appear early: the earliest attested so far dates to the early sixth century from Tiryns.[50] Treaties between states were put up rather later.[51] Lists of priests and public officials also seem to begin by the sixth century, though they were not kept systematically. The main evidence for some such lists are the later compilations like that of the Athenian archons. These often go back quite far and it is generally thought that these later lists would have been based on earlier records, though later 'elaboration' has certainly also occurred. A few lists of names have been found on stone from the second half of the sixth century,[52] but they may be lists of victors in the games. Public inscriptions occasionally seem to date

[49] *LSAG*: 58ff. is a very important survey.
[50] *LSAG*: Suppl. 1990: Tiryns 9a, *c.* 600–550 BC; *Archaiologike Ephemeris* 1975; 150–205.
[51] *LSAG*: 61: last quarter of sixth century, the earliest so far.
[52] *LSAG*: 60, 195: two from Sparta, two from Geronthrai.

themselves by naming an official: the existence of eponymous officials may imply the existence of a full list.[53]

Yet this is a good initial illustration of the different mentality of the archaic period. Does the dating by eponymous officials really imply a list of all such officials? Certainly later in Greece the cities had to date years by their own officials or by years in which Olympic Games were held. But in a society which relies almost entirely on memory, the eponymous official was himself a mnemonic aid, a short cut for identifying the year. Naming of officials might also have other purposes, like self-advertisement, or the recording of which officials took responsibility for a measure. So a list of officials would not be necessary here, and if anyone should need to calculate the number of years since a certain man held office, the official would probably be alive still (only a historian would want to investigate events further back). Memory is relied on at the expense of written record surprisingly often even in classical Athens – and it is always forgotten how much will disappear with time. Many of the lists of officials which historians would take as a fundamental basis for any chronology were probably only put together in the latter part of the fifth century by men with antiquarian and chronological interests.[54]

The case of written law is rather more complex.[55] Written law was widely regarded in the classical period as the basis for equality and justice (Euripides, *Supplices* 433f; Aristotle, *Politics* 1270b). Thus it is often thought that writing in archaic Greece was deliberately used to stabilize law and protect it from the arbitrary judgement of the aristocracy. Yet this idea is demonstrably most appropriate to classical Athens (see chapter 7). It is hard to believe that every citizen could or would read the early seventh-century laws, and the political history of the archaic city-states with written laws is not one of steadily increasing social justice, let alone democracy. Crete was far advanced in its publication of laws on stone (the massive corpus of laws inscribed at Gortyn in the middle of the fifth century, the so-called 'Great Code', is the culmination of a long local tradition), yet Aristotle singled out Cretan officials for their arbitrary judgement (*Pol.* 1272a36). Alternative theories have also been

---

[53] *LSAG*: 59–60; Jeffery 1976: 34–6.
[54] Especially Hippias: R. Thomas 1989: Appendix.
[55] For further detail, see my forthcoming article on writing and the codification of law.

suggested: for instance, that laws were written down as a conservative and aristocratic move, in order to forestall change.[56] The
problem is that most tend to regard the effects of writing something
down as obvious (e.g. justice, or stability), not seeing it in its social
and political context. Yet the effect of written law depends rather
heavily on the legal and political system it is part of, as well as
contemporary attitudes to writing. We need to ask who decided
which laws to write down, who enforced them, and what role
writing could possibly have in this very earliest stage of public
documents.

The picture is transformed by approaching these written laws
from the earlier world of extensive oral communication. These
communities had run on 'oral' or customary law, that is, generally
accepted norms of behaviour whose transgression would tend to be
judged (and punished) by the elders of the community (e.g.
Homer, *Il.* 18.497–508). In fact 'unwritten law' continued to be
respected and have a role in Greek society even as late as the very
end of the fifth century. When writing was applied to law in the
archaic period, not all these customary laws would get written
down: archaic written law often presupposes them and simply sets
out procedure and penalties if they are contravened.[57] We tend to
concentrate on the lawgivers, especially Solon, but most written
laws were probably not part of a 'code' at all. In other words, when
laws began to be written down, some oral law continued and there
can have been no sudden transition to the rule of written law. It is
still unclear how far the written laws ever reproduced what were
already accepted oral laws – for there is some evidence for oral laws
being sung and performed, and therefore already forming some
recognized set of rules. But the predominance of procedure in early
laws does suggest that writing was often used to record, fix, and
perhaps dignify the kind of rules that were not generally accepted
by the community.

However the written word cannot have been regarded simply as
a means for all citizens to have access to the laws, for a surprising
number of inscriptions (given our scarce evidence) betray considerable anxiety about the possible power of anyone who had control

---

[56] Eder 1986; or C. Thomas 1977: written law helped *create* a demand for equality; Gagarin
1986: 62. Camassa 1988 is an intelligent discussion.
[57] Gagarin 1986 stresses the extent of procedural law.

over the written records. The famous public curses from the city of Teos include curses against certain officials who 'do not read out the writing on the *stele* to the best of their memory and power', and they probably go on to curse anyone who does not write the words up, or who destroys the stone. Erythrai tried, probably in the fifth century, to curb the power of the secretaries and prevent them serving the same magistrate twice. These communities seem all too well aware that it was not enough simply to write up the laws, and that those in charge of writing could be very influential[58] (incidentally this also implies that few could actually read and write).

That they were right is confirmed if we consider more carefully who had responsibility for the records (written and unwritten). There is a significant continuity between the later period, when written law existed, and earlier times, and this should only surprise someone who approaches early writing purely from the point of view of later custom. Officials called *mnemones*, literally 'remembrancers', were probably fairly common. They crop up in inscriptions, therefore by definition *after* the *poleis* have started to use writing. But the name must reflect an early function of remembering. By the Hellenistic period *mnemones* are simply clerks,[59] but earlier *mnemones* were far more. Down to the classical period they were important officials and, most interesting, their role as 'remembrancers' continued even after writing began to be used. Thus in fifth-century Gortyn in Crete, the *mnemon* is closely attached to the judicial processes and acts alongside the judge as witness for a past case (*Gortyn Code*, Col. IX 31ff) – that is, his role was partly to remember court proceedings, for which there were no written records. Another inscription, from Halicarnassus in the first half of the fifth century, declares that 'what the *mnemones* know is to be binding' (ML 32.20–21). Even after the advent of writing the *mnemon* continued his role of remembering, and his memory was authoritative.

Closely related is the case of Spensithios, the scribe from a community in Crete, who was given extensive honours *c.* 500 BC.[60] The wider implications have been ignored, and attention has concentrated on his title of *poinikastas*, which refers to the Phoenician

[58] See Ruzé 1988; Teos: Herrmann, *Chiron* 11 (1981): 1–30, and ML 30; Erythrai: Inschr. v. Erythrai I: 2 and 17.
[59] Lambrinudakis and Wörrle: *Chiron* 13 (1983): 328–44.
[60] Jeffery and Morpurgo Davies, *Kadmos* 9 (1970): 118–54.

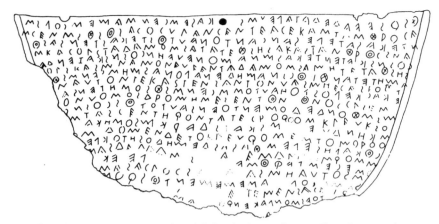

3. Inscription on a bronze mitra (abdominal guard) recording the grant by a Cretan community of extensive honours to Spensithios who is to be both scribe and 'remembrancer' for them. *c.* 500 B C (L. H. Jeffery and A. Morpurgo Davies, *Kadmos* 1970, fig. 1, side A.)

origin of writing and must mean 'scribe'. His duties are described as 'to write down and remember (*mnemoneuein*) the affairs of the city, both secular and divine'. The 'remembering' element recalls the *mnemones* elsewhere. So writing does not take over completely: the older office of 'remembrancer' overlaps with the new one of 'scribe', Spensithios continues to remember as well as to write. Moreover, he is also an exceedingly powerful man. It has become a platitude that in Greece writing was used by 'ordinary people', that Greece escaped the restricted 'scribal literacy' characteristic of the ancient Near East and that it lacked a scribal caste.[61] Yet here Spensithios is in control of all the records of the city, written and non-written, sacred and secular. He also has other non-scribal functions, extensive privileges, and his office is to be hereditary. The long cherished idea that Greece escaped the powerful scribe is fatally undermined.

Spensithios' community may be exceptional, or perhaps characteristic of Crete alone, and more evidence may yet change the picture. But even so, its implications coincide persuasively with these other instances to suggest that scribes and *mnemones* were often very important officials down to the fifth century at least, and that when the *polis* began to use writing, its officials continued some

[61] Classic statement in Goody and Watt 1968; see also Detienne 1988a, 1988b.

of the pre-literate functions and much of their authority. Writing drew its significance partly from the context and previous non-written methods of government into which it was introduced. Archaic city-states sometimes tried to supervise the powers of the officials connected with writing just like any other officials: they certainly did not trust to written record alone.

So why write down laws at all? There seems to have been an idea that writing down a law would record it in a manner that was publicly verifiable: even if most citizens could not read them, they could be read out, hence the anxiety about officials who failed to do so. Thus Solon could say (*c.* 594 BC) 'I wrote down laws alike for good and bad, fitting straight justice to each' (fr. 36 West, lines 18–20): written law seemed less amenable to manipulation than oral law (in practice it still needs interpretation). But to judge from the single laws we have on stone, an important factor was the need to record laws which were *not* universally agreed – laws about procedure, or laws controlling magistrates, like the one from Dreros, which especially needed public recognition. I suspect the act of inscribing them was to make a large public memorial of the decision. But neither this nor the public decision was quite enough to give the law effective authority. What is particularly striking is how many laws have religious sanctions, an oath, or a curse in the case of Teos, and several laws are actually dedicated to a god who is to ensure that no one transgresses them: 'May there be destruction on those who transgress it, but may the god (Pythian Apollo) be kind to him who observes it' (ML 13.14–16).[62] These archaic inscriptions are often put up near or on the side of temples. The writing itself was not thought sufficient to make the law secure, and there are attempts to associate the laws with the gods.

This places the written inscription in what is to us an alien or unfamiliar light. Some of the earliest private uses of writing were to mark dedications to the gods, as we have seen, and to write out curses (to make them more effective?). Writing preserved but it also exaggerated or dignified the act it preserved. The city of Teos actually propagated a law in the form of a curse and the officials who were to read out the inscription were effectively pronouncing a public curse on offenders. In a curious sense, then, we seem to find that the early written laws were also dedications and curses –

---

[62] Divine protection pointed out by Detienne 1988a: 51–3.

transferring the private manipulation of writing to the public sphere. The writing of a law on stone created an imposing memorial for all to see: it also created a physical object which could the more easily be dedicated to the divinity and put under his or her protection. Similarly, casting the written law in curse form was taking a well-known custom and adapting it to imposing monumental form. The monumental stone inscription was perhaps at first an attempt to give new political and procedural laws the weight and status – and, most important, divine protection – that was already accorded the unwritten laws. In this, the main and most prominent use of writing by the archaic *polis*, the impact of writing may initially have been largely that of lending monumental weight and perhaps religious authority to the new political organization of the developing city-state.

I have concentrated rather firmly on the specific evidence for the uses of writing in the archaic period – graffiti, private inscriptions, and writing in *polis* organization. This is to approach literacy from a more prosaic angle than is usual, avoiding for the time being the written products of literature. We do not see here the discovery of the self or development of rationality attributed by some to the effects of literacy. We find, rather, an enthusiasm for writing as a means of memorial, preservation or self-advertisement – enabling memory of the individual self to be perpetuated somewhat more easily. In more complex cases, writing is apparently seen as a way of magnifying or dignifying an action, whether a curse or a law. In others, the baffling unintelligibility of the written product leads one to think of magical or ritual use, or perhaps simply ineptitude.

These underlying aims were not particularly new, therefore not created by the arrival of writing. There had, for instance, been valuable non-written methods (oral and visual) of leaving memorials. Writing was at first enlisted as a further and perhaps a surer method, and it is grafted on to the customs already present. On a tombstone, as we have seen, the written message is part of the whole effect, visual, monumental, and symbolic. In the realm of law, written law is added to unwritten. It was perhaps hoped to extend the association of unwritten law with the gods to written law. In these cases what is perhaps most striking is the archaic manipulation of writing to create a physical object which can then be dedicated – the 'objectifying' of a curse, a law or a memorial.

This may be an unbalanced impression created by the fact that most of our evidence is of monumental writing on stone. The lead letters of the sixth and early fifth century recently found remind us that individuals were also writing simply to communicate over long distances – as in most other periods – and that this kind of communication could be extremely useful to commercial activity.[63] But we should not overlook the unusual or unintelligible facets of archaic writing.

Another recurrent theme is that most archaic writing was largely used in the service of the spoken word. In a straightforward sense, this means that our written evidence, which is anyway scanty, stands for just a fraction of what was actually transacted in antiquity entirely without written record of any kind. I hope to have shown in the case of archaic written law that beyond there lay a vast mass of orally conducted business, unwritten law, powerful officials whose memories alone were authoritative, not to mention attitudes to the written word conditioned by earlier beliefs, which combine to render the role and effect of written law very different indeed from what is usually thought. Written record and oral background are mutually interactive.

Archaic writing was also in the service of the spoken word in the sense that it was so often used either to represent poetry or to give inanimate objects the 'power of speech'. It would be tempting to try to trace the progressive development of writing away from the oral forms of speech – tempting, but difficult. Not only do we find graffiti from very early on which do not represent speech as such, but the written word continues in other spheres throughout the ancient world largely to reproduce the spoken word. One of the arguments of this book is that it is difficult, if not impossible, to make hard and fast distinctions between what is 'oral' and what is 'written' except in the most literal sense.

---

[63] Bravo 1974, on the lead letter from Berezan (translated in Austin and Vidal-Naquet 1977: 221–2), and *LSAG* Suppl. 1990: 429–430 for further refs.; note the lead letters apparently written by a merchant now found in Emporion: Sanmarti and Santiago, *ZPE* 68 (1987); 119–27; *ZPE* 72 (1988): 100–2; *ZPE* 77 (1989): 36–8; also *CRAI* 1988: 526–36.

CHAPTER 5

Beyond the rationalist view of writing: between 'literate' and 'oral'

I INTRODUCTION: BEYOND THE WRITTEN MESSAGE

It is frequently taken for granted that writing will be used to communicate and store information, to create documents and books which have obvious recognized functions, or generally that it will serve as a vehicle for rational thought. It is also assumed that writing simply conveys the message of its written content without any further meaning; or that written communication, almost exclusively now on paper (or disk), is predictably uniform in its significance. But such modern perceptions may not always be appropriate for the ancient world. The symbolic or non-documentary use of writing is often recognized in other cultures.[1] Scholars are strangely reluctant to see it in ancient Greece except in the unavoidable region of magic. This chapter aims to explore these neglected aspects of writing which do not conform to the straightforward (and modern) expectations of historians: one might perhaps call these 'non-literate' uses of writing, in order to underline their distance from what are usually felt to be the normal uses of literacy. Writing is not a neutral and autonomous medium.

I shall argue that Greek (and indeed Roman) writing has many forms and functions – symbolic and magical, for example – which take us beyond the message contained merely in the written content of the document; secondly, that the written word in the ancient world often has such a close relationship to the background of oral communication that it cannot properly be understood in isolation from that background; thirdly, that the use of written documents is dependent partly on experience, partly on the way writing is seen

---

[1] E.g. Clanchy 1979 on Middle Ages; Cressy 1986 (seventeenth century); Franklin 1985; Burke 1987.

by contemporaries, and partly on the very nature of oral communication: thus that the value and use of a written document (and even whether written documents are made in the first place) change considerably in the course of Greek history. It is the associations and context of writing which often determine its use, and this complexity above all which shows, as I have said, how inadequate it is simply to talk about the coming of 'literacy'.

It is perhaps particularly naive in the late twentieth century to regard all writing as having equal weight or as being purely functional. Handwritten, typed, and word-processed texts may subtly convey different messages. As Roger Chartier has recently underlined, 'form produces meaning':[2] the arrangement of a text on the page may help to emphasize the train of argument, its letter-forms convey a further interpretation. Readers may like to think they judge all printed books for their content alone, but publishers are well aware that type-face unconsciously conveys messages (avantgarde, authoritative, modern). Current attitudes, however, are crucial in determining meaning. The Nazis fostered Gothic script as a symbol of German nationalism, whereas in early modern England, Gothic type was the script of the common people, thought to be easier to read than non-Gothic. When the first printed books began to appear, certain monks were exhorted to copy them by hand, on the grounds that these printed texts were superficial and lacked the proper spiritual dimension of illuminated manuscripts.[3]

Variety of function and symbolic meaning exists even within a comparatively uniform educational system and a technology of printing which could reinforce uniformity still further. How much more should we expect it in the ancient world with its regional variety and the absence of any regular schooling for most of the population. In Greece the very alphabets remained regional until the Ionic one was formally adopted by Athens at the end of the fifth century and spread to other cities. The direction of the writing was not uniformly from left to right even in the fifth century BC. Rather than dismiss this archaic variety as the product of illiteracy, as did Havelock, it is more illuminating to look for other explanations. Archaic regional letter-forms, like regional dialects, were probably

---

[2] See R. Chartier, 'Meaningful forms', *TLS*, Liber no. 1, Oct. 1989: 8f; also McKenzie 1986; Barker 1981; Martin 1988; Chartier (ed.) 1989.

[3] K. Thomas 1986: 99 (Gothic); Clanchy 1989: 171–2, and 1983 (illumination).

a reflection of proud local identity; and the 'eccentricities' of archaic writing may rather express a refreshing creativity and imagination in writers' approach to the medium. Standardized script is by no means an obvious development and it may only become possible through some uniform method of teaching or desire for some particular form which is thought superior. The student of the ancient world must be particularly alert to this lack of uniformity because our printed texts impose the standard conventions of the modern printed page on texts which originally read from right to left, or top to bottom, or were written on lead, pottery or stone, carelessly or elegantly.[4] It requires an effort of will and imagination to conceive of writing in its ancient form.

A huge range of other functions must also lie beyond the script itself. If a written text has any other role than to be read and to convey straightforwardly the message written down – as I will argue inscriptions do and as we have already seen for the archaic period – then we are rapidly edging away from the severe rationalist view of writing and literacy so often assumed (chapter 2).

Ancient documents also have several levels of sophistication. This is most readily seen in what they leave out. Some documents (e.g. written contracts) presuppose knowledge which is simply remembered and not written down. So far from being autonomous, they cannot perform their task without backing from non-written communication. It becomes difficult to separate oral and written modes in any meaningful sense except in the most basic one (i.e. what was written down and what was not). It is surely only our modern confidence in and obsession with the written text which see documents as entirely self-sufficient.

It is therefore necessary to stress that there was a great deal of variation in the degrees of complexity in the production and use of documents. We have already seen early examples of this (chapter 4). But influential theories about the effects of literacy tend to reinforce an idea of literacy (and therefore its uses) as a timeless and neutral skill which has predictable effects. The teleological framework, in which all is tending towards a certain end, obscures the intricacies on the way. Modern attitudes to writing also interfere, and it is often hard to appreciate from the limited evidence just how alien some of the Greek uses of writing actually were.

---

[4] *LSA G*, for instance, is an exemplary production which has most texts photographed.

Here Clanchy's *From Memory to Written Record* (1979) is particularly enlightening – and it has now been joined by some other studies of the Middle Ages.[5] Clanchy traces the gradual change in medieval England from a general reliance on memory and oral communication in the early Middle Ages, to greater and greater trust in documents as proof. Medieval evidence survives of a quantity and type that have largely been lost for most of the ancient world, and we must take the implications of his subtle and intelligent study seriously. He reveals gradual changes in medieval attitudes to the written word which are reflected in the kind of written document made. Sometimes documents recorded the relevant facts very partially, either from lack of experience, or because they were relying on a background of memory and witnesses. Documents were sometimes made which were meant as records but did not actually contain the information that enabled them to be used as records later (e.g. the date). Clanchy even suggests that Domesday Book was in fact of very little use as a contemporary record despite its obsessive attention to detail: it was not referred to until it had become valuable as an antiquarian record of property ownership. Yet it had a great impact at the time as a monumental and no doubt awesome symbol of William the Conqueror's possession of England. A whole range of approaches to writing and orality emerge in which the use of writing is largely determined by contemporary attitudes to it and the associations it therefore bore, and these could sometimes give it more symbolic than practical force. Above all, the use of writing is determined as much by force of tradition as by inherent qualities belonging to the written word, and we may see how oral practices could continue alongside written ones even in a complex society.

Little study has been devoted to these kinds of questions for the ancient world, though the recent collection of papers edited by Detienne, for example, goes some way to change this.[6] But with the exception of the study of book production, changes in sophistication and use of writing have been analysed mainly as a means towards better dating of inscriptions, the relation of written documents to the spoken word barely at all.

---

[5] Particularly Stock 1983; Carruthers 1990 on memory; McKitterick 1989 on Carolingians; Saenger 1989 and 1980.
[6] Detienne (ed.) 1988; R. Thomas 1989; Svenbro 1988a.

2 THE NON-RATIONAL USE OF WRITING: SYMBOLIC, MAGICAL, AND MONUMENTAL

The visual effect of writing seems to be exploited fairly deliberately. One often gets the impression from archaic inscriptions, especially those on pottery or statues, that the writer regards the letters as an additional artistic element. An archaic sculptor was quite ready to add an inscription in large letters onto a fine statue (spoiling its appearance, one might think). But the fact that the inscription on the bronze dedication of Mantiklos, for example, is nicely balanced on the two legs in a couple of concentric semi-circles shows that artistry was being applied from a very early date to the writing as much as the sculpture (see opposite; *LSAG* p. 94, no. 1). Svenbro's interesting analysis of the interlocking imagery and meaning of statue, dedication, and language in another archaic memorial underlines how the archaic artist might be acutely aware of the whole ensemble. It is also quite usual to find the names of figures written in 'decorative antithesis', that is, one name written from left to right, the other from right to left. This may even have been extended to whole inscriptions facing each other across a path.[7]

There were often practical reasons for the choice of placing and direction of inscriptions (as Jeffery stresses, *LSAG* pp. 46–7). But the facility with which the archaic writer could turn from writing from left to right to retrograde, which used the mirror image of letters, rather suggests that the letters were conceived more like artistic motifs, shapes which could be turned either way like the motifs on vases. The system of *boustrophedon* (writing 'as the ox ploughs') did eventually die out in most places by the end of the sixth century, with conservative survivals in the fifth. This may have been from the 'natural' pressure of right-handed writers (*LSAG* p. 47). Yet it had still lasted over two centuries, and this must have been for other reasons than pure practicality. It is curious that this diversity and artistry are usually thought, if noted at all, to be simply characteristic of archaic inexperience; yet the aesthetic handling of writing surely continues into the high classical period and beyond.

Take magical manipulation through writing again. There is rich evidence for this in the classical period as well as the archaic.

---

[7] Svenbro 1988a: ch. 1; *LSAG*: 44–6; inscription layout suggested by Wilhelm 1909a: 31ff; Threatte 1980: 53.

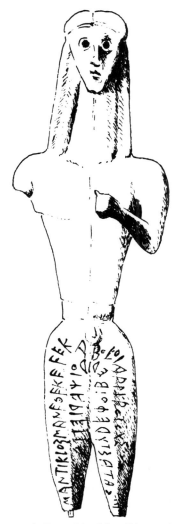

4. A large bronze statuette dedicated by Mantiklos to Apollo. The inscription, in *boustrophedon*, starts (outside leg) and ends (inside leg) in the bottom left-hand corner. It begins 'Mantiklos dedicated me' and hopes for some return favour from Apollo. From Boiotia, *c.* 700–675 BC (Drawing by the author after *LSAG* pl. 7, 1.)

Writing was used for public curses and for private curse tablets (or *defixiones*), which seem closer to magic spells. Curses, whether private or public, must date back long before writing was used for them, and the efficacy of the curse did not depend on its being written. They were usually spoken, like the horrific imprecations of Oedipus. In a sense, then, this was another case where writing was grafted on to an earlier (and continuing) oral feature. But why, then, write them down?

Curse tablets on lead of the fifth and fourth centuries seem to have used the written form at least to intensify the curse, and perhaps to make it even more effective. Writing enabled the ill-wisher to give visible and physical form to the curse, and that then created further possibilities: in an extreme example of such opportunities in the Old Testament, a curse was written out and then eaten. I know of no such examples from classical Greece, but in Byzantine times a ground-up icon might serve a similar purpose.[8] Many curse tablets had nails stuck through them, perhaps on analogy with the magical use of dolls. Greek curses also played around very imaginatively with the actual letters.[9] They did this far more than Roman ones, and it was probably the tradition of such varied forms and methods of writing in archaic Greece which suggested this kind of manipulation. Reversing, upturning or deforming the text of the curse in various ways, the writer may have been using this technique as 'sympathetic magic',[10] or more likely as a metaphor for what he or she hoped would happen to the individual being cursed. The very form of writing was being brought into the process of cursing beyond the actual words of the curse.

Public curses expressed and authorized by the community were fairly frequent in Greece.[11] Even in the sophisticated democracy of Athens, a political curse was proclaimed before meetings of the council and assembly (Demosthenes, 19.70). Demosthenes in the

---

[8] Numbers 5.23–4 (drinking a curse); other examples in ch. 2, pp. 19–20. cf. however, the woman in a Greek romance compelled to undergo a chastity test wearing the written text of the oath she had sworn, Achilles Tatius 8.12 (cited by W. V. Harris 1989: 219). Byzantine icon: Cormack 1985: 47.

[9] See the corpora, Wuensch 1897; Audollent 1904; additions in Jordan 1985, and 1980; Preisendanz 1972.

[10] But see Tambiah 1973; extreme examples in Wuensch 1897: nos. 77, 84, 85, 102.

[11] See Ziebarth 1895 and Vallois 1914, for the evidence; also Latte 1920: 61–88; Parker 1983: 191–206.

middle of the fourth century could call the foundations of democracy 'the curses and laws and safeguards' (*arai kai nomoi kai phylakai*, 20.107). Aristeides cursed those who medized in the Persian Wars (Plutarch, *Life of Aristeides* 10). The public curse was an attempt to use religious sanctions to protect the city, and though usually uttered by someone in authority, it tended to express the will of the people against a common danger. Some were inscribed on stone, though apparently not in Athens. The public curses from Teos are the most famous, uttered against poisoners, anyone who interrupted the corn imports, and various other offenders against the *polis*. They were engraved on stone well into the fifth century,[12] and the custom continued later.

But again, the formal inscription seems to intensify as well as to record the curse. When Delian magistrates in the middle of the third century BC put the same curse on both sides of a stone, they seem to assume that repeated writing would be doubly effective just like repeated spoken curses.[13] The Tean curses actually include imprecations against anyone who destroys the stone on which the curses are engraved. The inscription itself seems to be attributed with some kind of symbolic or actual power. Certainly Plato's image of a public curse on an inscription in his imaginary Atlantis really grants some kind of power to the inscription.[14] This is less surprising than it might appear, for stone inscriptions even without curses often seem to be regarded in a symbolic and monumental light (below), and this would have influenced the treatment of curses. An inscribed curse became a permanent, visible, and public object of warning and reminder.

Studies of writing in other societies often find (or assume) that writing is used in a magical way mainly by the illiterate or semi-literate, on the grounds that only they would regard the written word with sufficient awe.[15] This seems less appropriate for the ancient world – unless one categorizes the whole of it as semi-literate, which begs the question. The Tean curses were set out by the presumably rather educated elite of the city. As for private curses, 'judicial curses' were used in classical Athens against politi-

---

[12] ML 30, *c.* 470 BC; *SEG* 31.985D; Herrmann *Chiron* 11 (1981): 1–30, of *c.* 480–450 BC.
[13] Vallois 1914: esp. 250–2: other examples in Ziebarth 1895.
[14] *Critias* 119d–e: see Vallois 1914: 268–71.
[15] See e.g. Holbek 1989: writing for the illiterate is a particularly powerful kind of speaking: Burke 1987: 31–2 on the illiterate in early modern Italy. A subtle inversion of the usual argument in Harbsmeier 1988.

cal opponents and apparently by the upper classes.[16] So the magical or religious significance of writing is hardly confined to the lowest rungs of the citizenry and could coexist, in Athens at least, with a comparatively sophisticated ideal of the public visibility of the Assembly's decrees.

Moreover, a wide variety of writing materials was available and each kind probably had its own associations. The Greeks had several choices: pottery (broken or whole), papyrus, leather or parchment, lead, wooden tablets either whitened or with wax inlay, bronze, gold or stone – and in addition, the whole range of objects from marble pillars to bronze figurines that they chose to adorn with writing.[17] All are well attested, though gold is obviously very rare, papyrus survives mainly from Egypt, and wax tablets survive without their writing. But while we may regret their relative survival chances (and forget about those less durable than stone or pottery), it is also important to ask whether any logic lay behind the choice of any one material. Comparative examples make this extremely likely. More material is being excavated every year, and without any definitive study of this distribution, any remarks must be provisional. Yet we can immediately see some kind of symbolism and association.

Lead, for instance, was habitually used for curse tablets from at least the sixth century onwards. This was perhaps because it was cheap, foldable, and could be re-used. But, like the jumbled letters of the alphabet common in curses, its very cheapness probably had further metaphorical value for the curse. It could be folded and thus 'sent' to the Underworld like a letter, buried or left in a crevice. But it was perhaps the idea of the foldable letter which was dominant in the use of lead. It was used for private letters (now attested from the sixth century), perhaps important ones which needed folding, and also for questions delivered to the oracle at Dodona, plaques recording loans in Corcyra (*c.* 500 BC), and for the curious records of horses from the Athenian 'cavalry archive'.[18]

---

[16] See Faraone 1985; Jordan 1980 and 1985.

[17] See Turner 1968: ch. 1 and *LSAG*: 50–8 for general picture; for papyrus, Turner 1968, and N. Lewis 1974.

[18] Lead loans: Calligas, *Annual of the British School at Athens* 66 (1971): 79–94: Corinthian calendar: *BCH* 100 (1976): 600; lead letters: see *LSAG* Suppl. 1990: 429–30, and esp. Bravo 1974; for letter from Emporion, see references in ch. 4, n. 63 above. Cavalry archive: R. Thomas 1989: 82–3, and Kroll 1977.

Letters could also go on potsherds: these were used extensively for any casual pieces of writing, from lists, notes, graffiti, abuse, and labels, to the Athenian institution of ostracism.[19] Pottery was, as we have seen, the ancient equivalent of our scrap paper, for it lay around in quantities. Whatever the truth is about the price of papyrus,[20] we can at least be sure that such imported material was far more costly than potsherds and used with comparative care. Even in Egypt where papyrus was produced, private 'archives' written on sherds are common. One of the earliest texts so far found of a fragment of Sappho's poetry was on a piece of pottery from Egypt dating from the third century BC (fr. 2, Lobel–Page, *Poetarum Lesbiorum Fragmenta*).

Wooden tablets (*pinakes*) are more elusive, as their written texts have been lost.[21] Wax tablets were used for schooling, and we would expect their content to be totally ephemeral.[22] Whitened boards (*leukomata*) were common, traditionally used in Athens for proposals of decrees to go before the assembly; they may also have been the tablets which eventually went into the state archive (how many decrees went up on stone is unclear).[23] Wooden boards were important for many public notices, and a passage in Plutarch's *Life of Pericles* about the tablet holding the notorious Megarian decree of perhaps 433/2 BC (*Per.* 30.1–2) may suggest that they could be used for publicly visible records as well as inscriptions. The fifth-century Erechtheum accounts note the purchase of 'two boards on which we inscribe the accounts' (*IG* I³ 475, 476). For all we know, wood may have been used more extensively instead of stone for inscriptions in early times, since Solon's laws were on wood, just as early statues were in wood, later to be replaced by stone.

But the most impressive documents went on metal or stone. Gold was reserved for precious religious texts: gold leaves have been found in graves of the fourth and third centuries, inscribed with instructions about the after-life.[24] Bronze also seems to have had some religious associations – though, as with lead, its use was quite

---

[19] See the collection from the agora, Lang 1976.
[20] See most recently, W. V. Harris 1989: 94–5, 194–5.
[21] Though see Turner 1968: 7, for rare cases where the writing can be read.
[22] It is surprising to find that they are attested in the Roman archives: Williamson 1987: n. 15; cf. the receipts on waxed tablets from Pompeii, Andreau 1974, Finley 1985: 44.
[23] For some refs. to *pinakes*, *sanides*, Wilhelm 1909a: 240–249.
[24] *LSAG* Supplement 1990: 429; Janko 1984; S. G. Cole 1980.

varied. Bronze plaques were used widely for public decrees in certain areas of Greece, the Peloponnese, western and central Greece, Thessaly, but not Athens. In Athens, decrees of *atimia* (deprivation of full citizenship) often went up on bronze *stelai*, as did copies of international treaties which were to be erected at the sanctuary of Olympia.[25] But stone was above all the material of memorial: used for funerary monuments from early on, stone became the medium for permanent documents which were to be displayed publicly. However, it was more than permanence that the stone *stele* offered. The testimony of ancient writers combines with the overwhelming evidence of surviving inscriptions to suggest strongly that their symbolic significance was also fundamental.

Inscriptions survive in massive, though uneven, quantities from the ancient world. Apart from papyri from Egypt, they are the historian's main documents. Their texts are published neatly according to modern printing conventions, and they come to seem just like any other documents. Most publications give the dimensions of an inscription, but it is easy to ignore their appearance, height and bulk; and since few give photographs, the visual arrangement of the text on the whole *stele* is often lost. Yet stone was only one of several materials for writing, inscribing was expensive, and some cities used inscriptions far more than others. Why were they used?

This is a question surprisingly seldom asked, or if asked, seldom answered. Little work has been devoted to the precise role of inscriptions,[26] which is indeed usually taken for granted. We can dismiss the idea that they were simply used in proportion to the local availability of marble. But it is always important to notice what kinds of texts go up on stone (as well as what is never written down at all). The details of the inscriptions themselves, and the way Greek writers treat them, make it clear that they were often thought of primarily as symbolic memorials of a decision rather than simply documents intended to record important details for

---

[25] As in Thuc. 5: see L. Robert *Collection Froehner*, I, *Inscriptions grecques* (1936): 47–8, and *Hellenica* x (1955): 289–90; Stroud *Hesperia* 32 (1963): 138–143, esp. n. 1; Franciscis 1972, for bronze tablets in the Locrian Olympieion.

[26] See however, R. Thomas 1989: ch. 1.2, mainly on Athens; Detienne (ed.) 1988; Klaffenbach 1960; and on the Roman side, Williamson 1987; Macmullen 1982; Meyer 1990; Corbier 1987 (and epilogue below).

administrative purposes. It is striking that even fourth-century Athenian politicians may refer to a treaty or a decree of the Assembly in its stone form – not in the abstract, nor to the archive copy. Moreover, they seem to refer to the stone as if it actually *were* the treaty or decree. If the inscription is erected, the treaty is in force. To take down the stone would be to annul the treaty (Dem. 16.27, on a treaty between Athens and Thebes); if a decree is revoked, the public inscription must come down. If a new decree supersedes earlier ones, the inscriptions of those earlier ones must go: hence in an Athenian law about coinage of 375/4 B C, it is added, 'If there is any decree inscribed anywhere on a *stele* which contravenes this law, let the secretary of the council pull it down'.[27] Even if there are copies in the archive, the public ones on stone are what matter. A form of *damnatio memoriae* may also operate which extends to any copies in the archives (e.g. as specified in the decree of Patrocleides, Andocides 1.77–9; cf. *IG* II² 11.13–15, names on register and copy). Many inscriptions actually forbid their own defacement, most famously the Tean Curses we have already encountered.[28] Inscriptions sometimes record why they are put up. An honorific decree from Erythrai in the 330s declares that two *stelai* are to go up 'so that all may know that the People knows how to return appropriate thanks for the benefits conferred on it'.[29] In classical Athens it is important for something to be inscribed in stone 'so that anyone who wants may see it'. Here is the Athenian idea of democratic accessibility and accountability. But in one inscription we find the surprising idea that the oaths and the alliance should be inscribed on a *stele* 'so that the oaths and alliance should be valid'.[30] The public erection of the inscription was part of the treaty. Attributing 'symbolic significance' can often be very vague, but we see here rather precisely how the inscription is a monument or memorial whose public presence and very existence guarantee the continuing force of the decision it records. Hidden archival copies are simply not enough.

[27] R. S. Stroud *Hesperia* 43 (1974): 157–88, lines 55–6; for further documentation, p. 185 and R. Thomas 1989: 45 ff.
[28] Other threats against defacement: M L 17 (*c.* 500 B C), Mitsos *BCH* 107 (1983): 243–9 (fifth-century Argive); see also M L 49 (*c.* 445 B C).
[29] *Die Inschriften von Erythrai u. Klazomenai* I (Bonn 1972), eds. H. Engelmann and R. Merkelbach, no. 21.
[30] Tod 1946–8: II 142, treaty of 363/2 B C.

This last observation leads us into treacherous waters, firstly because the Greek system of archives varied considerably from state to state and in different periods, secondly because the value of the documents in the archives has been controversial. This is yet another case, though, where modern presuppositions about documents are simply unhelpful. Finley has pointed out certain features of the ancient treatment of documents which make them inadequate for modern economic analysis (1982). But most modern scholars assume – partly from later practice which may not be relevant – that the copy in the archive is obviously the 'original' and most important (e.g. the epigraphist Louis Robert).[31] Yet in classical Athens, which offers most evidence for what contemporaries thought of documents, not only do politicians cite inscriptions as authoritative records, but the same attitude to the inscriptions persists even after a central archive has been established at the end of the fifth century. In other cities and certainly down to the fifth century, it is quite probable that the inscription was the only official copy kept of a law or decree (and why make a frail papyrus the authoritative copy when you had the law on stone?). The image of the 'stone archives of the Greeks' is not inappropriate, at least for the archaic and classical centuries. It was essential that these documents be publicly visible so that someone could read them if necessary.

I would not want to deny that the written contents of inscriptions were read if they were needed. But this is not incompatible with their having a monumental and symbolic role as well. Some otherwise curious features of inscriptions fit into place if we see them as more than merely documents: for instance the visual element already noted, or, more fundamental, the very selection of what went up on stone. It is well known, for example, that the famous fifth-century 'Athenian tribute lists' recorded in minute detail, not the total tribute collected from the Athenian empire, but the one sixtieth dedicated to the goddess Athena. In other words, the lists were for the goddess and were inscribed for some kind of sacred reason. Similarly with the immensely detailed building accounts, or the equally intricate inventories of temple treasures which could well go up on stone every year and are not quite inventories in our

---

[31] E.g. J. and L. Robert, *Bull. Épigr.* 1961, 154 = *REG* 74 (1961): 140–1; Robert 1961: 459; Wilhelm 1909a, cf. Posner 1972: 99 for a good example of confusion.

sense.[32] Are these seen as public records of the performance of public duties which are accountable to the people or to the gods? The notorious 'Coinage Decree' issued at the height of Athens' empire has elaborate instructions for its propagation by herald: the stone copies were therefore not merely to give information (M L 45). Or note the way so many Athenian inscriptions record exactly the decree as it was read out in the Assembly, and then the amendments just as they were added: an exact record of what was decreed orally, whether or not the amendment contradicts the bulk of the decree.

The very habit of using inscriptions seems to have grown out of a context where stones began as monuments or mnemonic aids. Inscriptions were not always thin slabs of stone covered with writing on one side. Some of the very earliest inscriptions are short stubby pillars which look more like boundary markers and have writing on all four sides.[33] It has been suggested tentatively that stone pillars were a development of the use of natural standing stones.[34] Many early inscriptions are tall and narrow and taper at the top. In fact, the use of boundary markers and the later but very primitive 'mortgage *horoi*' of fourth-century Athens with their minimal inscriptions (see below) seems to confirm that the use of stone slabs to bear writing grew out of the earlier use of large stones as non-inscribed markers or mnemonic aids. We should also remember that certain written texts were often added to temple walls (as in seventh-century Dreros), or even natural rocks (Thera), which may have helped the transition to flat stone slabs. Other early legal texts were put on marble columns (*LSA G* p. 55), so that again the written text was added to some other object (which might bear its own significance), not given its own separate 'document'. The written text did not stand on its own.

The early development of the inscription does not of course necessarily determine its later use, but the later classical inscriptions clearly do have a certain monumental quality. It is also important to emphasize that there is by no means a straightforward progression in Greek inscriptions towards greater legibility.[35]

---

[32] Inventories and accounts: see Knoepfler (ed.) 1988; Burford 1971; Georgoudi 1988: 234–5.

[33] E.g. from Crete and Kleonai: see *LSA G*: 52.

[34] *LSA G*: 52.

[35] For punctuation of any kind: e.g. Immerwahr 1990: 168; Threatte 1980: 52–73 (arrangement of texts), 73–84 (for the many possibilities for punctuation, some simply decorative).

Some of the earliest have careful word-division (perhaps a Phoenician legacy[36]) as well as punctuation, and are easy to read. But regular word-division seems to die out, and the fashion of inscribing the individual letters in a grid or chessboard pattern (*stoichedon*), which developed in the later sixth and fifth centuries, meant that the end of the line seldom ended with the end of a word and words would be divided very strangely. The effect, especially in the high period of the Athenian empire, is highly ornamental, impressive, and monumental. Little attention has been devoted to the implications of these various changes in layout, certainly nothing comparable to recent discussion of the implications of layout in the printed works.[37] Yet surely the main aim of *stoichedon* was monumental, and it came to be associated with certain kinds of inscription, perhaps, as the prestige script of Athens, with the Athenian Empire itself. It may be no coincidence that the first state decree of Athens surviving on stone is partly in *stoichedon* (*I G* I^3 1), the next extensive one (*I G* I^3 4) in full *stoichedon*.[38]

The monumentality and longevity of stone lent certain associations to the stone inscription. The Greeks were quite well aware that an inscription was valuable and impressive, hence the occasional attempts to limit them. Citizens in Athens from *c.* 500–*c.* 430 BC seem to have been forbidden large funerary inscriptions and monuments unless they had died in war, Sparta forbad written named tombstones for all except those who had served the state by dying in war or childbirth.[39] This would further suggest that in the classical period at least there were attempts to associate the inscription still further with the *public* activities of the state.

3 ORALITY AND THE WRITTEN WORD

We have already encountered cases where the written word cannot satisfactorily be separated from oral communication (chapter 4). This chapter has argued so far for what one may call a 'non-literate' use of the written word (in an attempt at least to dis-

---

[36] Martin 1988: 66–7, citing James Fevrier.
[37] See Martin 1988, and works cited in n. 2 above.
[38] For *stoichedon*: Austin 1938; Threatte 1980: 60–4; for irregularities, M. J. Osborne 1973; and for democratic associations, D. M. Lewis 1984.
[39] See Stupperich 1977: 71–86; Richter 1961: 38–9: 53–5; Cicero, *De Legibus* 1.26.64. Plut. *Life of Lycurgus* 27.3, and Cartledge 1978, n. 71.

tinguish our own expectations of literacy): features in the use of writing which are not dependent on the simple content of the writing alone, but where other elements, symbolic, religious, visual, contribute to the function of the written text. Oral communication can be seen to influence the use of writing more specifically, and these cases underline still more how misleading it is to separate the oral and literate, to use 'literate' as if it were self-explanatory, and to see literacy as antithetical to 'orality'.[40]

Oral modes of proof, memorial and communication, as we have seen (chapter 4), did not cease with the coming of writing, and actually influenced its adaptation. The Greeks marked graves long before writing was introduced, and the mound and grave-markers are effectively non-written types of memorial or mnemonic aid. Writing was added to these as presumably yet another marker, but the earlier system was not eliminated altogether. With tombs and dedications, the written element merely adds a further and probably more efficient way of remembering the individual or marking the gift. Oral methods continue to be trusted, just as oral tradition was considered the perfectly normal source for the past at least till the fourth century and to some extent beyond. Similarly with contracts, which would have witnesses. A non-written means of security, they were probably the most important and trusted part of the contract, to which writing was only an additional safeguard. One can trace fairly exactly a gradual change in fourth-century Athens by which the written part of the contract begins to be trusted more, though it is not until the later decades that we find a written contract completely without witnesses. This would confirm that earlier the written part of the contract had been a minor element (or absent altogether). An Athenian speaker can complain of a written agreement made in court, in which witnesses only had been taken for certain points, that his opponents 'affirm the validity of the parts to their own advantage even if they are not in writing, yet deny the validity of what is against their interests unless it is in writing' (Isaeus, 5.25). This underlines rather neatly, through the rhetorical manipulation, that an agreement was built up partly from the memory and security of the witnesses, partly through the written document.[41]

---

[40] Most forcefully argued in general terms by Finnegan 1977 and 1988.
[41] For further detail on contracts, Pringsheim 1955; R. Thomas 1989: 41–2.

The two main points which emerge here are first that the written element is inseparable from the non-written (the stone, tomb, witnesses); and secondly that the use and function of the written element are influenced by the earlier (non-written) custom and the continuation of the oral methods of memorial and proof. This is a particular case of the general argument that the use of literacy is affected by current customs and beliefs, as propounded by Street and Finnegan (see chapter 2).

This influence can also be seen quite concretely in the very content of written records. Perhaps the most extreme example, where we have enough literary evidence to explain the background, is that of the notorious 'mortgage stones' (*horoi*) put on a man's land to mark debts borrowed on the security of that land in fourth-century Athens. The stones' very presence is proof of the debt, but they bear short and enigmatic inscriptions identifying creditor and sum of money but neither the debtor nor (usually) the date. As documents, therefore, they are badly incomplete, but then the written text was not the sole proof. The whereabouts of the stone identified the debtor, the witnesses could fill in the rest. Hence the written element could be extremely brief[42] (by contrast, the lead loan-tablets from Corcyra do mark the name of the debtor (see n. 18)).

Similarly one may compare the almost total absence of dates on any written texts (of laws, decrees, treaties or epitaphs) before 500 B C and many thereafter: for even when officials are named, as they are on Athenian decrees, they are not always the ones which would most easily identify the year (e.g. the eponymous archon). At the time, officials and citizens knew when a law or decree was passed, and why would they need the date anyway? (In the inscriptions of other cities, inclusion of 'dating' formulae is even more haphazard.) But in any case the officials of each year were themselves, if need be, mnemonics for the year, not the other way round; a further explanation for what appears to be lack of interest in dating as such. Our own obsession with dating is partly the product of an antiquarian and record-conscious society which thinks it *may* possibly need the date one day – or else does not think of persons as mnemonics. Archaic inscriptions are particularly compressed and enigmatic: they presumed that everyone knew – and would

[42] See further, R. Thomas 1989: 55–9; Finley 1952.

continue to know – what they were talking about. Whether memorial, mnemonic aid, or record of a law, the written text was not thought of as the sole and complete record of its subject matter.

Often, documents may have (for us) a curiously incomplete and frustrating form, not so much because they presupposed a non-written background, but because they exactly reflected what contemporaries thought was the aim of the inscription. For example, the bare lists of the war-dead erected in the Kerameikos by the Athenians each year give (to us) extraordinarily little information about the circumstances of death. Their meagre 'factual' content is usually noted only as a curiosity, if at all. But the form of these inscriptions in fact exactly corresponds to the official ideology of the city expressed in the ceremonial speeches delivered at the public funeral: this includes an ahistorical and heroic anonymity which demands little attention to the precise circumstances of the campaigns, or to any individual acts of bravery.[43]

The practical implications are extensive. What we have to envisage is a world in which most activities were carried out without writing – from the dirges at funerals to the conduct of everyday business; when writing was added to these it was usually in a subordinate and supplementary position. It might add an extra form of proof, preserve some information more exactly against the vagaries of memory, or record parts of a business transaction.

The commonplace that the written word in the ancient world, particularly the written record of literature, was meant to be heard rather than read silently may be a related issue. In one sense the written word was subordinate to the spoken, thus perhaps rather a mnemonic aid for the recollection of what was to be communicated orally than a text to be read in its own right. Even when exact and accurate transmission of a literary text was intended in the late fourth century, the tragic texts in question were read aloud by the secretary of the *polis*:[44] that is, the written text was apparently transmitted orally, a possibility little discussed in the controversy about the transmission of oral poetry totally without writing.[45] It can be argued that the production of Greek books was commonly effected by means of dictation.[46] A Greek often read a text in order

---

[43] For this ideology, Loraux 1986, and R. Thomas 1989: ch. 4.
[44] Plut. *Lives of the Ten Orators, Lycurgus* 841F.
[45] Ch. 3 above; Finnegan 1977; Goody 1987: chs. 3 and 8.
[46] From the presence of phonetic errors: Skeat 1956.

to memorize it, particularly if it was a poetic work. The concept of 'phonetic literacy' used by Saenger for the Middle Ages may be useful as I suggested (pp. 9, 13): that is, the possession of enough reading ability to puzzle out the syllables aloud in order to learn a text by heart, or to say prayers aloud, but not to read silently with immediate comprehension.[47] Or as Flory has pointed out, an analogy with the modern use of a musical score to learn a piece seems appropriate[48] – reading to learn by heart and recite aloud was surely fairly common. There may be further similarities with the Middle Ages, where literacy was very often an aid for reading and even memorizing what a person was already fairly familiar with (e.g. the Bible). It is not often noted that Plato's famous description of primary-school teaching, usually cited to show the teaching of literacy,[49] actually says that the children are given poems of good poets to read and learn *by heart* (*Protagoras* 325e). Rhetorical speeches, which certainly got written down and published from the late fifth century, were meant to be learnt by heart: orators and litigants wished to give the appearance of speaking extempore,[50] and the written text was therefore only an aid to recollection and memorization. It is in Aristotle first that one finds extensive discussion of literary and philosophical works in terms of the written text.[51]

If certain kinds of written texts really were thought of primarily as mnemonic aids for what the people concerned knew already or were going to learn by heart, that might explain why written literary texts were so unhelpful to the reader right down to the Hellenistic period (they were not, in fact, dissimilar from inscriptions). Without word-division, accents or much punctuation, even poetry was written out as if it were prose (as we know from the fourth-century papyrus of Timotheus).[52] It was not till the work of the Alexandrian scholars in the third century that accentuation and better punctuation were devised, and the now traditional arrangement of poetry, showing the metrical units on the page, was

---

[47] Saenger 1989; see also Carruthers 1990 for wider context of memorization.
[48] Flory 1980: 20–22, taking the musical analogy from Hendrichson 1929: esp. 184; see also the examples in Harris 1989: 86–7; and illustrations on pottery, Beck 1975.
[49] E.g. by Knox 1985: 13.
[50] Hudson-Williams 1951.
[51] Knox 1985: 11.
[52] For books, see Turner 1952, 1968, and 1971 (2nd edn 1987); Kenyon 1951; Immerwahr 1964.

invented by Aristophanes of Byzantium (*c.* 257–180 BC). Even so, it is doubtful that books with full punctuation were ever widespread in antiquity.[53] We should be very wary indeed of assuming that our own difficulties in reading ancient texts were shared by the Greeks and Romans, but I would tentatively suggest that it is no coincidence that such techniques to help the reader were developed in the highly scholarly milieu of the Alexandrian library and very little before; and that the comparatively unhelpful features of earlier written texts (including documents) were closely related to the fact that they had rather different functions – as monuments, documents for possible reference, or mnemonic aids for works which it was assumed would be heard and read aloud rather than read silently. Turner has tentatively linked the extreme variability and inaccuracy of our earliest papyri (i.e. early or middle of the third century BC) to a carelessness about exact quotation in a culture which was used to 'the cut and thrust of oral dialectic'; respect for the authority of the written text grew with the Alexandrian scholars and the Roman period.[54] We can perhaps go one step further. For the silent reader and scholar, the written text is all-important, because there is nothing else.

4 DOCUMENTS VERSUS RECORDS?

Finally we return to the question of documents and records in their own right. I have stressed the monumental or symbolic features of the written word and its interaction with oral communication, in order to get away from the modernizing and over-literate approach which is so common. We may now see that when we speak of ancient 'documents' these must include a whole range of texts, such as inscriptions, whose primary functions might not have been 'documentary' and administrative. But symbolic use hardly rules out other functions – as many seem to assume. Many documents were made in the Greek world which had some kind of administrative use and archives became increasingly common to store them. The Athenian inscriptions themselves had to be consulted. Even

---

[53] The question is controversial: see Turner 1968: esp 90–92; Pfeiffer 1968: 178–81; N. G. Wilson, *CR* 19 (1969): 371; Marrou 1965 (6th French edn): 602 n. 30 – punctuation mainly for educational purposes; for Latin, Wingo 1972, G. B. Townend, *CQ* 19 (1969), 330–3.
[54] Turner 1968: 107–9.

the most administratively functional types of document sometimes seem to lack crucial elements, yet we can hardly assert that they are all totally 'symbolic'.

The phenomenon we seem to be dealing with here concerns the variability of documentary forms and practice: what is written down in the first place, how it is used, how it is regarded, and how it is set out. Clanchy's study of medieval England reminds us that the practice of making documents may develop considerably in intricacy and attention to detail; it is not necessarily immediately obvious what to put in a text and how to arrange it. As his study makes clear, there is a crucial distinction to be made between records and documents: making documents and using them later were quite separate stages which by no means followed inevitably from one another. Documents might be – and were – written out which became useless as records, either because the habit of using written records was slower to develop than the habit of making documents, or because the documents themselves (e.g. early charters) had been laid out in such a way that they lacked the information necessary for them to be usable for future reference. (Compare the growing elaboration of texts and their formats which can be discerned in detail in the ancient Near East.[55]) The creation and use of documents are as variable, and as dependent on contemporary attitudes to the written word, as I have argued the use of literacy is in general.

This variety is immediately and crudely visible in the ancient world (indeed it parallels the wider variety in the use of writing): the gulf between the Spartan state (which kept almost no records) and Athens in their use of writing is as large as that between classical Athens and Hellenistic Egypt under the Ptolemies. Sparta's distrust of writing may partly have been in conscious reaction to the extravagant proliferation of inscriptions created by the Athenian democracy. Or compare fifth-century Gortyn in Crete, renowned for its extensive 'law code' engraved on its theatre wall and a long tradition of legal pronouncements on stone, with Corinth whose oligarchy has left almost no public documents at all, or Paros which in the third and early second centuries had a complicated system of keeping records but also a severe problem with their falsification.[56] Ptolemaic Egypt, on the other hand, had a

---

[55] Larsen 1989; esp. 137.
[56] Lambrinudakis and Wörrle 1983; see further ch. 7 below.

highly sophisticated system of record-keeping: yet this was hardly surprising, for Egypt had had a scribal tradition and a complex and centralized bureaucracy for many centuries before the Macedonian conquest (the impression of greater complexity cannot simply be the result of the fact that papyri tend to survive only in Egypt, for *ostraka* – which would survive elsewhere – were also used with the same elaborate proficiency).

But we also need to keep sight of the level of complexity or sophistication in the very *use* of documents once they have been made. When so much has been lost from the ancient world, historians tend to be grateful for any documents preserved (usually on stone), and may assume that they simply have a tiny random sample from a mass of documents which were once made and carefully stored. Certain information must, it is thought, have been preserved in archives, and the city officials would surely have been able to look up the relevant documents in a manner recognizable today. A useful synoptic work on ancient archives, for example, tends to interpret according to modern archival ideas and take for granted that ancient documents were stored and used in a perfectly recognizable (though slightly more primitive) modern manner.[57] A picture of reasonably effective and blandly modern archive-keeping in the ancient world can thus be produced through quite well-meaning assumptions about the keeping of records when the ancient evidence gives out, or through misinterpretations of what evidence there is. Yet if certain documents simply were not made at certain periods in the Greek world, or were made but not used later, the whole edifice collapses. We can occasionally be fairly sure that certain pieces of information were either *not* written down or recorded only in ephemeral form: for example Athenian officials kept records of debts owed to the state only until the debt was paid, then the record was erased and there was simply no further evidence of that debt (Aristotle, *Athenaion Politeia* 47.2–48.2). Even in the most complex system of all, that of Ptolemaic and Roman Egypt, the theory could easily break down in practice: the immensely complicated system of officially made and registered contracts, receipts, and duplicate copies was evaded occasionally

---

[57] Posner 1972: e.g. (despite his own proviso) 156: 'In the best tradition, Zenon must have realized the wisdom of clearly identifying each letter before filing it'; contrast Finley 1982 (repr. 1985: 34–6). Georgoudi 1988 has intelligent discussion of the danger of anachronism.

by alternative methods, or vitiated by the corruption and negligence of the officials themselves.[58] It was the Athenian example which underlined Finley's polemical article (1982) on the sheer non-existence of certain kinds of documents and therefore economic data in the ancient world. He was mainly concerned to show that ancient governments simply did not keep records for the purposes of economic or statistical analysis. But one can see this as part of a much wider pattern. More attention could also be given to the consequences of such a dearth of documentation, to what it meant (say) to rely entirely on your own witnesses and the private record of a debt.

Take the case of Athens. Here, as I have shown elsewhere,[59] there is a quite definite increase in the production of written documents (not merely inscriptions) in the first half of the fourth century as Athens became more 'document-minded'. By the middle of the fourth century politicians seem to show a new awareness of the value of the documentary record which can be found also in the works of historians and in Aristotle's concentration on the written text (chapter 5.2 above). So though Athens' democracy had been making documents since _c._ 507 BC, they had been kept in a certain disorder for many decades. A 'central' archive was created only in the last decade of the fifth century, and yet still politicians and historians did not make impressive use of its contents (nor were these particularly well organized) till rather later. The 'rule of law' was heavily dependent on individual memory and commitment. Athens became 'document-minded' before she became 'archive-minded'. The evidence from Athens enables us to form a comparatively refined picture of this development, but we should surely look for similar (or dissimilar) processes elsewhere.

If making a document is a quite different (and simpler) process from using it again, then we should expect to find many documents made which were not actually of much use as records. I suspect this is the case at least with some of the numerous Athenian decrees which in the fifth century were recorded and distributed in such a haphazard way that they helped necessitate a revision of the laws at the end of the century. There was no adequately organized system of storage or routine system of checking to ensure that new decrees

---

[58] See (e.g.) Turner 1968: ch. 8.
[59] R. Thomas 1989: ch. 1.2.

did not contradict even older ones (this was left to individual citizens). Quite apart from that, 'unwritten law' was also prestigious and valid. Even in the fourth century, politicians still tended to rely on memory and oral communication where one might have expected written proof. Was this because the records (decrees, for example) were still of an inappropriate form for easy reference, or because documentation was still not regarded as the most impressive form of proof? Probably both, since both factors are related to the overall degree of sophistication in the use of written texts (and having appropriate personnel looking after the records must also be important: in Athens they were slaves). Either way, there is a clear gap between the making of records and their reuse.

So when a large body of documentation is found to lack crucial details or a sensible order – as with the temple inventories – or when a massive body of records appears not to be referred back to as one would expect, it is not necessarily a sign that the texts in question were purely symbolic. It may rather be the result of inexperience and ineptitude in making the text in such a way that it tells one what one may want to know at some future date (and the ancient world certainly did not keep records of everything indiscriminately, as we sometimes seem to do). Compare the gaps and problems in the so-called Gortyn Code which show how far it is from being a code; or in the Roman sphere, the curious deficiencies of the records of the Arval Brethren.[60]

A great deal probably depends on the degree of professionalism involved. The intricate and impressive labelling and filing system in Egypt which could cope with huge numbers of documents was kept running by professional scribes and a system which had grown up over centuries. One of the cases where the system broke down involved the negligence of the superintendents of the depository of records in the Arsinoite nome (or administrative district) in the late first century A D.[61] These were unpaid officials performing the job as a liturgy, and this use of non-professional officials may have been a widespread problem in Roman Egypt.

The general problem of accessibility and reuse is closely related to the internal organization or appearance of documents. What are

---

[60] Beard 1985.
[61] Corrected by Mettius Rufus in A D 90; Turner 1968: 143–4, P. Lugd.-Bat. vi, Nos. 14, 15, 17, 24. See N. Lewis 1986: 123.

the implications or intentions behind changes in format? The format may determine the future effectiveness of a document, and lay-out may affect the way the reader interprets the text, as recent studies of the printed presentation of literature suggest – where the progressive breaking up of the page into paragraphs and indentations have served to make the flow of argument immediately visible on the page.[62] In the ancient literary world, as we have seen, it was not until the appearance of professional scholars in the third century B C that helpful alterations were made to the appearance and arrangement of written literary texts. These alterations presumably aimed at greater clarity and efficiency (even if changes in punctuation were piecemeal and mostly used for educational purposes). But scholars are reluctant to speculate on their implications and on earlier procedures.[63] It may be significant that the principle of listing in alphabetic order, so useful in so many spheres, was almost certainly developed by literary scholars, and apparently not used much by administrators in Egypt.[64] As for ancient documents, as opposed to literary texts, we must unfortunately rely mainly on inscriptions for the classical period, but then the stone texts probably reproduce written texts which were actually used, and papyrus documents begin to appear in Egypt from the late fourth century. This kind of analysis has been done in some areas, particularly that of Athenian decrees, but more often as a way of charting, organizing, and dating the evidence than with any further sociological questions in mind.[65] It is time the wider implications were assessed.

Some features of inscriptions are suggestive. For instance, the fine tradition of legal inscriptions at Gortyn in Crete seems to show a development of punctuation and layout, of which the 'Great Code' is only the culmination.[66] Athenian decrees become increasingly formulaic in the fifth century as the democracy set such store by the recording of its decrees, and have an increasingly standardized number of officials at the head of the decree. Athenian *polis*

---

[62] Martin 1988, on the printing of texts from the sixteenth to eighteenth century; Clanchy 1979 on medieval manuscripts.
[63] But see Flory 1980.
[64] Daly 1967: 45–50.
[65] E.g. Threatte 1980; Immerwahr 1990; Henry mainly looks at formulae and language: 1977, 1979.
[66] Gagarin 1982: esp. 129–30.

inscriptions are notably more regular in their alphabetic, linguistic, and orthographic usage than private inscriptions, and a recent study of Attic script finds that it is only in the fifth century that a distinction between public and private script develops.[67] This regularity seems to be the result of greater professionalism and greater familiarity with documents, and may have made the retrieval of decrees from the archives a little easier. Yet it can be exaggerated: there was no absolutely uniform system of prescripts, nor of abbreviations in Attic inscriptions until the Roman period; and if there was a shortage of space the last letters of a word would simply get left off by the stone cutter.[68] It is still difficult to believe that they were very easy to find again in the archive, given the possible variations in prescripts, and the arrangement of the archives.

The brevity, terseness, and sheer obscurity of archaic laws must have made it easy in later generations to argue about the meaning of the law. The lack of word-separation made verbal ambiguity quite possible, and interpretation of such ambiguity became a regular subject for rhetorical discussion at least in the Roman Empire.[69] The ancient habit of setting out accounts not in double entry form, but in the form of narrative must have made it hard to measure profit and loss, if that were ever the aim.[70] The Athenian convention of setting out a decree and then adding further proposals and amendments without altering the substance of the decree (mentioned above) – not to mention the use of *stoichedon* – may reveal something about their view of the role of the written record: it also makes the process of finding out what decision was eventually taken even more elaborate. One is reminded of the Domesday Book, so impressive, so complete, yet so difficult to use for reference at the time it was made.

On the other hand, the elaborate system in Egypt seems to have facilitated the reuse of documents, partly because the Ptolemaic kings insisted on the use of professional scribes to draw them up, and the ubiquitous scribal system in Egypt is generally regarded as the cause of formulaic uniformity and clichés in so many docu-

---

[67] Immerwahr 1990; see W. V. Harris 1989: 50, 77 for evidence of official secretaries.
[68] Threatte 1980: 99; Henry 1977. W. C. West (1989) argues for greater organization.
[69] Russell 1983: 69–70.
[70] Mickwitz 1937 accordingly argued that the main aim was to record transactions accurately and reveal any negligence or dishonesty; cf. de Ste. Croix 1956; Macve 1985; Rathbone 1991, rather differently, on Roman Egypt.

ments and letters. It would again be interesting to see just how far the presence of professional scribes was responsible for refining and extending the sophistication of the written document.

This is a vast and complex area, but the possibilities are very rich, and so far as I know, little work has been devoted explicitly to these problems from a perspective that does not take for granted a fairly standard modern and 'document-minded' approach to written texts.[71] Yet the idea, for example, that writing and literacy further political control and economic exploitation (Lévi-Strauss) needs exactly this kind of detailed attention if it is applicable to the ancient world (or anywhere else). If we do not know what documents were made and how those that were made were applied, such a statement can only have the most general value, if any at all.

[71] See however, Ruzé 1988, Georgoudi 1988; W. V. Harris 1989.

CHAPTER 6

Orality, performance, and memorial

What does the prevalence of oral communication imply for later Greek culture? In what way does it really change our understanding of the ancient world? Is orality a useful tool of analysis? Is it largely specific to a given culture, like literacy (as I tentatively suggested for the field of Homeric epic)? Much recent work on Greek orality has been connected with the stylistic study of specific Greek authors. But it is time to get beyond stylistic analyses and move into areas more difficult to discuss but equally important to any understanding of oral communication, that is, the performance and context of Greek literature (and attention is increasingly turning to this). We need also to consider more sympathetically how oral communication may have affected not so much individual style or mentality, but our own evidence and judgements. Many of our problems in understanding Greek culture stem simply from the lack of accurately preserved material.

I ARCHAIC AND CLASSICAL ORALITY: ORALITY AS A TOOL OF ANALYSIS

Most discussion of orality and oral communication in Greece after the period of the Homeric poems suffers from an inability to detach itself from the lines of debate used for Homer, and accordingly concentrates on formulaic style. This approach even affects the chronological period for which orality is presumed to be relevant.

Thus a dominant strand in work on post-Homeric orality has taken literary style as the main feature – or result – of orality and oral composition (the distinctions are sometimes left unclear). Though the identification of formulaic style with pure oral composition can, as we have seen, be seriously undermined, such features continue to be identified in early Greek literature, notably in the

Homeric Hymns, Hesiod, and Archilochus.[1] Debate then revolves round the problem, which is probably insoluble, of when these early poets began to write down their works, and how far they improvised in performance. On a slightly different level, the historian Herodotus is also analysed as an 'oral writer', on the grounds of his style. Fluent and leisurely, it has certain archaic features (like ring composition) which some have seen as specifically 'oral'.[2] The 'oral context' of Herodotus has bulked large, for instance, in a recent important collection of papers on Herodotus, and his position at the 'transition from oral to written form' has been suggested as the most profitable direction for Herodotean studies[3] – apparently mainly envisaging stylistic analysis.

Much of such analysis is extremely interesting on the literary level. But what seems to deserve more critical questioning is whether these stylistic features can simply be attributed to 'orality', the 'oral context', the prevalence of performance – all fairly vague terms – or to the literary and stylistic tradition then dominant. The pursuit of an oral style deflects attention away from other features: for example the nature of the performance itself (which is very hard to determine, but as recent work shows, extremely important); the character and role of the audience; the relation of the written text to the performed version; the social and political context.

The coming of literacy has also been linked with a change in mentality, reflected again in the grand sweep of Greek literature: the oral gives way to the literate at least by the time of Plato in the fourth century.[4] In this scheme, Homer represents the anonymous oral epic, traditional and lacking in a sense of poetic individuality or creativity. Hesiod's didactic poetry shows more sign of the self, a corollary of literacy, for he mentions his own affairs and personality (though the kind of poetry Hesiod was writing was probably as old as the epic genre[5]). The flowering of self-consciousness, the expression of individual feelings and views, are to be

---

[1] Janko 1982 makes a particularly good case for development of language over time; Notopoulos 1964 failed to distinguish sufficiently. cf. Brillante, Cantilena, Pavese (eds.) 1981. For Hesiod: Gentili 1988: 19ff; Hoekstra 1957; Jensen 1966; see also G. P. Edwards 1971, arguing with caution that Hesiod's style is oral; M. L. West 1981, based on a somewhat subjective idea of what a literate style looks like. For Archilochus: Page 1963.

[2] E.g. Flory 1987: 16.

[3] Connor in *Arethusa* vol. 20 (1987): 259; also Lang 1984, Flory 1987; Nagy 1987, for Hdt. 'the *logios*'; cf. Murray 1987, 1988.

[4] Most influentially argued by Havelock 1963, 1982; see also Gentili 1988: esp. chs. 1 and 3.

[5] Griffith 1983, against Havelock 1963 and 1982.

seen in Greek lyric, especially Sappho and Alcaeus. Literacy, it is argued, tends to develop a sense of the individual and the individual artist. Contrary to the anonymity of an oral society, it creates introspection and self-consciousness.[6] This schema is reminiscent of Snell's *The Discovery of the Mind* (1953), except that it attributes the changes to literacy. The similarity reminds one that, like any 'history of ideas' drawn from the great works of ancient thought, it is applicable (at best) only to a very small portion of the population. It also suggests that orality, once discovered, is in danger of becoming a ready-made explanation for all previously noted developments in ancient literature. This is all the more regrettable when Goody and other scholars in non-classical fields now insist that literacy is not a sufficient explanation for mentality by itself.

We need not dwell anew on the shortcomings of this view of the effects of literacy. Most seriously, the crudity of these schemes is made clear by their inability to accommodate the fact that practically all ancient literature, however compressed in style (e.g. even Pindar or Thucydides), would have been heard and not read silently. They also tend to ignore the continuing importance of oral communication after Herodotus (or alternatively, Plato). There seems to be an almost irresistible tendency to start from the length of time writing has been available and to read into the available material the appropriate degree of orality and literacy (features of archaic style like paratactic structure are therefore assumed to be expressions of orality simply because they coincide chronologically[7]).

In the sphere of prose writing the fallacious argument is particularly striking: Herodotus, as I have said, is credited with an 'oral style' but with little discussion of what this might mean, or how we know (or alternatively seen as representative in some way of a transition from orality to written form).[8] Yet Thucydides' prose-style (and I concentrate on style, not content) is usually classified as the product of writing and a different 'literate' mentality, intended to be read rather than heard like Herodotus' *Histories*. His famous claim to have produced 'a possession forever' has been taken as a sign that he was relying on writing.[9] Yet Thucydides

---

[6] Goody and Watt 1968; Ong 1982; some criticisms of this view in Andersen 1987: 38–41.
[7] E.g. Gentili 1988: ch. 3, esp. p. 48.
[8] But cf. Lang 1984.
[9] E.g. Knox 1985: 8; also Hartog 1988: 285–6, 304.

cannot have been referring to anything so basic as a reliance on written texts (hardly new in the late fifth century). While he might think he was writing for future generations, so did the earlier poets (below), and Herodotus' preface also suggests he was trying to preserve memories of the Persian Wars before they faded. I am aware that any comparison with Herodotus may be thought contentious, since Thucydides' style was notorious for its denseness and difficulty even in antiquity, and it is hard to believe it could be readily understood on a single hearing (or perhaps even after several). But on the other hand, his complex antithetical style is closely akin to that of the contemporary Sophists, for example Antiphon and Gorgias, and they most certainly set great store by performance and recitation. Scholars do not usually, in this context, discuss rhetorical prose (Sophistic and fourth-century oratory), designed for oral delivery but largely developed later than Herodotus, so one can only guess that mere chronological sequence is being allowed to influence the analysis. Is Herodotus credited with an oral style primarily because his sources are mainly oral, and because in both historiographical and chronological terms he is seen as Thucydides' predecessor?[10]

More generally, any crude vision of the relationship between orality and mentality seems too schematic to help us really understand what it was like to live in a society which relied so heavily on performance and the living voice. These features of orality have also deeply affected our own perception of the ancient world, because they have determined what has been preserved. Awareness of the oral side of Greek culture reminds us of what was not written down, the selectivity of the written texts, and thus the context (social, political or cultural) of the Greek literature still extant, which is curiously easy to forget. It helps to strip away too 'bookish' an approach to the written texts,[11] and to re-emphasize the value and circumstances of the performance. It reminds us of the musical element in ancient poetry which is almost impossible to recover and which was itself transmitted largely without written record. It thus gives our picture of the Greek world an extra depth and dimension which it would not otherwise have.

[10] E.g. S. West 1985; Nagy 1987; Lang 1984; Flory 1987: esp. 16 where he says that since Hdt.'s approach is largely oral we need 'special poetics'.
[11] See esp. Gentili 1988: ch. 1.

One example where appreciation of orality is particularly valuable concerns the survival of literature. Our literary texts are the result of two levels of selection, most obviously the process of selection by which so much ancient literature was lost in the Middle Ages. But at an earlier level of selection much was never written down in the first place. Some form of oral poetry (oral at least in the sense that it was not written down) continued long after Homer but simply never got preserved at all.

The many oral poems composed by contemporaries and predecessors of Homer are frequently regretted. But they cannot be the only songs lost to the evanescence of the spoken word. Even epic poetry apparently continued to be composed and recited well into the Hellenistic period,[12] but little is preserved and much was probably not written down at all, either because it was bad, or taste had changed, or, more likely, because these later poets performed to a more popular audience. High literature had moved on to other genres. Modern practitioners of 'oral history', working from extensive interviewing, remind us that even now the views and experiences of lower reaches of society are often not represented in written documents at all; many oral historians see their task as preserving what these people have to say which would not otherwise have been graced with written record.[13] In the very different social context of the ancient world, even more was simply never recorded in writing.

Certain magic spells, for instance, were not written down until the first century BC, but they must have existed earlier.[14] Popular literature is especially tantalizing. At funerals for instance, lamentations (*gooi*) were always sung, usually improvised by the women. The few fragments we have are a mere drop in the ocean. Even the more formal *threnoi* or dirges would mostly have remained unrecorded: the *threnoi* we hear about are by famous poets like Simonides who were commissioned by aristocratic families, and took care to preserve the texts.[15] The mass of dirges, composed simply by the female relatives of the dead, were unrecorded. The extensive 'oral composition' by Greek women is unrecognized in the written literary record. We hear about work songs in Homer: those of women at the loom (*Od.* 5.61; 10.221) or at the vintage where a boy

---

[12] Jensen 1980: 125 on wandering epic singers in the fourth century.
[13] See P. Thompson 1988.
[14] Winkler 1990: 173.
[15] See Davison 1962 and Herington 1985: ch. 2, for ideas about how texts were preserved.

sings to the workers (*Il.* 18.570–72).[16] Numerous 'hymns' of ritual significance must have been performed in the shrines all over the Greek countryside. The whole substratum of what is usually called folk-poetry, folk tradition, or popular poetry, remained largely unrecorded except for a few curiosities noted by antiquarians. A more aristocratic example, the drinking songs of the symposium, were usually totally ephemeral and improvised on the occasion by the participants. A few were written down and published – perhaps for their political nature or especial popularity. But of course most disappeared without trace.[17]

These poets and singers remain anonymous for the prosaic reason that they did not produce written records: not because oral poetry is by its nature traditional and anonymous, a romantic and rather arrogant notion of modern scholars. Oral poets seem to be quite conscious of their creative individuality as singers: witness the Yugoslavian singers who are quite aware both that they are telling traditional tales, 'singing the same song', and that they are embellishing them according to individual skill and taste.[18] But however conscious their composition, these men and women left only memories behind when they died and must have merged rapidly into a half-forgotten blur – and that is the real problem. Written records can be forgotten too, but reliance on memory alone to preserve artistic achievements or the past is almost always less effective than reliance on the written word. For it depends on the many fallible links in a human chain, all of whom have to remember accurately and pass on the tradition for it to be preserved. The works of a dead poet were not preserved easily, and certainly not accurately, without writing: therefore 'anonymity' is the result of bad memory rather than lack of individual consciousness.[19] What gets written down is also partly determined by social and political factors. Poetry that celebrated a *polis*, for instance, was surely more likely to be preserved by the *polis*. Pindar's ode for Diagoras of Rhodes (*Olympian* 7) was written up in golden letters in the temple of Lindian Athena:[20] the chances of an individual poet's texts

[16] Redfield 1975: 30; note also the *threnos* at *Iliad*, 24.720–2; paean to Apollo, *Iliad*, 1.472–5, 22.391; hymn at *Iliad*, 18.493; *linos*, 18.570; marriage song of some sort, *Odyssey*, 4.17–19. cf. marching songs at Sparta (in text p. 121). See Alexiou 1974 for modern Greek laments.
[17] cf. Aly 1921, and Trenkner 1958 for folk-tales and popular story-telling.
[18] See ch. 3 n. 53 for refs.
[19] Against anonymity of the oral poet, Lord 1960: ch. 2, Finnegan 1977: 201–6.
[20] Gorgon *ap.* schol. Pindar, *Olympian 7 init.*

being lost were that much smaller. Patrons surely had a share in preserving the works they helped finance and the more prominent the patron, the more chance that copies of the texts could circulate.[21] In the realm of modern field research, the perceptions and omissions of the researcher may be to blame – as it has been put succinctly, 'anonymity' is usually the result of the folklorist not having collected the songs.[22]

There is also an opportunity to appreciate the features of 'orality' especially characteristic of Greece (avoiding any prescriptive view of orality), but which may not be part of our own experience of oral communication. For orality must be culturally specific, its manifestations largely if not entirely formed – like literacy – by the specific nature of the society in question. There remains the tension, as with literacy, between the characteristics which may be generally applicable, and those specific to the Greek world. But the implications and expressions of 'orality' in the Greek world deserve individual attention in their own right. If we take the example already mentioned, the complex, antithetical, and rhetorical displays of the fifth-century Sophists, a typical modern reaction would be (as it certainly is for Thucydides) that these pieces were far too complex to be taken in and appreciated by listening alone. Yet we know quite well that many of them were performed to listening audiences who apparently loved the convoluted and extravagant stylistic devices: Gorgias' style took Athens by storm in 427 BC, and Thucydides makes the politician Cleon chide his Athenian audience for their excessive liking for 'clever speakers' (3.37). The Athenians, characteristically, seem to have thought themselves more experienced in rhetoric than other Greeks (e.g. Dem. 18.149). Perhaps they missed certain subtleties only appreciable on the written page, but the evidence indicates that ancient audiences were more attuned to listening carefully to complex prose (or poetry) than we are.

It would be most valuable to explore further the *specific* expressions of Greek oral communication. Indeed to see it in this way may perhaps clarify the whole topic. Geoffrey Lloyd has pointed to the public and competitive nature of so much of Greek life, in order to help explain the peculiar development of Greek thought and science.[23] One could go further and see these as characteristic

[21] See Herington 1985: ch. 2, and Appendix 6, who collects the evidence.
[22] Jensen 1980: 14.
[23] Lloyd 1987: 70–8; 1979: ch. 4; note also Andersen 1987.

elements of Greek orality. It was not just that Greek debate, poetry, discussion were oral: they were also couched in an intensely competitive atmosphere which was both public and open. Highly characteristic of oral communication in archaic Greece are the performance and singing of poetry, Herington's 'song-culture' (1985); this seems to give way to a greater emphasis on oratory (and in a political context). One could say that expressions in performance of Greek orality shifted from poetry to oratory – for neither is any more 'oral' than the other. The social or political context also changes: there may be a slight shift from the private symposium as a milieu for oral performance and the transmission of memory of the past to the public sphere (agora or public festival).[24] Another central element may be the vivid awareness of the importance of the memorial, whether poetic, oral, written, or stone, for preserving the memory and fame of individuals – and this too changes in emphasis and expression. Beyond this there are further specifics to explore, the continuing stress on improvisation in oratorical performance, the relation of performance to written text, the precise role of the written texts alongside the oral discussions in the philosophical schools, the role of memory and memorization.

2 ORAL TRADITION

Certain features of oral transmission are seen most vividly in the realm of oral tradition. They underline strikingly the problems of preserving information without the help of writing, thus they illustrate how some of the features which may seem characteristic of societies without writing are features, not of any generation in the present, but of the past as seen by the present, an effect of the progressive wearing down of memories.

Oral traditions are traditions concerning the past, according to one definition, which have been handed down for more than one generation. Everything we know about oral traditions in the modern world suggests that they are extremely unstable unless there are specific, formal or ritual mechanisms to preserve them accurately. Everything we know about ancient Greece suggests that it had very few such formal mechanisms.[25] As for the character of

[24] Rösler 1990 (making a connection with the origins of historiography).
[25] On oral tradition generally, Vansina 1985, Henige 1974 and 1982, Miller 1980. For Greece, R. Thomas 1989 (where further documentation can be found); Murray 1987, and now Evans 1991. Van Groningen 1953 is also interesting.

the traditions, one cannot produce hard and fast rules, but what has emerged from the vast and sophisticated anthropological literature on oral tradition is that oral traditions, dependent on their human transmitters and on human memory, do not get passed on accidentally: the reasons for remembering them and passing them on are fundamental. They select the tradition and may well change it in the process: the reasons for change can be cultural, social, political, or ideological. Similar effects have been analysed by psychologists working on human memory.[26] The process of selection and change is a complex interweaving of social, political, and presumably psychological factors. For instance, if a society sets very great store by the possession and identity of mythical ancestors, memory and traditions will attempt to record such ancestors, and the prestige attached to them will exert conscious or unconscious pressure upon those transmitting the traditions. For aristocratic families in Greece, it was precisely the legendary ancestors who brought most status, and who were accordingly most susceptible to manipulation. In the Athenian democracy, undemocratic and therefore unsuitable ancestors were quietly set aside and eventually forgotten. If traditions are fundamental to the current social and geographical organization of a group (tribe, city, family), anthropologists find that they may change with alarming rapidity when the social divisions themselves change. For instance legendary genealogy is often assumed to mirror the present-day social structure exactly, and when that structure changes, so do the genealogies in the tradition, a process attractively called 'structural amnesia' (the classic example is among the Tiv of Nigeria).[27] 'Memory' may be a dynamic process. The character, content, and rate of change of oral traditions are therefore intimately related to the society transmitting them, as they are constantly refined, honed or 'deformed' by the beliefs, needs, and values of the society. Both oral tradition and memory are culturally determined, and that, again, forces us back to the specifics of Greek culture.

How and what did the Greeks know about their past? The remote past, the past of legendary and Homeric heroes, was visible everywhere, preserved in the Homeric epics and other poetry, and

[26] Baddeley 1976 and 1983 are good introductions; Bartlett 1932; P. Thompson 1988 has interesting discussion of the implications for history; Halbwachs 1950 on the collective memory.

[27] Bohannan 1952; Goody and Watt 1968: 31–2.

represented in art. It was the legends and heroes of individual cities and aristocratic families which were sung in poetry, at festivals, cults, competitions. But for the recent, non-legendary, past (not a distinction often made by Greek writers), there was very little beyond the loose oral traditions. The specialized story-tellers or 'official remembrancers' who have preserved traditions in African states simply do not seem to exist in Greece – Greek *mnemones* remembered other kinds of information, and there was a much looser series of stories, myths, traditions, and anecdotes passed on by various groups and individuals, certainly, but with little official control.[28] Until Herodotus, writing in the third quarter of the fifth century, the recent past seems not to have been regarded as an obvious or common subject for prose or poetry – though it now appears that historical subjects were the themes of elegiac poetry,[29] and Athenian tragedy had occasionally dealt with recent events (notably Aeschylus' *Persae*). The shadowy prose-writers who were the predecessors of Herodotus seem to have concentrated their energies on legendary traditions.[30] Either the recent past was simply not thought as worthy of literary record as the remote legends, or the Greek cities were content to rely on general memory and tradition for their history.

Herodotus states in his preface to his *Histories* that he is publishing his researches 'so that the memory of what men have done shall not be destroyed by time, and that the great and wonderful actions of the Greeks and Barbarians should not lose their due fame'. It is possible that the Persian Wars themselves were the catalyst for the development of historiography (as we would call it). The Wars changed the political configurations of Greece and did much to influence the formation of Greek identity. It was perhaps only once the Greeks had a recent and largely communal achievement that ranked in Greek consciousness as equal to the Trojan Wars and was an important factor in inter-state rivalry that they began to realize recent memories were fading and that recent history was worthy of literature. Herodotus' *Histories* set themselves quite consciously in the Homeric and poetic tradition of recording and giving fame (*kleos*). But it was only now that this could be done outside the realm of poetry and oral tradition.

[28] See for the problem of 'logioi' and Herodotus as a 'logios': Evans 1991: 95–104.
[29] See Bowie 1986 and now Rösler 1990.
[30] See e.g. Fornara 1983, Drews 1973.

What, then, were the Greek oral traditions, and what kind of memories did they preserve? This is a deceptively simple question. It is obviously very difficult to uncover oral traditions: we hear only about the ones which were lucky enough to get written down, and the very process of recording them may have involved structuring and reshaping them. But for all that, evidence of traditions can be found in the poets, plays, orators, and historians – Herodotus, of course, being the most energetic collector. On the general level there were all kinds of stories, folk-tales, gossip, which look like oral traditions. Murray (1987) has stressed the Ionian story-tellers (of which he sees Herodotus as an offshoot). Men boasted of their military prowess in the messes at Sparta, or the private symposia elsewhere. One of Xenophanes' poems evokes a scene in which they sit around over wine and food, and ask 'How old were you when the Mede arrived?' (fr. 22 Diels–Kranz). But these were often casual reminiscences which might not survive long. For more resilient traditions, as anthropological work shows, it is helpful to isolate the main groups or institutions which would transmit and preserve the traditions. The traditions that get passed on will tend to be those attached in some way to those groups or institutions with sufficiently developed identity and power to foster traditions: thus traditions were attached to aristocratic families, cults, festivals, and city-states. Each group remembered selectively and passed down even more selectively. Families tended to remember their most prestigious forebears. Cult traditions clustered around their foundation legends.

City-states seem to have concentrated on their legendary past, until the Persian Wars created another focus for *polis* pride and competition with other cities. Political struggles against earlier tyrants were also a powerful symbol of *polis* identity. Military achievement, especially in the Persian Wars, bulked large (and, of course, survives in Herodotus' narrative). Athens may have been exceptional in having a democratic forum to air and preserve traditions, but even at Athens we find a predominantly militaristic and patriotic emphasis in the official traditions. It was a recurrent theme of the Greek *polis* to stress collective achievement above that of individuals. It was therefore left to aristocratic and other families to preserve their own individualistic traditions. Even Miltiades, the victorious general at the battle of Marathon, was not given the hero's official glorification at Athens that we might have expected.

This *polis* ideology consistently obliterated individuals and individual achievement.

To the Greeks living in this kind of world, then, their image of the past was, from our point of view, much simplified and rather shallow. Beyond the remote legendary past, whole centuries had simply dropped out of the collective memory, chronology was exceedingly fluid, and periods, events and individuals could get merged together. There is little evidence to suggest that many traditions concerning the historical past went back more than three or four generations: there was a narrow band of tradition for the very recent past and little more.[31] The selectivity and re-formation of memory ruthlessly smoothed down the traditions which managed to survive. Those that had the best chance were the ones most important to the Greek *polis* as a whole and most favourable to the collective beliefs and values of its inhabitants. In the course of time, oral traditions therefore tended to express collective myths of identity.

For an historian like Herodotus, researching the past from oral sources, the most accurate sources were therefore eye-witness accounts. Once you moved beyond these, you entered a realm of traditions which might, or might not, have been remembered accurately, which might have been elaborated by fantasy and the techniques of story-telling, and which were very hard to verify. Herodotus tells us that his principle was to record 'what was said' (*ta legomena* 7.152.3), whether or not he believed it. Serious historians in the ancient world tended to concentrate on the history of their own times.

We should not underestimate the existence and vitality of individuals' memories of recent events. They survived long enough for Herodotus and Thucydides to collect a vast wealth of information for their histories – presumably mainly eye-witness accounts. For a generation or two a mass of recollections and anecdotes was available for anyone who wanted to collect them. Nor should we underrate the speed and efficiency with which information *can* pass around within a population. This is worth dwelling on since I have been stressing the changeable nature of oral tradition. A recent modern survey gave documents to a randomly selected group of people and instructed each to get the document to a 'target individ-

---

[31] See R. Thomas 1989: esp. ch. 3.

ual' by sending it to the person he or she knew who was most likely
to know the target and instructing that person to do the same. The
target individual was reached in between two and ten intermediate
links (five being the most common).[32] This shows how fast information (especially confidential information) can spread through a
modern population. We can probably expect to magnify this rapidity for the ancient city-state where even the largest, Athens, had
only 30–40,000 adult male citizens and a total population of
c. 250,000, and where political discussion was conducted in an open
Assembly of citizens – and of course for a society in which the
spoken word was in any case the usual way of spreading news.

But oral tradition itself tended towards the expression of collective uniformity and collective memory. This was primarily the
inevitable result of the ruthless selectivity and cutting down of
memory as it was passed down from generation to generation.

3 POETRY, MEMORY, AND PERFORMANCE

The poet

The poet in archaic Greece was both sage and philosopher, preserver of memory and performer. His position might range from
that of resident bard living in a nobleman's house, like the Homeric
Demodocus, to that of the peripatetic poet visible at panhellenic
festivals and dependent on commissions (like Simonides). Or he
might be an independent aristocrat, like Solon of Athens who presented his poetry as influential lawgiver and thinker. Audience,
patronage, social position, and the changing political atmosphere
of Greece must all have affected the nature and context of their
poetry.[33] But the main point, for our purposes, is that until prose
works began to be written towards the end of the sixth century,
verse was the medium for anything worth preserving. Even in the
fifth century the early Greek thinkers Parmenides and Empedocles
put their arguments into verse. This illustrates not only continuity
of expression, since verse continues to be used for the beginnings of

---

[32] Cited by Paulos 1989: 29–30.
[33] See remarks in Gentili 1988, chs. 8 and 9; Detienne 1967; Jensen 1980: ch. 4; Nagy 1989;
also Nagy 1990, on Pindar; Goldhill 1991.

philosophical thought, but also the centrality of poetry, and therefore of performance, in archaic Greek culture.

This may partly be explained by the importance of poetry for
immortality in a world of predominantly oral communication
which we have already encountered. Ancient writers are acutely
aware of the importance of memory. As Plato implies in the *Phaedrus*, verse was particularly useful because it could be easily memorized.[34] In other words if something was worth remembering and
passing on, it would be better remembered if it was in verse. Sappho's confidence in the survival of her poetry lay in its continuation
in song, not in its existence as a written text (fr. 193 L–P; fr. 55 L–
P).[35] Indeed it is a commonplace in the study of oral tradition that
anything passed on in verse has a better chance of accurate transmission.[36]

Poetry also provided fame or *kleos*, a much-repeated idea. Ibycus
says to Polycrates the tyrant of Samos that he will gain undying
fame through song,[37] though, as Goldhill shows, the context and
nature of this kind of claim should be differentiated more carefully.
If you have done great deeds, you will deserve to be the subject of
song,[38] and it is presumably your only chance of fame and memory
after your death. Poetry is assumed to confer this, surely, because
the poet's treatment lifts a subject above the mundane and commonplace into the realm of literature, and the poet sings of your
deeds, therefore (provided the poetry is good) they are spread
around. Poetry was itself also memorable and memorizable. It is
interesting that poetry is several times contrasted with sculpture as
a better kind of memorial, for it moves around. Pindar claims that
he is superior to a sculptor because his song can move around
announcing the victory:

> I am no maker of statues
> Who fashions figures to stand unmoved

---

[34] *Phaedrus* 267a, 'indirect censures, which some say [Evenus] put into verse to help the
memory'; see Plut. *De Pythiae Oraculis* 407f–408a, similarly.

[35] Andersen 1987: 39f.

[36] Modern Somali nomads regularly put complicated messages into poetic form: I. M. Lewis
1986: 139.

[37] *PMG* 282 (a) 47f. See M. L. West 1988, and p. 153 for other refs; Goldhill 1991: ch. 2.

[38] '*aoidimoi*': see Redfield 1975: 32–5, 38 generally on *kleos* and song; Goldhill 1991: ch. 2
(with further bibliography); cf. *Od.* 3.203–4, Telemachus, of Orestes, 'The Achaeans will
carry his *kleos* far and, for men to come, his song': *Od.* 24.192–202 on Penelope and Helen
who will be a 'hateful song'. The songs themselves may have fame.

> On the self-same pedestal.
> On every merchantman, in every skiff
> Go, sweet song, from Aigina
> And spread the news that Lampon's son,
> ... has won the wreath.
>
> (*Nemean* 5.1–5. Bowra's translation)

Isocrates uses the same idea when he claims that good deeds are better than statues, for statues must stay put, but speeches (or words – *logoi*) may be published (*exenechthenai*) throughout Greece (*Evagoras* 73–4).[39]

The language here is that of words, announcements and oral means of communication: it is striking that the written word itself is not mentioned as giving fame or immortality. This cannot be pressed too far: it is undeniable that by Pindar's time poets did keep written texts of their songs (though probably not many,[40] and Pindar may repeat a tradition that Homer gave the *Cypria* to his daughter as a dowry (fr. 280 Bowra). But the quality, performance and circulation of poetry are what gives fame. For what it is worth, a poem of Simonides mocks the idea that a stone inscription would last for ever (fr. 581 *PMG*), when even a human hand could so easily destroy it. The implication is that only poetry can ensure the fame that Kleoboulos so desired.

Poets are also seen as transmitting and preserving the truth. As Detienne (1967) (among others) has pointed out, the word for truth, *aletheia*, means literally the opposite or lack of forgetfulness (*lethe*). This etymology helps elucidate the complex of ideas around memory, the Muses, and poetry. For it has been noted that both Homer and Hesiod call on the Muses not for inspiration, as later Hellenistic poets do, but for the *facts* of what happened.[41] Homer opens the Catalogue of Ships in *Iliad* book 2 with a call upon the Muses (2.484ff.):

> Tell me now, Muses, dwelling on Olympus,
> As you are heavenly, and are everywhere,
> And everything is known to you – while we

---

[39] cf. Pind. *Nemean* 4.13ff, where Pindar says that the victor's father, if still alive, would repeat the present song accompanied by the lyre, to celebrate his son's victory; *Ol.* 9.1, on reuse of ancient encomiastic songs like Archilochus' hymn for Heracles in celebration of new occasions. Theognis, 237ff, the poet's word flies swiftly over sea and land.

[40] See Davison 1962; Pöhlmann 1990.

[41] Detienne 1967: esp. 9–27; cf. Cole 1983; Jensen 1980: ch. 5 esp. 79–80; Gentili 1988: ch. 4.

Can only hear the tales and can never know –
Who were the Danaan lords and officers?
(transl. R. Fitzgerald)

It is the Muses, as goddesses, who know and are present, while the humans know nothing without their help. They seem to be guardians of the facts, the details difficult to remember. The elaborate invocation at the beginning of this most difficult of lists suggests strongly that the poet calls on them to help his memory, and invokes them as guardians or guarantors of those details of the past which mere mortals could not know if it were not for memory and poetry. The Muses are often invoked before a particularly difficult passage or catalogue.[42] The bard Demodocus in the *Odyssey* is praised fulsomely by Odysseus (8.487–91) because he has sung everything that the Achaeans did and suffered, 'as though you were there or heard the story from one who was': he must have been taught by the Muses or Apollo. Singing it as it really happened is the highest praise: thus the poet is clearly seen as preserver of the past, preserver of truth which would otherwise be forgotten.[43] (Hesiod recognizes that the Muses can also say false things which seem true, but they may also speak the truth (*Theogony* 26–8).)[44] One cannot help being reminded of the claims of the Yugoslav poets to sing things exactly as they happened, without any alteration: some people understood them to mean that they had not altered any words, but this is probably too literal-minded. Surely what the singers were emphasizing were the events of the stories themselves, which they believed were true happenings from the past.[45]

To say (with Havelock) that Homer's epic was a 'tribal encyclopedia' and little else, is going too far: this is over-teleological, reading back from the extreme prestige Homer had in later centuries. But poets were in an important sense the preservers and transmitters of their cultural heritage – of the myths and legends which were regarded as historically true, the tales of the Trojan War, the local tales and origins of the Greek cities and shrines. In a world where so much did depend on memory and oral transmission, and

[42] cf. also Hesiod *Theog.* 1ff, 104–15, (also 966, 1022); Homer, *Il.* 2.761–2; Jensen 1980: 79–80.

[43] Herodotus, Prologue, sees himself as doing the same thing.

[44] cf. *Theog.* 99–101.

[45] See refs. at ch. 3, n. 53; there is an interesting discussion at Jensen 1980: ch. 5, esp. 62–9.

where anything important was in verse, poetry was a better way of preserving for posterity and communicating to the Greeks of the present. Poetry conferred fame, and was fitting for those 'worthy of song'.

The performance

Most Greeks would have experienced their literature as something recited or performed. But it was not simply a matter of hearing, rather than reading or seeing it on the written page. There were, of course, a wide variety of modes of performance, from the recitation of the rhapsode, to the rhetorical performances of orators who strove to give the impression of improvisation, or the 'readings' attributed to historians like Herodotus. Most important for us to grasp is that a large proportion of poetry was accompanied by music – and even by dancing – as an integral part of the experience. The implications are vast but extremely difficult to pin down: music, intonation, modes of performance, are exactly the elements which are barely recorded by our written sources. But some indications are there, and though it also requires vivid imagination to envisage the performance of Greek poetry, it is perhaps, as Herington has recently said, one of the most urgent tasks of all for the student of Greek poetry.[46]

Ideally we should read all ancient literature aloud – still better, attempt to recite or 'perform' it. As an example of what we are missing in the realm of prose, take the extreme example of the Sicilian orator Gorgias. His rhyming and extravagantly antithetical rhetoric was said to have captivated his Athenian audiences. Strange enough to read silently, it must have been vastly different when performed and heard.[47] Or compare the famous defence speech made on his own behalf by the orator Antiphon at the end of the fifth century which Thucydides praises so highly (8.68): the few fragments we still have give little impression of brilliance, yet perhaps this should just remind us of how much the written text alone fails to convey. The habit of hearing, rather than reading, must have focused attention on the sound and on those qualities best appreciated when heard – an aspect which deserves careful

---

[46] Herington 1985: 50: a most stimulating discussion.

[47] cf. observations in Segal 1962: 99–155, on Gorgias' theory of the power of speech; I recommend the translation (and layout) of a section of his funeral oration, in T. Cole 1991: 71–2 for an English intimation of his Greek style.

attention.⁴⁸ It is exceedingly hard to know what the aural and
visual impact might have been, yet in order to appreciate the whole
performance, that is exactly what one needs. There is little work, so
far as I know, which attempts to capture the entire experience of
ancient literature.

Occasional ancient descriptions give something of the spectacle
we are missing in the sphere of poetry.⁴⁹ In the early fifth century,
Pindar alludes to the combination of song, lyre, *aulos* (oboe-like
reed instrument) and dance in the epinician ode:

> The garlands placed like a yoke on the hair exact from me payment
> of this sacred debt: to blend together properly the lyre with her
> intricate voice, and the shout of oboes, and the placing of words.
> (*Olympian* 3.6–9)

> Lyre of gold! . . . to you the dancers listen, as they begin the
> celebration; and singers obey your signals, each time you
>   fashion,
> on your quivering strings, the opening notes of the preludes.
> (*Pythian* 1.1–4)

Poets who wrote choral lyric, like Pindar, Bacchylides, and Alcman, had to act as chorus trainers for the singing and dancing. It is
not known how the singing would have been divided up among the
chorus, if at all, or its relation to the dancing, but clearly the
composing of the words was only one element of the poet's task. As
for non-choral lyric poetry, that of Sappho and Alcaeus, monodic
lyric, would certainly have been accompanied by the lyre (played
by the singer). Elegiac poetry may have been chanted, not regularly accompanied by an instrument. As for the rhapsode, he performed poetry without musical accompaniment, but his manner of
delivery is better described as 'chanting' than simply reciting: he is
described in Plato's dialogue the *Ion* (named after the rhapsode
Ion) as gorgeously dressed with golden garlands, standing before a
huge audience of more than twenty thousand people, and so over-
come with emotion as he relates some of the most moving scenes
from Homer that he is, as it were, possessed, filled with fear or
misery.⁵⁰

---

⁴⁸ See for Homer, Packard 1974; Nagler 1974, ch. 1.
⁴⁹ All ancient descriptions of performance are collected and discussed by Herington 1985.
  For a general introduction, Bowra 1961; Fränkel 1975.
⁵⁰ Plato, *Ion* esp. 530b6–8, 535b–e.

This must mean that the written texts of the poetry, certainly made in the archaic period, recorded only an element of the total performance. They were merely an *aide-mémoire*, a silent record of a much richer experience, hardly something to be relished and read on their own. As I suggested in chapter 5 (p. 92), their unhelpful nature, since they were written out without word- or even verse-division, may reflect the comparatively mechanical role they played as simple memorials of words which were to be learnt by heart as soon as possible, and transmuted into a far richer experience.

Beyond the style of performance, we should also remember the audience, the circumstances or occasion of performance, and the role of the poet. Studied from written texts, Greek poetry tends to be seen in terms of genre. Later Hellenistic scholars classified it into strict genres, and Hellenistic and Roman poets followed those conventions. But while this later poetry may have had no relation to any specific occasion or ritual, the various poetic forms of the archaic and classical centuries cannot have been merely literary conventions, unrelated to audience and context. Uncovering the circumstances of a poetic performance, which become obscured by the written texts alone, is not easy. But as Gentili has reminded us, earlier Greek poetry was designed for a specific occasion or type of occasion and a specific audience.[51] Literary genres are based originally on ritually and socially distinguished occasions at which songs were sung. It is again hard, but crucial, to try to uncover these occasions.

Thus the highly complex choral odes of Pindar, baffling to the modern reader with little knowledge of Greek society, were performed to music and dancing to honour and celebrate victors in the major games. At the panhellenic festivals at Delphi and Olympia and other major sanctuaries, the participants were the flower of the Greek aristocracy, the games the focus of Greek inter-city rivalry and some of the rare occasions when Greece laid down its weapons in panhellenic unity. The songs would be performed publicly by the victors' cities to a large and patriotic audience,[52] then almost certainly re-performed. They honoured the city and family of the victor as much as the victor himself.

---

[51] Gentili 1988: esp. chs. 1, 3, 8–9; p. 37 for Alexandrian division into genres; M. Davies 1988 on the 'tyranny of the handbook'; see also M. L. West 1974, Most 1982, on the context.

[52] Lefkowitz 1988 is a recent discussion of the details.

Greek choral lyric in general, a specific category of poetry which will get separate treatment in the manuals, tended to be sung and performed by choruses at most of the major events in Greek society. Extant poems are usually highly elaborate, obscure, their contents subject to long scrutiny by modern scholars. Yet they cannot have been so opaque to their original audiences, for whom they provided poetic and musical celebration at the major ritual occasions in Greece: hymns to the gods at public religious festivals, paeans in honour of Apollo, victory odes at the games, processional songs (*prosodia*), songs praising individuals (*encomia*), and songs at marriages and funerals – marriage songs (*epithalamia*), maiden songs (*partheneia*), and dirges. They cover most of the central activities of Greek life.

Alcman's Louvre *Partheneion* or maiden song (*PMG* fr. 1), sung by a girls' chorus in the seventh century, is a case in point: highly obscure to us, it may have been part of some archaic Spartan ritual surrounding initiation into the *thiasoi*, or perhaps a marriage hymn (*epithalamion*) chanted ritually at dawn.[53] We can only be certain that, unlike the later Hellenistic and Roman imitations, it was a song of genuinely religious and ritual significance, probably quite clear to its original audience. The ancient scholiast's comment about marriage songs underlines the complexity of the system of ritual marriage hymns alone:[54] 'of the various sorts of *epithalamia*, some are sung during the evening and are liable to go on until the middle of the night; others are *orthia* (sung at dawn) and are called reveille songs'. The poet composed music, words, and dancing as well, and each type of occasion had its conventional metre – and presumably music. Characteristically, Plato tried to regulate *choreia* or dancing as well as poetry (*Laws* 653e–657b). Reading the written text alone may not be quite as limited as reading the libretto of an opera without music or performance. But we are clearly missing a fundamental aspect of some of the most moving and awesome events in Greek life.[55]

The longer elegiac poems may also have been performed at public festivals. Indeed it has recently been argued that elegy in

---

[53] E.g. Page 1951; Gentili 1988: 73–77; Griffiths 1972 (an epithalamium).

[54] Schol. on Theocritus 18 (p. 331 Wendel), cited by Griffiths 1972.

[55] For dance, see Webster 1970 on archaeological material; Mullen 1982: esp. chs. 1–2, attempts to reconstruct the dance from metre; Calame 1977; Goldhill 1986: 264–74 (tragedy).

general – another major category of verse – was performed not primarily at funerals but at symposia and public festivals. The evidence is fragmentary and tantalizing but one should at least ask where the long poems about a city's mythical past might have been performed – for instance the shadowy *Smyrneis* by Mimnermus about Smyrna's legendary origins, or Xenophanes' poem on the foundation of Colophon. Their local patriotic (and parochial) character would fit exactly the public festivals and rituals where the citizen body would be assembled.[56] But the symposium, or private drinking party, also seems to be an important arena for the performance of elegy and other types of poetry – not merely the rather trite 'drinking songs' or *skolia*.[57] It would also be at the symposium that poems would be re-performed, thus fostering their continued transmission in a living, musical context.

Where was Tyrtaeus' poem *Eunomia* originally performed? Dating to the seventh century, it consisted largely of exhortation to fight bravely for Sparta and must have been addressed to the citizen-body as a whole. At least we know that his poetry had a long after-life: according to a later source, Spartan soldiers on campaign were summoned to the king's tent to hear Tyrtaeus' poems, and chanted them after dinner themselves; we also hear about 'marching songs' (*embateria*) to which Spartans apparently marched.[58] They may also have been sung at public festivals and symposia.

The poem of exhortation by Athens' great lawgiver Solon to fight for the island of Salamis in the early sixth century had a similarly political message, perhaps addressed to the citizens in the Assembly: 'I came as herald in my own person from lovely Salamis, putting the glory of verses in place of public speech'.[59] We would also dearly like to know the occasion and audience of the poems in which Solon justified his far-reaching reforms – Diogenes Laertius, the only source who gives a context, sees him rushing into the agora to declaim before the citizens (1.49.), but this may be sheer imagination. Whatever the answer, it must affect our interpretation of Solon, as well as the manner in which contemporary Athenian

---

[56] See Bowie 1986: 13–35.
[57] See Murray (ed.) 1990, esp. papers by Schmitt-Pantel, Bowie.
[58] Lycurgus, *Against Leocrates* 107; Philochorus, *ap.* Athenaeus 14.630f; see Herington 1985: 33; cf. Bowie 1990.
[59] Frag. 1 *W*; Plut. *Solon* 8.1–3 (cf. Diogenes Laertius 1.46) says Solon declaimed it unlawfully, pretending insanity. cf. Dem. 19.251–5.

politics worked. Unfortunately many of these questions, so easy
with live performances, are extremely hard to answer from written
texts and ancient testimony alone.[60] But the effort needs to be
made, and though, ironically, this side of Greek literature has been
stressed most by those interested in *oral* poetry, it is relevant to all.
The performance and appearance of Greek tragedy, which is still
being produced today, have received much more attention:[61]
perhaps we should now look to the modern performance of non-
tragic Greek poetry.

One further question bears upon any examination of oral and
written preservation: the extent of later performance after the
initial occasion. It raises in acute form several problems which are
very relevant to our discussion. As ancient references make fairly
clear, archaic poetry did continue to be performed well into the
fourth century, and indeed beyond – and it was performed along
with the music and accompanying dance. The ancient writers
clearly think that it was the original music that was being followed,
alongside the original words. Yet it is almost certain that musical
notation had not been invented before the late fourth century, and
in any case any notation, when it appeared, was very crude. How
could they be following the original music of (say) Sappho? As
Herington has suggested,[62] we may have to envisage the transmission of the music and dance accompaniment to poetry through
performance alone: that is, the words were transmitted with the
help of written texts, but the rest was passed down purely through
the continuity of performance, the teaching of one generation by
another. If this is correct, then here is an element of oral transmission which continues alongside the existence of a written text,
well into the fourth century and long after the words have been
committed to writing. It is true that pupils do seem to have learnt
the delivery and music of the poetry they read in school, poetry
being inseparable from music, and repetition would be both con-
strained and helped by the metre of the verse. But it may be
implausible to expect absolutely accurate transmission of music in
this way. One only has to look at the modern fashion of playing
baroque or early music 'authentically' to realize how, even with

---

[60] For the possibilities in other societies, cf. Finnegan 1977: ch. 6–8.
[61] Taplin 1978; 1977; Bain 1977; Goldhill 1986: esp. ch. 11.
[62] See Herington 1985: ch. 2 for detailed discussion; see also Comotti 1989 for a lucid
introduction to Greek music.

very detailed musical notation, performance of music is inevitably influenced by current fashion and taste. One wonders if the transmission of Greek dance and music would not have been equally susceptible to change, even if the performers were unconscious of it.

The performance of poetry ceased to be so central to Greek life in the late fifth and fourth centuries. But why stop looking for performance or orality beyond the sphere of poetry, or after Herodotus? Historians habitually delivered their work through recital or performance, and as Momigliano has pointed out, the evidence for this gets better, not worse, after the fifth century – public delivery certainly does not die out with Herodotus.[63] There is no simple transition from a 'song culture' to a book culture.[64] Plato still seems in the *Laws* to equate the uneducated with the '*achoreutos*', the person not trained in the chorus or dance (654a). The art of rhetoric, the ultimate performance, is only just beginning to be formalized in the last third of the fifth century, and it was being developed just at the time when the mechanisms of the direct democracy at Athens demanded more than ever that politicians should be able to persuade. There is evidence about the manner and implications of rhetorical performance in the fifth and fourth centuries, though it has received surprisingly little attention.[65] Even in the Roman Empire, Greek oratory and 'declamation' were being developed to still greater levels of sophistication, with characteristic techniques of presentation, gesture, performance, and even dress.[66] This too could be seen as another typically Greek manifestation of orality, rather than dismissed as the decadent antics of a now meaningless art.

Performance and the written text

This brings us back to the role of the written text. Written texts of the words existed for most of the types of literature we have been discussing. So what was their relation to performance, recital, or composition? When one looks more closely, there appears to be a

---

[63] Momigliano 1978: 59–75. See also Parke 1946.
[64] As Herington, for example, sees it (1985).
[65] See Kennedy 1963; most recently, T. Cole 1991: ch. 7 on written texts and their function; Ober 1989: 138, 147 collects references to audience participation in the Attic orators.
[66] See Russell 1983.

rather fluid connection, and it is, in some respects, reminiscent of certain features (and controversies) of the Homeric and oral composition of a much earlier age.

In the sphere of archaic and classical poetry, as we have seen, the written text often recorded only one element of a complex combination of words, music and dance. But what is more, the written text may be the final record made only after careful composition in the poet's head. All we have to go on are the few ancient descriptions of poetic composition, and in these the poet did not necessarily write down the poem until fairly late in the process of composition – the image of the poet in the throes of composition given in Aristophanes does not include pen and paper.[67] This should not be surprising in a society which cultivated the skills of instant improvisation in the symposium. Improvisation has, of course, mainly captured the attention of those interested in Homeric poetry and the oral epic, yet it was so far from being confined to societies totally dependent on oral composition and transmission that it continues in good health in Greece in those later centuries when written texts of sophisticated literature are produced quite regularly.

In public oratory, Greek orators fostered the appearance of improvisation and spontaneity, even if they had a text. A work by the early fourth-century writer Alcidamas, *On Those Who Compose Written Speeches*, has much good advice, some still bitingly appropriate today, on the virtues of speaking without a written text. Political speeches were supposedly never written out; forensic speeches might be, but were delivered from memory. There was considerable prejudice against written speeches in the fifth and fourth centuries, fuelled by a suspicion that someone who had written out his speech carefully might neglect the truth in favour of artifice. It also seems to be related to prejudice against the Sophists who, from the later fifth century, both taught rhetorical technique and (still worse) produced written handbooks. Demosthenes' speeches, which, notoriously, he wrote out, were said to 'smell of the lampwick', but even he managed to improvise.[68] The texts might then

---

[67] A point made by Herington 1985: 46–7: the two passages are *Acharnians* 383–479 and *Thesmophoriazusae* 95–265.

[68] Plut. *Life of Demosthenes* 8.2; generally, Hudson-Williams 1951; Dorjahn 1947 on Demosthenic improvisation; Kennedy 1959 on rhetorical handbooks; see Ober 1989: ch. 4, part C, sections 1 and 2 and pp. 278–9 for rhetorical use of such prejudice.

be revised further before publication and the versions we now read are the creations of this final revision (this is particularly true of Demosthenes' speeches). But in that case we again have a process in which the eventual published text is the result of a long gestation – preparation, perhaps written record, and memorization before delivery, then performance accompanied by improvisation and all the accoutrements of a living spectacle, then finally, possible elaboration for the literary publication of a text. So far as I know, the most explicit discussion of this kind of elaboration from delivered to written, published speech, occurs in the Roman writers Pliny and Quintilian, but these belong, of course, to a rather different age.[69]

This makes one wonder about the nature of the 'readings' given by historians. Would they be content simply to read out a text – the text we still have – or would they attempt more of a performance, perhaps even recital from memory? The possibility of 'performance' in its dramatic sense on the historian's part has not received much attention, and perhaps rightly. But it is worth considering whether the prejudice against written speeches, and the habit of memorizing them if they were written, might have affected the historian at all.

One scholar has recently explored the possibility that Herodotus engaged in extensive 'pre-publication' for his *Histories*: that is, extensive 'publication' of various sections through readings, recitals or written texts, before the whole work was completed. Oswyn Murray's idea that Herodotus was the last Ionian story-teller envisages a somewhat similar situation – a series of tales told separately and in series, but woven finally into the written text we have.[70] Murray's version presents an Herodotus more firmly rooted in the archaic period. I would add a third possibility, on the principle that oral performance or recital is by no means confined to an earlier 'oral' age, that Herodotus' readings might have been akin in some ways to the performances of the Sophists which became fashionable in the latter half of the fifth century. At any rate, this was a world where performance was the most effective way of making your work known. So a picture of numerous performances before publication of the final written text is attractive.

[69] E.g. Pliny *Ep.* 3.13.5; 3.18.1; 9.13.14; 13.23; Quintilian, *Institutio Oratoria* 7.2.24; 10.7.30–32; cf. 11.2.11–51.
[70] Evans 1991: 90, thus cutting through some of the controversies about when his work was 'published'; Murray 1987.

It helps explain the way Herodotus refers to his audience's scepticism about his earlier account of Persians debating whether to institute democracy – an idea Greeks found preposterous.[71] It avoids the anachronistic idea of an author labouring away for years without releasing any of his achievement until the final printed publication, and it conjures up a delightful image of Herodotus trying out certain of his more contentious views on an amazed or antagonistic audience.

How far this precise picture could be extended to other historians is uncertain, but three main points remain. If an historian gives readings (or recitals) from his work, they will inevitably be excerpts, so that we have the same problem encountered (with such different reactions from scholars) for the Homeric epics. A somewhat fluid relationship between written text and oral performance seems increasingly plausible, though the written text enables the author to keep exactly to the words as written if he wishes. And it would be unnecessary, in fact positively unwise, in the classical period, to rely entirely on the final published text for propagation of your life's work – when the perilously few copies that were made could, unsupported by any public libraries after all, be lost at sea, copied out badly, eaten by worms, or otherwise become totally illegible.

A further and rather different relationship between written text and non-written 'performance' or transmission is offered by the philosophers. I have already mentioned Plato's distrust of written texts because, by themselves, they were inadequate for purveying the truth: what was needed was teaching and discussion, and written words were only an image of knowledge. Plato's views may have been extreme, and he came, in the *Seventh Letter* attributed to him, to espouse the view that the truly important philosophical doctrines should not be written down at all, for fear that they get into the hands of the ignorant multitude. But though the evidence tends to concern the later philosophical schools of the Hellenistic and Roman periods, there was a strong current of thought holding that the written texts of works by philosophers could only really be

---

[71] Hdt. 3.80.1; 6.43.3 (other possibilities, Evans 1991: 100). They considerably strengthen Evans' argument about re-publication.

understood as an adjunct to the teaching of the great man or his followers. The texts were reminders, mnemonic aids, for what was more accurately propagated and understood through the living performance, from the teacher himself.[72]

[72] Alexander 1990; Edelstein 1966; see Epilogue, below, p. 161–2.

CHAPTER 7

Literacy and the state: the profusion of writing

I INTRODUCTION: LITERACY AND POWER

The modern state is inconceivable without its extensive record-keeping, its administration and bureaucracy. Information for and about the population is amassed in large quantities. The collection of taxes involves enormous paperwork. Economic, social, and political decisions may be based on elaborate data collected and stored with the aid of writing. Not surprisingly, indeed, it has been said that writing is essential to the definition of the state and its power. More cynically, as we saw, the anthropologist Lévi-Strauss once claimed in a famous passage that writing was an essential tool of empire and expansion, since it 'seems to have favoured the exploitation of human beings rather than their enlightenment', and that 'the primary function of written communication was to facilitate slavery'.[1] In ancient Mesopotamia, writing was indeed used from early on for bureaucracy and exploitation: in fact it was used exclusively for administrative records and lists for its first 600 years, and its role as an instrument of power and control in China and Egypt also may suggest that the development of complex state-structures is at least related to, if not closely bound up with, the development of literacy.[2]

When we look more closely at such theories, however, the relation of writing to 'power' or to the state is often left extremely vague.[3] Or else what is envisaged seems actually rather closer to the bureaucracy of the modern state than anything else (not all states or empires have even had writing: witness the Incas, though

---

[1] *Tristes Tropiques*, transl. by Weightman: 392–3.
[2] Larsen 1989: 136–7; also Larsen 1988; Eyre and Baines 1989 on early Egypt.
[3] cf. Goody 1986: 91: Lévi-Strauss 1976; Gledhill, Bender and Larsen (eds.) 1988 examines the question rather inconclusively: note esp. papers by Larsen and Harbsmeier.

they did have in the *quipu* a kind of recording system using knots in a series of strings which could store certain information very efficiently). One such analysis examines the component parts of what is in effect the modern bureaucratic state. Jack Goody has argued that writing makes possible communication at a distance and increasingly formal procedures: these could effect more authoritative control by a state, make possible accounting and more complicated systems of taxation, and therefore more control of expenditure. Institutions could gain more autonomy through the use of writing.[4] Effectively this is singling out the potential of writing (a) to facilitate communication over long distances and therefore control over larger areas, (b) to make commands more authoritative and unchangeable, and (c) keep records of large numbers of people and taxes. One could add a further function, the use of writing for display or propaganda, which deserves distinguishing from the use of writing for administration.[5]

For the ancient Greek world, such issues, though suggestive, sometimes seem curiously remote. As so often, writing turns out to be a many-edged tool, with diverse implications. The bureaucratic use of writing does not appear in ancient Greece, though it does in Egypt under the later, Ptolemaic and Roman, rule. In the Graeco-Roman world generally, the state did not make documents in order to collect information on the population or guide policy.[6] However, the absence of this kind of extensive record-keeping and 'control' through written records is illuminating in its own right, and helps draw attention to the peculiarly Greek uses of writing in the service of the city-state (as well as the peculiar nature of states without extensive records). Two further factors are important. Firstly, the Greek *polis* is a different form of 'state' from those envisaged above. There seems to have been little idea of 'the state' as a separate entity from its citizens: the *polis* was its citizens. Citizens might even have the privilege of not paying direct taxes.

Secondly, writing plays a very different role, both in actual administration and in the ideals voiced by Greek writers. Athens produced a profusion of documents from the beginning of her radical democracy in the 460s, yet even she had nothing resembling a bureaucracy, and the bureaucratic documentation of the ancient

[4] Goody 1986: ch. 3; Goody 1977. cf. critique by Larsen 1988: 176 ff.
[5] Larsen 1988: 187 ff.
[6] Finley 1982.

Near East is as alien to Athens as it is to any other Greek state. Considerable distrust of writing is visible or openly voiced, and the Athenians were painfully aware that documents could easily be tampered with.[7] But nowhere, so far as I can see, is writing distrusted as an arm of the state, as a tool in an impersonal bureaucracy, a mechanism of 'Big Brother', or a means of propaganda. This idea does in fact appear in Roman writers: Virgil idealizes the countryside as free from (among other things) the *populi tabularia* or public archives, but this seems far removed from the Greek experience.[8]

When ancient writers do express views about the role of writing in the *polis*, they draw a rosier picture: writing down the laws helped ensure justice and fairness (Aristotle, *Pol.* 1286a 9–17; 1287b 5–8; 1270b 28; Euripides, *Suppl.* 433), 'written laws (*nomoi*) are the guardians of the just' (Gorgias, *Palamedes* fr.11a, 30), writing is useful for managing a household, money-making, learning, and political life (Aristotle, *Pol.* 1338a 15–17).[9] However, even despite this ideal, the *polis* itself was not necessarily defined by its inhabitants in terms of writing. What we tend to find, certainly, is that the *polis* was generally associated with the rule of law, and thereby contrasted with Eastern and non-Greek regions: the 'law-abiding *polis*, though small and set on a lofty rock, outranks mad Nineveh' (Phocylides fr. 4). But the law mentioned here is not explicitly *written* law: also included was customary law, the 'laws of the gods' or 'unwritten law', prominent in Greek thought and politics. Aristotle argues in the *Politics* for the rule of law, but includes customary law (1287b 5–8). Sparta was widely admired as a city-state run on 'law', but the laws were unwritten. It was with Athens that written law itself came to be associated.

What emerges starkly is that writing as such is not thought an important defining characteristic of the Greeks or the Greek *polis*. For Herodotus in the middle of the fifth century, writing tends to be associated with barbarians, especially the Egyptians and Persians, or with tyrants who have a propensity to send messages which are secret and sinister.[10] It was later in the Hellenistic period that literate education seems to become more closely associated with

---

[7] Calhoun 1914.

[8] *Georgics* 2.501–2, cited by Georgoudi 1988: 244; see also Ovid, *Metamorphoses* 1.90–1.

[9] cf. the later eulogy of Diodorus Siculus 12.12.4, who stresses literary culture.

[10] Hartog 1988: 277–81.

being Greek, and it may be no coincidence that this was a period when Greek culture was often thinly scattered amongst alien cultures. But one cannot detach literacy as such here from the wider features of Greek culture and education (*paideia*).[11] In the Hellenistic and Roman periods high culture was also much more closely associated with books, and it is notable that the eulogy of the virtues of writing produced by Diodorus Siculus (first century BC) emphatically includes its ability to preserve literature, philosophy and *paideia*.[12]

As for power, the city of Sparta wielded enormous military power and influence for centuries with a use of writing that is almost invisible. She had no written laws and few public documents of any kind. Yet she was certainly no less of a 'state' than others, and controlled citizens, helots, and allies through other means, being one of the most effectively cohesive of the Greek city-states. One reason why states without writing seem unable to reproduce themselves (as Lévi-Strauss suggested) may indeed be that the evidence for the way the state held together has, being unwritten, simply vanished: the problem is thus one of the beholder. Other Greeks thought (wrongly) that Spartans were illiterate. But they were in no doubt about Sparta's power.

I therefore intend to concentrate on the role of writing in the city-state, its changing use, its associations, and any possible connection with certain political systems. It is exceedingly difficult to answer even the simple question 'how did the Greek *polis* make use of the written word?' But some of the difficulties we encounter may tell us something positive about the role of writing.

There is surprisingly little modern discussion so far. This may stem from an uneasy awareness that there is a yawning gap in the evidence.[13] We are almost entirely dependent on inscriptions.

[11] W. V. Harris 1989: ch. 5, esp. pp. 137–9. For a perhaps similar effect of New World discoveries on European valuation of literacy, see Harbsmeier 1989; K. Thomas 1986.

[12] 12.12.4: introduced in connection with a law enforcing universal literacy attributed to the very early lawgiver Charondas, which is seldom believed.

[13] Note, however, the articles in Detienne (ed.) 1988, esp. those by Maffi, Detienne, Georgoudi; R. Thomas 1989: ch. 1; for studies of written law, see n. 59 below. Note also Finley 1982, more generally on collection of information. More obliquely, see the important studies: F. D. Harvey 1966, Cartledge 1978, W. V. Harris 1989. For the data on archives: Weiss 1923: esp. chs. 8, 9; Wilhelm 1909b collects much of the evidence for the display and storage of documents (but his arguments have been much criticized); Klaffenbach 1960: 5–42; also Boegehold 1972, Stroud 1978a; Lambrinudakis and Wörrle 1983 collect much useful evidence in their commentary.

These represent only the few documents that went on stone or bronze, and it is difficult to know how many others were made, but lost. Yet these difficulties are not completely insurmountable, and they are less formidable for the classical period when archives were more primitive than later. There is a wealth of evidence from Athens about the making of documents, largely embedded in the inscriptions recording the decrees themselves, which has not been systematically collected.[14] Nor need we always be left helpless by the image of vast numbers of 'lost' inscriptions. Sometimes it is even fairly certain they were not made at all. For example, it is now almost beyond doubt that the reason so few inscriptions have been found in ancient Corinth before Roman times (before 146 BC) is that very few were put up in the first place.[15] There may actually be some relation between the extent of records and the political system. This is recognized in the case of democracy, but little explored. For Corinth, the gap in the record may well be connected to the oligarchic or tyrannical nature of her government throughout most of her history. Thebes, another major city, and leader of the federal Boiotian League, poses a similar problem (though it has produced more inscriptions). Most Greek cities were probably nearer to Sparta or Corinth in their official use of the written word (as well as in their constitutions) than to Athens. That is, there does seem to be a correlation between the number of public documents in a *polis* and the degree to which its constitution was democratic. Thus there is no simple general answer to the question about the *polis'* use of writing, but there is a further political dimension which we will return to below.

2 RECORDS, LAWS, AND ARCHIVES

The city-states varied widely in their use of writing, but overall it is far more haphazard and far less geared to record-keeping and administration than we would expect. I would say (though provisionally) that very little was strictly for administrative purposes.

If we can assume for the archaic and classical periods that inscriptions were the principal copies of the decisions they

---

[14] See R. Thomas 1989: ch. 1.2 for some.
[15] Dow, 'Corinthiaca', *HSCP* 53 (1942): 89–119, esp. 113–18; Kent, *Corinth* vol. VIII *part* III *The Inscriptions 1926–1950*; the debate has recently been reopened.

embody,[16] then most Greek cities used writing mainly for the public recording of laws, sacred laws, and treaties. There might also be records of letters, lists, calendars, and accounts which were not displayed in public. In the course of the classical period, there appears to be a slow and steady increase in the amount of written documents produced, both public and private. From the late fourth century and during the Hellenistic period, archives appear more often in the sources,[17] and city or temple archives are used for preserving the documents (contracts, for example) of private individuals. Certain kinds of inscriptions disappear as if records were now being preserved in archives instead of on stone. At Athens, for example, stone inventories of temple dedications, documents of the *poletai* (financial officials), and temple accounts disappear by the end of the fourth century.[18]

But how complex was classical record-keeping? Some older studies give the impression of a neat system and extensive bureaucracy. But it is not at all certain how far Greek states made copies of documents which were then simply destroyed, or kept records in archives rather than publicly displayed on stone inscriptions; or whether they actually used documents later, once they were made. We discussed this more theoretically in chapter 5.4, but such problems are very pertinent to the issues here. The bureaucratic image of the Greek state to be found in many studies is created partly by an anachronistic interpretation of the ancient evidence, and partly by amalgamating evidence from many different periods and areas (analogies with Ptolemaic Egypt are particularly dangerous). The composite view of Greek record-keeping can produce strange and anachronistic results.[19]

One vivid example of this anachronistic approach will suffice, that concerning the habit of registering private documents under state protection in the city archives. This custom becomes fairly

---

[16] R. Thomas 1989: 45–6, and Klaffenbach 1960, to show inscriptions are regarded as authoritative; also Georgoudi 1988.

[17] For the Hellenistic period: Klaffenbach 1960: esp. 37ff.; Posner 1972: chs. 3–5; Lambrinudakis and Wörrle, *Chiron* 13 (1983) (primarily about Paros); W. V. Harris 1989: 118–24 on Hellenistic bureaucratic arrangements; Sherwin-White 1985, on Priene, is suggestive.

[18] Klaffenbach 1960: 37 (suggesting Persian influence); Posner 1972: 117.

[19] E.g. Wilhelm's useful collection (1909b) of evidence for the publication of Greek documents cites cases from the Roman empire and fifth century BC; cf. Lambrinudakis and Wörrle 1983: 320, combining Parian practice of the second century BC with second century AD Thasian; Posner 1972.

regular in the later Hellenistic world. It is usually thought[20] that most city-states began the practice earlier, though how much earlier is left unclear: Aristotle notes the existence of officials who were in charge of registering private contracts (*symbolaia*) and judgements of the law courts in various cities (*Pol.* 1321b 34–40).[21] But this procedure seems not to occur in Athens itself till much later, and this would make Athens much less advanced than other cities. Athenians continued to place private stone markers (*horoi*) on their land to record loans on the security of that land until the second century BC when they disappear; one presumes that Athens too has now joined the rest of Greece in registering private documents in the city archive.[22] But can all this be right? The evidence from Athens is comparatively rich next to that of other cities, and only for Athens has there been sustained and detailed examination of changes in archival practice.[23] (Incidentally, it also suggests a rather gradual change in habit towards depositing private documents with officials, for some individuals before the second century both erected a stone marker and left a copy of the text with the archon, or chief official of the city.[24]) So we have a curious situation in which the city for which evidence is by far the most extensive is regarded as having a more primitive archival practice than states for which much less is known. I suspect that the comparative wealth of Athenian evidence reveals arrangements so crude that scholars instinctively take them to be unrepresentative and imagine more advanced arrangements in other parts of the Greek world.

We also need to be wary of anachronistic terminology, whether ancient or modern. Ancient terminology related to writing and documents seems suspiciously – and significantly – unsystematic, and crucial words change their meaning. There may be a trend towards more uniform terminology, but a Halicarnassian law of the middle of the fifth century, for example, actually refers to itself in three different ways, only one being *'nomos'* (law) (ML 32). Words

---

[20] E.g. by Posner 1972: 93, from Weiss 1923: 391–425; W. V. Harris 1989: 120 is refreshingly sceptical.

[21] *Pol.* 1331b6ff. is much vaguer; see also Pseudo-Aristotle, *Oeconomica* 2.2.12.

[22] Fine 1951: 52–4.

[23] See Boegehold 1972 and 1990; Wycherley 1957; Stroud 1978a; Kahrstedt 1938: appendix; though see now the discussion of archives on Hellenistic Paros, Lambrinudakis and Wörrle 1983.

[24] Note that loans elsewhere might be on other material: see the lead copy of a loan from Corcyra, *c.* 500, Calligas 1971.

frequently change their meaning, like the *mnemones* who switch from being oral recorders to clerks. The word *anagraphe* tends to denote public inscription in the classical period but registration in an archive in the Hellenistic – or even both at the same time.[25] These changes are interesting in themselves, but what they suggest is that the Greek treatment of documents and archives is much less systematic, less formalized, and less legalistic in its terminology than a modern observer would expect. Indeed different kinds of document are very often collected together with the simple term 'writings' (*grammata*). It is tempting to impose a system which may simply not have existed in the Greek world.

Modern terminology is particularly misleading when it comes to the very material and status of ancient documents. The source of the confusion pinpoints some interesting and central features of the Greek approach to record-keeping. One modern authority, for instance, describes the whitened boards or *leukomata* used all over Greece as 'wooden bulletin boards', which suggests a crude and temporary posting; but they were primary documents in their own right and might be deposited in archives.[26] It is difficult to believe that the stone inscriptions could be official, authoritative documents, yet, as we have seen, they clearly were.[27] The modern observer finds it hard to imagine an original document that is not on paper and carefully stored away in an archive. Inscriptions often include instructions about deposition in archives and other information which seem appropriate only for the 'original' document, but that simply makes it more plausible that inscriptions were the ultimate and authoritative documents.[28] Certainly some documents went into archives without being put on stone. But we cannot go to the other extreme and suppose that everything a modern citizen would expect in an archive would be in an ancient one. It has been suggested that a whole range of appropriately official documents kept on papyrus in archives and official registries, on precisely the grounds that inscriptions could not be authoritative themselves. This seems to be a circular argument, and it generates

[25] See Georgoudi 1988: 225 on ambiguity of this and other words; other refs. and bibliog. in *Chiron* 13 (1983): 361 and n. 392; Robertson 1990: 55.
[26] Posner 1972: 110; cf. 'archival agencies', p. 108.
[27] See ch. 5.2 pp. 84–6.
[28] An objection of Wilhelm 1909b: 279; *contra*, Klaffenbach 1960; further argument from Athenian material in R. Thomas 1989.

a picture of extensive record-keeping which is certainly not borne out by close examination of the evidence. The presence of seemingly extraneous information in inscriptions shows how different they are from modern documents, and suggests some further unexpected functions (see chapter 5). The possibility of extensive documentation on the part of the classical Greek city-states collapses.

Practices of making and keeping documents are extraordinarily varied: there is no regular overall pattern in the use of writing. The diversity is startlingly revealed by the disparate evidence collected in the most detailed studies,[29] and it is illuminating to explore the characteristic functions of writing in different city-states. Let us look in more detail at two cities which have been studied reasonably carefully, Sparta and Athens.

Ancient Sparta seems to have had almost no state records at all.[30] Officials wrote letters and dispatches, the kings kept records of Delphic oracles (Hdt. 6.57.4). Copies of certain international treaties were erected on stone at Olympia, Delphi, the Isthmus, Athens, and the sanctuary of Apollo at Amyklai just south of Sparta (Thuc. 5.18.10). But only one such classical document has been found in Sparta, a fifth-century treaty with Aetolia,[31] and the only other surviving state inscription is a list of contributions to a war fund (*IG* v 1.1 = M L 67). They had no written laws on principle, trusting rather, as Plutarch says, to their educational system (*Life of Lycurgus* 13.3). Nor, apparently, were any written records of judgements produced; Aristotle criticizes the ephors for not judging according to written law (*Pol.* 1270b 28). The very early *rhetra* or law about the constitution (Plut. *Lyc.* 6) presumably got recorded before the embargo (or else was not regarded as a 'law'). There is no evidence for other records such as citizen-lists, and in the more private sphere named tombstones were generally forbidden. Classical Sparta was a state which seems to have run in all essentials without the help of writing, let alone archives. She managed to enforce strict control and uniformity very effectively through other means, mainly her stern way of life.[32] Our evidence suggests a public use of writing only for the recording of international treaties.

---

[29] Wilhelm 1909a, 1909b and Klaffenbach 1960 for evidence of diversity.
[30] See Cartledge 1978 and Boring 1979.
[31] ML Addenda, 67 bis; Cartledge *LCM* 1 (1976): 87–92.
[32] For which, see e.g. Cartledge 1979, 1987, Hodkinson 1983.

It can be no coincidence that most public inscriptions in Laconian script have been found outside Sparta,[33] as if the Spartan state bowed to wider Greek practice only outside the territory of its own state.

Classical Athens, especially from the 460s, lies at the other extreme. Reinforced by her democratic ideals, her extravagant erection of stone inscriptions was probably in conscious opposition to the customs of her main rival, Sparta. The range of documents, especially those on stone, is well known: decrees of the Assembly and council, laws, accounts of the various treasuries and officials, temple inventories and building accounts, calendars, treaties, public dedications. The individual demes or villages followed suit in their more parochial manner. The surviving Athenian decrees of the fifth century alone number 229 in the standard corpus (*I G* 1³). Public lists of traitors and public debtors were visible on the Acropolis to anyone interested, and other lists of offenders existed. As Boegehold points out, by 405 a decree (of Patrocleides) concerning Athenians who have been dishonoured or disenfranchised is couched in terms of public lists.[34] Isocrates (*Antidosis* 15.237) gives a recital of other incriminating lists on wooden boards, detailing public offenders and sycophants, malefactors and their instigators, private offenders and initiators of unjust complaints. We catch glimpses of other records not put on stone, for example, accounts, lists of metics, lists of deme members, and perhaps of those who could attend the Assembly, the last two kept separately by the demes.[35] Public inscriptions and the production of written documents increase steadily in the fourth century.

But despite this apparent wealth of documentation, there is little to suggest an 'archive mentality'. Many of these records were impermanent, destroyed when they were no longer needed. Others were made but apparently not used,[36] and many served a symbolic and exemplary rather than administrative purpose (e.g. the Athenian tribute-lists: see pp. 86–7). The amnesty decree of Patrocleides of 405 (Andoc. 1.76–9) enfranchised several groups and

---

[33] Cartledge 1978: 35.

[34] Andocides 1.76, and 77–9 for decree itself, with Boegehold 1990.

[35] Metics: Whitehead 1977: 83. Assembly: M. H. Hansen 1986: ch. 1.4; Whitehead, 1986: 35 n. 130, 103–6; for others, Boegehold 1990.

[36] R. Thomas 1989: 82–3 for an example; see Finley's stress (from a rather different angle) on minimal documentation, 1982 (repr. 1985).

provided for the obliteration of their names on certain damaging documents.[37] This meant *total* obliteration of their 'criminal record', and was the opposite, as it were, of *damnatio memoriae*, for it was meant to preserve a man's reputation rather than destroy all memory of him. Many kinds of record were probably never made at all. There was no land register, no central list of citizens, no list (so far as we can tell) of all those eligible for liturgies other than the trierarchy, no record of the entire tax revenue or entire expenditure of Athens gathered together in one document (accounts of separate funds did exist). Such information as was recorded was more often fragmented amongst all the various official boards, temples and demes, and information pertaining to 'the state' was therefore scattered. The Metroön or 'central archive' established in the last decade of the fifth century in the classical period mainly housed the decrees and laws. It was not the only archive housing public material: the decree of Patrocleides suggests other locations, and the Aristotelian *Athenaion Politeia* mentions an official who guards the keys to the temples where the money and 'the documents of the city' are (44.1), thus introducing yet another place of deposit for what were clearly regarded as 'public papers'. The decrees and laws, prominently displayed around the Acropolis and agora, and mostly on stone, were perhaps the most important written records of the 'state'.

Nor were the records very remote from the citizen-body. Ordinary citizens participated, at least in theory, in the drafting and passing of these decrees, and at deme level they were even closer to the official activities of the deme. It was up to citizens in general, not officials, to watch out for the infringement of laws, and it was only with the establishment of the board of *nomothetai* ('law-givers') in (probably) 403/2 that there was any official and automatic mechanism to control the making of new laws and to ensure they did not contradict earlier ones. As for the later use (as opposed to storage) of the decrees in the archives, this seems to have been minimal before the late fourth century.[38]

So although Athens boasted a wide range of official documents compared to some other cities, even the Athenians were not

---

[37] Andocides himself takes it that whole decrees are being obliterated (1.76): for discussion of details, see Boegehold, *Historia* 1990.

[38] R. Thomas 1989: 60–83.

seriously overshadowed by the written word, at least in the administrative sense. There was neither the state apparatus to achieve this, nor appropriate exploitation of the potential of written records. (For non-citizens it may have been different: resident aliens, for instance, who had to pay a direct poll-tax, were all listed.) There was a serious dearth of permanent record-keeping of the kind that could be used to record the lives of the citizen population: archives were not store-houses of information on the citizen body. However, there was a very effective system of vigilance by neighbours, ever watchful for any leverage at all against their enemies, and this did not always need written documents. There might be no written record in the classical period of who owned what land, for instance, but in this fairly traditional society everyone knew anyway. The stone markers were enough to signal debt: they were placed on your own land and neighbours would notice if you attempted to dig them up. It was perhaps in the areas of life where local and personal knowledge was not enough – for instance, where they were not bound by cult[39] – that distrust drove people to demand additional proof in writing.

But the hand of the community or city was dramatically visible in the public inscriptions and records. Writing might not be used extensively for administration, but one could say that public writing was used in effect to protect and confirm the values of the city. Citizens in debt to the state *were* recorded, however temporarily. Permanent offenders were listed on the Acropolis and elsewhere, as were traitors. There was a list of public benefactors, and people tried to bribe their way onto it. These lists are treated as if they were a well-known spectacle. One man was accused of being a traitor, literally of 'being inscribed on a *stelee*' (*steletes*), and he tried to argue in his defence that if his hatred of the people had really been inscribed in stone, the Thirty Tyrants would have trusted him more (Aristotle, *Rhetoric* 2.1400a 32–6). Athenians went up to the Acropolis to look at the public lists for information incriminating their enemies.[40] Like the stone lists of those who died fighting for the city (e.g. ML 48), these were exemplary texts displayed for the improvement and encouragement of the rest of the citizenry.

What is striking is the very public and visible nature of this kind of written record. Writing was indeed used in the service of the city,

[39] J. K. Davies, reviewing Connor, *New Politicians* in *Gnomon* 47 (1975): 376.
[40] R. Thomas 1989: 64–6 for public lists.

by its own citizens (who were responsible in the Assembly for passing decrees about erecting inscriptions). But it seems to have been more by means of public display – exemplary lists and decrees – than by written records kept behind the scenes. Inscriptions served also for the display of authority: the Greek states which had to pay tribute to the Athenian empire were listed carefully according to their contribution (or rather the one sixtieth given to Athena) in the Athenian tribute-lists on the Acropolis. Rather than administrative record, public, exemplary, and monumental inscriptions were probably the most characteristic public use of written record in the service of the classical city-state. This is, I think, precisely the use of written record that one might expect in a society so dependent on public reputation and public honour (as opposed to mere private approval). In a society intensely conscious of public reputation, it would be the open and visible signs of honour, appreciation, and conversely, treachery or dishonour, that would hold the most meaning.

What were the archives actually for, then, if the publicly visible records on inscriptions were so crucial? I do not want to suggest that Greek archives were of trivial value. But it is tempting to overestimate their functions and sophistication, and therefore the extent of state 'control' of records. I discussed certain features of ancient archives more generally in chapter 5: the distinction between documents and records, the slow development in Athens of an 'archive mentality', the anachronistic modern interpretations of archives. All this has an obvious bearing on the question of state control of records – or of the population through records. Further issues arise here which bear precisely on the city-state's treatment of records. This involves a partial foray into the Hellenistic period, which provides some particularly useful evidence, though the political system was now very different. Hellenistic archives have usually been thought rather sophisticated, but this may be anachronistic.[41] The evidence is often confusing and not easily accessible, and in lieu of any comprehensive recent study, I can only make tentative suggestions here.

For instance, we have encountered the registration in public archives of private contracts (for business, marriage or lease) which

---

[41] cf. R. Thomas 1989: ch. 1, concentrating on classical Athens; Georgoudi 1988 is suggestive. For Hellenistic practice, n. 17 above.

is so prominent in the Hellenistic period. This suggests that the cities were now responsible for protecting records, private as well as public. Yet even in the Hellenistic period such registration may not have been absolutely necessary to make the document valid.[42] The evidence starts appearing by the third century BC, but while Aristotle implies that registration was necessary (*Pol.* 1321b 34–7), it is not clear that registration was always compulsory. Much later, in the second century AD, Dio Chrysostom mentions that a contract receives maximum validity if it is entered into the public archives (*demosia grammata*) (31.50ff.). The passage is often cited to show the importance of public archives for the validation of private contracts,[43] but what he in fact says is that public registration makes the contract *more* valid. In other words archival protection was only an additional guarantee. Even in Egypt, where far more documentation was needed than elsewhere, it was still possible to make unwritten contracts.[44] The later habit of depositing private documents in a public archive certainly shows that attempts were made to keep them safe – mainly from falsification. But it remains quite obscure what proportion of documents would still be given to trusted individuals rather than a public archive. Nor is it certain that registration of the sale of property was compulsory everywhere in the Hellenistic period, though it was in Athens.[45]

When we come to the question of whether it might be easy to get access to the archives, the actual organization of records is obviously relevant. The arrangements of archives we know much about seem fairly unsystematic or even haphazard. The details of organization in the Athenian Metroön in the classical period do not suggest particularly easy (or frequent) access, or much awareness of their potential value till the middle of the fourth century – and in any case, official documents were still spread around the offices and temples of Athens.[46]

A long and important inscription recording a reform of archival

---

[42] W. V. Harris 1989: 120, with refs. there; Arist. *Pol.* 1321b34ff. does imply compulsory registration; Lambrinudakis and Wörrle, *Chiron* 13 (1983), sect. 8.1.2 (322–8 on private contracts); Weiss 1923: 243–354. Some helpful discussion (mainly on Egypt) in Burkhalter 1990: 203–8.

[43] Posner 1972 (rather misleading); Georgoudi 1988: 246, along with Gernet 1955: 223ff. (on private contracts and the city).

[44] Taubenschlag 1955: 301–3.

[45] W. V. Harris 1989: 121; Pringsheim 1950: 134–42.

[46] Above, pp. 96–7, 138; R. Thomas 1989: 72ff.; Wycherley 1957 for evidence; W. C. West 1989 now argues for a more regular system of organizing decrees.

practice in Paros in the second century BC proclaims that there should be public access to the copies of the documents (private and possibly public also) put in the sanctuary of Hestia,[47] and the principle of accessibility may have been generally upheld. But in Paros before the reform there were apparently separate collections of private documents kept by the *mnemones* as individuals (inhibiting public access?), and it was only after the reform that these *mnemones* had to deposit the documents in their charge in the Python, the sanctuary of Apollo, Artemis, and Leto. The editors of the inscription stress the optional and piecemeal approach of the Parians to these documents.[48] In addition, the system they were now initiating meant that copies of all documents had to go into a second temple archive (in the temple of Hestia, perhaps the 'city archive'), so that, effectively, there were now (and perhaps before) two archives containing the same kind of records and two sets of what are apparently equally authoritative documents duplicated in each collection.[49] We only hear so much about the Parian archives because documents were being tampered with.[50] Perhaps the public proliferation of inscriptions was often matched by similar confusion in the archives which succeeded them.

Other problems seem to revolve around the concept of 'state archive' itself. The frequency with which archives, like laws (and indeed, treasuries), are placed in the safety of temples should give pause for thought. Even the comparatively late Parian archives are placed in two temples and their integrity protected by a public curse.[51] The gods are being enlisted for support and security, and the practice of depositing records in temples which we dignify and 'bureaucratize' with the description 'state archive' seems to have less and less to do with protection by the state itself.

The very existence of a 'central state archive' which houses all public documents (and private contracts into the bargain) is questionable in the ancient world.[52] Medieval material shows how very

[47] *Chiron* 13 (1983): 283–368, lines 65ff.; Georgoudi 1988: public records as well as private.
[48] *Chiron* 13 (1983): 283–368, sect. 8.3.
[49] Georgoudi 1988: 244. For other examples of official duplication, Lambrinudakis and Wörrle 1983: 360ff., Georgoudi 1988: 240ff.
[50] cf. later reforms of Q. Veranius in the Roman province of Lycia and Pamphylia in Claudius' reign, in Borchhardt (ed.) *Myra* 1975: 254ff., esp. 279–85; and numerous problems with decaying or falsified papyri in Egypt, Posner 1972: 151–3.
[51] Other examples of curses, *Chiron* 13 (1983): 310–13; other temple archives, 303–4.
[52] Such an institution may only emerge in the sixteenth century: Georgoudi 1988: 226ff.; Nora 1988.

gradually, if at all, documents were gathered together in a single place rather than left distributed amongst relevant individuals.[53] In the Greek world, collections of the relevant records tended to be kept by the corresponding officials in their offices – for instance the cavalry archive at Athens, or the many kinds of list mentioned in the decree of Patrocleides (above). Even the Metroön was more an archive for the Assembly and council decrees than a central state archive (above p. 138). In the Hellenistic period different collections of documents still existed in their separate storage places (often wooden chests or *kibotoi*), as we see in the case of Paros, and fourth-century Delphi had a highly mobile archive of this kind (here called *zugastra*).[54]

The term 'archives' also dignifies what were often haphazard mixtures of records on a variety of materials ranging from wooden tablets to bronze or lead. It may be significant that one of the most common Greek phrases to designate 'archives' is *demosia grammata*, a phrase which strictly refers not to the building itself but simply (and literally) to 'public writings'.

Obviously the classical and Hellenistic cities did collect certain kinds of records together and did have a concept of 'public writings or documents', but we probably still overestimate the extent to which they were centralized – and underestimate the prevalence of various miscellaneous collections of documents kept by individuals, even officials. It has been noted how blurred the distinction between public and private documents is in sixteenth-century Italy, and how commonly officials could 'treat official documents as their private property and pass them on to their heirs'.[55] The rich evidence from highly bureaucratized Graeco-Roman Egypt shows that even there officials often did not turn their papers in at the end of their term of office.[56]

So, of course, archives housed and protected important documents, accounts, contracts, decrees, and laws. But the much admired extension of public archives to private documents apparent from the late fourth century[57] seems to be less indicative of

---

[53] See Clanchy 1979.
[54] *Chiron* 13 (1983): 346–50 has more refs. to *kibotoi*; for Locri, de Franciscis 1972; for Delphi's mobile archives, full of *pinakes* relating to the temple rebuilding, Georgoudi 1988: 235, Roux 1979: 111–12, 117.
[55] Burke 1987: 36.
[56] Turner 1968: 137, and *CAH*[2] VII, pp. 147–8.
[57] Posner 1972: 95.

state protection or 'state endorsement' of records than has sometimes been thought. Only some types of private document, in some
cities, had to be registered with the archives, and the archives were
very likely to be merely collections of documents, kept fairly hapha-
zardly, and permanently manned only by slaves. Divine protection
is seldom far away from public records (or private ones entrusted to
the archives), and this must alter our emphasis.

3 POLITICAL CONSTITUTION AND WRITTEN RECORD

Let us return to the possible links between a city's political system
and its use of written record. The case of Athens enables us to look
more closely at (a) the link between democracy (or any political
system) and extensive public written texts, (b) closely related, the
political implications of written law, and (c) the factors behind
Athens' growing reliance on writing. As we shall see, there seems to
be no immediate identification of public written record with
democracy: this emerged slowly in response to specific historical
developments.

For it is widely recognized that there is a rough correlation
between ancient democracy and extensive display of public
records: democracy fostered an ideal of public openness and accountability which demanded easy access to the records and laws,
whereas an oligarchy (such as Sparta or Corinth) neither made nor
publicized state documents and cultivated secrecy.[58] This was
probably the main reason why Athens spent so much money on
inscribing the minute details of Assembly business, and expressed
the intention to put up certain inscriptions 'so that anyone who
wants may see'. But this schema is still fairly crude and more must
be at stake here than political orientation alone. These monumental inscriptions of decrees had symbolic purpose as well as providing information and enabling justice to be done. The huge tribute-
lists, and the decrees erected in the territory of a subdued city at the
latter's expense, were, as we have seen, meant to impress and
impose the weight of Athens' authority, not simply to inform.

Much revolves around the Greek conception of law and its relation to writing. Many inscriptions of a public nature in the
archaic and classical Greek city are laws of some kind. Athens may
have erected copies of her decrees partly because she believed that

[58] Classic statement in Detienne 1988a.

laws as such should be publicly displayed. Modern as well as ancient writers have seen written law as a bulwark against arbitrary judgement and inequality, and it probably is at least a necessary first step in checking arbitrary judgement and ensuring consistent treatment. Democracy is closely associated with written law. The idea that written law fostered justice had been voiced already in Athens by her early sixth-century lawgiver Solon (fr. 36 West).

However, writing down the laws cannot be enough by itself to produce certain political results, as commentators tend to assume.[59] As we saw (chapter 4.4), the early Greek communities' use of written law had ambiguous implications. Certain Cretan cities had a tradition of publicly inscribing laws, yet they were hardly democracies and their leaders used arbitrary judgement just the same. Given that evidence for literacy of any kind in Crete is minimal, Gortyn's impressively inscribed laws were perhaps aiming at 'mystification':[60] their dramatic monumental presence was meant partly to impress inhabitants with the ineluctable authority of the laws and those who administered them. Even in Athens, law was not seen as exclusively written law until the end of the fifth century, nor were laws distinguished from decrees passed by the Assembly until the early fourth[61] (and not always then). As Finley has remarked, the legal and political system behind the written laws has to be democratized too before written law can be effective and available for all citizens.[62]

Officials' authority is important for implementing even written law. Officials might retain considerable latitude in their giving of judgement, untempered by the presence of written law (e.g. M L 32, from above, chapter 4.3). The Gortyn Code refers obsessively to the necessity of abiding by 'what is written' in the law. But if, on the other hand, the law does not provide an answer, the judge is to 'decide on oath', and the official *mnemon*'s personal knowledge also plays a part (col. 9.31ff.). Even if written law is meant partly to form objective, unquestionable rules which hold for everyone, there are gaps in the authority of the written law and room for interpretation, as well as official procedures, into which the personal authority and status of officials can be inserted.

---

[59] Eder 1986; C. G. Thomas 1977; Gagarin 1986; Bonner and Smith, 1930, vol. I, p. 67.
[60] Stoddart and Whitley 1988: 766.
[61] M. H. Hansen 1978.
[62] Finley 1983b: 30. cf. Finkelstein 1961 for Babylonian law codes.

Even those drafting laws seem to foresee problems in enforcing their authority. Many laws and treaties that survive on stone are dedicated to a divinity or explicitly protected by one, and this is by no means confined to the archaic period. Almost wherever one turns, laws and treaties have some kind of divine guardian. The recently discovered Parian inscription of the second century BC provides a Hellenistic example.[63] There is little question of democracy here, but rather attempts by various communities to make and enforce law that would have as much authority as possible. Similar stratagems are used in the Near East.[64] If we note that the kind of laws involved are controversial and political ones, the legislators' problems become apparent. Writing is therefore being used partly to fix these often controversial regulations, but also to fix them in an impressive and monumental form and to enlist, through their dedication to the gods, the kind of divine protection which was assumed for customary (unwritten) law but was desperately lacking for the kind of political and procedural regulations that the developing city-states required. Written law was not enough by itself – and many Greek states knew it was not enough – to achieve fairness, or even the most basic control of the city's officials. That is presumably why secretaries were watched as carefully as any other officials to check abuse of power.[65]

The identification of written law exclusively with justice and the democracy seems more likely to have been a product of late fifth-century developments in Athens. The reasons for this change are complex, but what is particularly interesting is how written law was not identified immediately and uncompromisingly with democracy.[66]

In the period from 410 to 400/399 BC Athens revised her laws. In part this was necessary because of the ever-growing number of laws and decrees. It was no longer clear which were still valid, which were superseded: contradictions could be observed, and greater organization was clearly needed.[67] This must have been important

---

[63] Lambrinudakis and Wörrle, *Chiron* 13 (1983).

[64] E.g. Goody 1986: 98 (invocation of gods' anger for those who disobey a treaty).

[65] Ruzé 1988. See W. V. Harris 1989: 50, for evidence for important sixth-century secretaries at Athens.

[66] This argument is developed at more length in a forthcoming article.

[67] E.g. Boegehold 1990; on the revision: Ostwald 1986: 369–72, 404–9, 414–20, 509–24; Harrison 1955; Fingarette 1971; Robertson 1990 presents a radical new interpretation; generally, Goody 1986: esp. chs. 3–4.

for practical reasons, and to preserve an uncontradictory legal system. But there was a political and intellectual dimension to this reorganization, and it occurred in a period of political upheaval in which the democracy was overthrown twice by oligarchic coups.

Unwritten laws (or the 'laws of the gods'), such as the imperative to bury the kindred dead, were still prominent, frequently mentioned and respected in the late fifth century.[68] But the relation of the unwritten laws to the written laws, or the laws of the state, comes under discussion in the second half of the fifth century in the climate of Sophistic debate. This is most vivid in Sophocles' *Antigone*, produced in 441 BC.[69] 'Unwritten laws' (as opposed simply to 'law') only begin to be distinguished as such in the second half of the fifth century, and this presupposes the development of written law as a recognized and separate category. The word *nomos* could still denote custom as well as law. Euripides is the first tragedian to articulate the notion of specifically written laws (*nomoi*) as a protection against injustice (*Suppl.* 433).[70] But the concept of 'unwritten law' seems to have been manipulated by some of the late fifth-century Sophists – indeed it was perhaps an inherently slippery notion – and become increasingly distrusted. When democracy was restored in 403 after the brutal oligarchic regime of the Thirty, it forbade magistrates to apply an unwritten law (Andoc. 1.85 and 87). The manipulation of 'unwritten laws' (not to mention written ones) by the late fifth-century oligarchs may be the political background to this. Some of the Sophists had oligarchic sympathies themselves. Written law had presumably become closely associated with the democracy through the Assembly's creation of law by its decrees in the fifth century. But it took the intellectual and political turmoils of the late fifth century to crystallize the connection firmly.

Written law, then, may be a necessary condition for judicial fairness but it is not a sufficient one. The social and political context determined the efficacy of written law in ancient Greece as elsewhere, and it could equally well have conservative or aristocratic as democratic force. Its associations with democracy developed gradually in the specific political climate of Athens.

[68] Contrast Ostwald 1973; see also Gagarin 1986, for whom law is by definition written.
[69] cf. also Xenophon, *Memorabilia* 1.2.40–6; 4.4.13.
[70] See Ostwald 1973 on unwritten law, and 1986, ch. 5, esp. 250–66 for intellectual debate on *nomos*; but he does not see it so much in terms of conflict between written and unwritten law.

Why do written documents increase in Athens during the fifth and fourth centuries? Our immediate answer would be that fifth-century Athens was developing an ever more complex administration to run her empire: the Assembly was dealing with more business, passing more decrees, and the empire involved Athens in more alliances and more punitive settlements. But a problem with this is that the extension of the empire did not necessarily require sophisticated written records. The decrees (as they stand on stone) are not all useful administrative documents, and the huge monumental inscriptions had other functions as well. While the proliferating inscriptions partly reflected the growing power of Athens, the city was in one sense simply producing more of the traditional kind of written record – laws and treaties – rather than radically different types of document. Of course the Assembly saw itself as passing laws, which tended by convention to be made publicly visible on stone. It is at least worth asking whether Athens' use of writing here was not still an extension of the idea that laws passed by the democratic Assembly should be in written, publicly visible, preferably monumental, form.

In addition, many inscriptions seem intended to impress Athens' authority over her empire – for example the imposing *stelai* recording punitive settlements after an ally has revolted, set up in Athens and in the disobedient city at the latter's expense. (Lists might also be kept, not on stone, of individual citizens once they had taken the oath of obedience to Athens. As the Chalkis decree declares, 'The oath shall be administered ... and they shall write down (*apographsai*) the names of the Chalkidians who swear it', M L 52.36–9). We have here the use of writing for a punitive – and exemplary – purpose, rather than a strictly administrative one. These are surely not primarily administrative documents but perform something like Finley's 'police function', but with an additional exemplary and symbolic force.[71]

But matters are rather different in the fourth century. The written word is, as we have seen, increasingly accepted as proof and it is added to certain procedures in the courts.[72] Athens was becoming more 'document-minded' and the state was in effect demanding more written documentation. This was not an automa-

---

[71] Finley (police function) 1952: 14, and 1982.
[72] Calhoun 1919; Pringsheim 1955.

tic development, but involved a changed respect for the written word. Witnesses and oaths had long been sufficient, and the development cannot have been inevitable, a simple progression towards greater sophistication.

The forceful identification of written law with democracy by now may have had some influence, perhaps extending greater respectability to written proof by association. It is also likely that the impetus for greater documentation comes originally from those making contracts or loans, and from the individuals who were likely to sit in the jury courts for contested cases, or pass decrees in the Assembly. In that case the encroachment of writing may have been the result of the ever-present distrust in an increasingly complex society, the impetus to ensure as much proof as possible for any transaction coming from individual citizens rather than the 'state'. A written document is comparatively permanent, and more easy to check in a dispute: without standardized format, forgeries were very easy, it is true, but witnesses were still used, and attempts were made to guard documents by sealing them in jars. (The lid of a jar containing documents for a fourth-century trial and found in the agora reads: 'Of the written copies, the following four are inside: testimony from the arbitration, law on the abuse of heiresses, challenge of testimony, oaths of litigants. Antenor put the lid on'.[73]) In the increasingly commercial and therefore mobile world of the fourth century, writing perhaps seemed more stable and trustworthy than witnesses whom you might not know and might never see again. Thus written contracts were almost universal in the risky area of maritime loans.[74] As the orator Aeschines said in the middle of the fourth century, 'We make written contracts with one another through distrust, so that the man who sticks to the terms may get satisfaction from the man who disregards them' (1.161); on this, at least, Demosthenes agreed with him: 'the law requires people to give evidence in writing so that it is impossible to remove any part of what has been written or add anything to it' (45.44).

There is therefore no straightforward relationship between political system and the written word. Athens certainly used written records

---

[73] Camp 1986: 113, fig. 86 (Agora Inventory P 28470).
[74] Finley 1952: 22 and n. 61.

more than her contemporaries largely because of the democratic ideal of publicity, accountability, and then the explicit identification of written law with democracy and justice. But what is interesting is how gradually that identification crystallized out of specific social and political conditions in Athens. The ideal did not *in itself* entail extensive administrative use of written documents, and was compatible with other uses of at least public written texts for monument, example, and authority, which are reminiscent of the practice in other Greek cities. Writing was used in the service of the city-state, and in Athens, at least, the impetus and precise details came from the citizen body itself, in the citizen-assembly.

4 STATE, INDIVIDUAL, AND WRITTEN RECORD

No one would want to deny the fundamental role of writing in preserving and communicating information, nor the role of the written literary texts in the culture of the elite, particularly from the fourth century on. It is much harder to determine how far Greek citizens actually needed to read and write themselves, and to what extent they were debarred from the major activities in their society if they could not. The important recent study by Harris (1989) has shown exhaustively how little evidence actually exists for extensive literacy in the ancient world. Should we assume that the relevant evidence is simply unavailable, or do we envisage a society in which only a tiny elite were able to read and write, and thus participate fully in Graeco-Roman culture? For the purposes of this chapter I concentrate mainly on the sphere of government.

Yet we need to distinguish the products of literacy (documents, written texts) from a person's need to be literate himself. Ancient writers tend to praise the uses of writing rather than the skill of being able to write. We probably should assume that comparatively few had very complex literate skills.[75] In a scribal society like ancient Mesopotamia, the kings could rely on trusted servants to perform the physical act of writing while benefiting from its products. In early modern England, the products of literacy (and its benefits) could spread far beyond the comparatively narrow circle of those who could read them: illiterates did not live 'in some sort of mental darkness'.[76] In classical Athens, someone who did not read

---

[75] I use this vague phrase deliberately: see ch. 1 and below.
[76] K. Thomas 1986: quotation p. 105; Stock 1983.

literary texts would not necessarily be cut off from them entirely, since they would be performed – whereas in the more bookish Roman culture this would be harder. There is much more at stake here than literacy. In the Roman period (not to mention later) many illiterates were quite unimpeded by their illiteracy from pursuing successful careers. A famous wealthy businessman at Pompeii, P. Annius Seleucus, was illiterate.[77] Social status was a great deal more limiting than illiteracy. It is far from clear that literacy could contribute to social mobility in the ancient world.

There is a further question, seldom tackled, of the relation of the extent of literate skills (of any kind) to need. Modern experience of literacy underlines that the extent to which people can read and write is often a function of necessity and that literacy is forgotten if there is no reason to use it. Did so many people in the ancient world remain illiterate or 'semi-literate' because it did not matter to them? Some of the people officially classed as 'slow writers' in the documents of Graeco-Roman Egypt may have been in the process of forgetting what little writing skills they had learnt at school.[78] Alternatively, could the prevalence of illiteracy have in fact limited the powers of the 'state'?

The case of Graeco-Roman Egypt offers an extreme example of this set of problems, and its custom of classifying people according to their ability to write offers ample evidence of a kind we lack elsewhere. In Egypt under Graeco-Macedonian rule (332–30 BC) and then Roman (from 30 BC), written record does indeed seem to form a powerful bureaucracy, for it was used intensively for administration, taxation, business receipts, contracts, official memoranda (much of this bureaucracy may have been inherited from the Pharaonic system).[79]

The modern reader would assume that anyone unable (or barely able) to read and write would be at a heavy disadvantage in this morass of paperwork. Only the literate could write private letters and memoranda themselves. Yet it is precisely for the more formal

---

[77] For Annius Seleucus, W. V. Harris 1989: 197–8 and refs. there; cf. Youtie 1971a: 172–3 for people in responsible positions in Egypt unable to write a word (incl. Aurelius Isidorus); early modern examples, K. Thomas 1986.

[78] Youtie 1971b: 252.

[79] On bureaucracy in Graeco-Roman Egypt: Turner, *CAH²* VII ch. 5; Cockle 1984; Burkhalter 1990; Pierce 1968; Welles 1949; Montevecchi 1988; Posner 1972; Husselman 1970; Boak 1923; Raschke 1974; Seidl 1962. cf. Hopkins 1991

documents used for business or marriage contracts, loans, and sales
that the functional division between literate and illiterate becomes
more blurred. Many of the details are unclear, but under the Ptolemies agreements had to be drawn up by a professional notary and
be registered (*anagraphe*) at a public office. The Romans extended
the system, and some of the huge mass of papyri dealt with by the
local village writing office (the *grapheion*) have been found. They
insisted that an individual could only produce documents in court
if these had been drawn up by a notary – or, if not, if they had been
given publicity by being deposited (two copies) in a state registry
office in Alexandria.[80] This developed system of registration, storage, and retrieval was capable of checking records over the space of
several years. Here indeed was the state imposing its demands for
standard, authoritative documents to be produced by officials for
all private individuals involved in certain (rather common) activities. Both literate and illiterate individuals were drawn inevitably
into this system.

Yet the existence of a highly sophisticated scribal system meant
that illiterates were not quite as disabled as we would think, and
the fact that everyone had to go to a scribe for certain documents
perhaps reduced the social stigma (if there was one) of being
unable to write. Indeed, Greeks even used the services of the scribes
for private letters they were perfectly able to write themselves, so
they seem to have set no premium on the personal contribution of
the sender himself (who only added a short greeting at the end).
Incidentally, the scribal office had its own influence on the written
products of Egypt: people dictating letters were inhibited by the
publicity of the office from describing private matters, and even
letters written by private individuals reveal the influence of the
scribal style.[81]

Illiterate people turned to literate friends and relatives to add the
'subscription' (a sort of signature) at the bottom of the document
on their behalf[82] – an example of how one literate person could, as
it were, go a long way. Illiterates were sometimes prey to deception,
unable to check the documents they were party to, and an important study by Youtie admits that a total illiterate would only be

---

[80] Turner 1968: 134–5; Cockle 1984: 106–22, esp. 114–15.
[81] Turner 1968: 83, 130.
[82] See esp. Youtie 1975; also Youtie 1971a and 1971b; Calderini 1950; Majer-Leonhard
    1913; Turner 1968: 82–4, for illiterates generally.

completely secure from fraud if he or she had a literate person prepared to examine the document carefully on his or her behalf.[83] We probably cannot insist that the illiterate was not disadvantaged in any way.[84] But the degree of disadvantage is a function of the system as a whole, and cannot be separated from the social context. Youtie was concerned to stress that the illiterates in these documents were not cut off from their society as illiterates would be today, and that they do not seem to suffer any social stigma. Yet some of his evidence reveals that illiterates and their literate helpers do tend to be economically and socially inferior, borrowers rather than lenders, for instance, and that the social elite, members of the gymnasium, were expected to be 'literate'.[85] The scribal system helped the illiterate to participate easily in all activities which needed writing, but it bore most heavily on those least able to pay the scribal fee (the modern use of lawyers may be a good analogy). In fact, simpler types of agreement (the *cheirographa* and *hypomnemata*) continued to be drawn up by private individuals rather than scribes, so, again, all that was needed was someone trustworthy who could write. But any procedure was less burdensome on those more prosperous and familiar with documents.

In the case of women, the ability to write seems to be comparatively immaterial to their status compared to other factors. Women with the privilege of acting without a *kyrios* or guardian are sometimes literate, sometimes not. A famous example of a woman petitioning for the *ius trium liberorum* (privileges for women with three children) stresses that she is also literate: but others with the same privilege are sometimes illiterate, even though they could act without a guardian.[86] Literacy might be useful, but it was not central. This is underlined rather neatly by a particular case of a literate woman who has an illiterate male guardian. Her guardian has to get another man (not, of course, the woman, who was under tutelage) to add his subscription for him. A woman never added a subscription for someone else, even her own husband.[87]

We thus get the impression that degrees of literacy were related

---

[83] Youtie 1975: 205–7.
[84] W. V. Harris 1989: 141ff.
[85] Youtie 1971a: esp. 173–5; 1971b: 260–1.
[86] See Youtie 1975: 221 n. 62, altering his previous view (1971a: 166–8); Sijpesteijn 1965; Pomeroy 1984.
[87] Youtie 1975: 213.

to social status, but literacy did not bring status itself. The real disadvantage came from social class and origin. Illiterates would tend to be of a lower social class (or native Egyptian), and so would be disadvantaged anyway. This is perhaps to be expected in a society where writing was often left to slaves.

There are further social factors hidden behind these arrangements. The documents make careful distinctions between those who can write, those who were 'slow writers', and those 'without letters' (*agrammatoi*). But this hierarchy of literate skills applies exclusively to literacy in Greek. Most of the population was Egyptian. Plenty of Egyptians were functionally illiterate from the point of view of the administrators, but could read and write in Demotic (Egyptian).[88] Moreover, it tends to be forgotten that these definitions are not only ethnocentric but made precisely for the purposes of signing and validating contracts (that is, a function of the bureaucratic system). Only one aspect of literacy was needed for that, the ability to write simple sentences, and I would doubt if it told one about, say, someone's ability to read. In most periods of history, the skills of reading and writing have been separate ones, and it is worth suggesting that some of the 'illiterates' and 'slow writers' may have been able to read, even read Greek.[89] Individuals might be functionally illiterate in one context but not in another. The differentiation of skills in using writing meant that many would be effectively excluded from certain 'literate' activities.

That brings us back to the relation of literate skills to the demands made on individuals for written documents. If recent indications from Roman Egypt are correct, a rather high proportion of the inhabitants could sign their names and add subscriptions.[90] We do not (yet) know what else they used their skill for, but even if it was narrowly limited to the needs of authenticating documentary transactions, one may well suspect that such a level of literacy was a direct response to the perceived importance and usefulness of the written word in a highly bureaucratic society.[91]

---

[88] See Youtie 1971a.

[89] There may be slight evidence that more Greeks in Egypt could read but not write in the fact that subscriptions to documents occasionally mention that the literate helper also *read out* the document to the illiterate party (examples in Youtie 1971b: 254 (AD 212), though Youtie takes them to show that 'slow writers' could not read either (he never separates writing from reading).

[90] See K. Hopkins 1991.

[91] A merely practical accomplishment: Youtie 1975: 220–1.

Equally important, there was a degree of familiarity with documents in everyday life which was quite unusual in the ancient world. On the other hand, the governments of Egypt were surely only able to achieve this intensity of bureaucracy because they inherited an established scribal culture (not to mention a tradition of bureaucratic record keeping) which actually enabled them to demand appropriate written documentation from all. Illiterates could be expected to provide it because of the scribal system, and if they learnt to write, they would learn a mode of literacy suited to this particular bureaucratic context.

In classical Athens, by contrast, the average Athenian citizen in the fifth and even fourth century was not required to produce written documentation so regularly, and much more stress was laid on oral agreements and witnesses. With the ubiquitous heralds and secretaries to read aloud in the Assemblies, the Athenian who was unable to write would not be totally unable to participate in political and social life. Yet one suspects – and can only suspect – firstly, that more Athenian citizens had a rudimentary knowledge of how to read or write than was the case in the rest of the contemporary Greek world; and secondly, that while the illiterate individual could get someone to write a formal document for him (or a ballot for an ostracism, Plut. *Aristeides* 7), he would (paradoxically) find it a great deal harder than in Ptolemaic Egypt, where there were the props of an elaborate scribal system. But literate skills of some kind were probably more extensive in Athens. The graffiti found in the Athenian agora testify to a large amount of miscellaneous and casual scribbling, notes, lists, owners' marks. Their very presence contrasts with the situation in (say) Crete, where no such informal writing is found.[92] A joke in Aristophanes' comedy, *The Knights*, may reflect the educational level of the mass of the citizenry who did not usually achieve much political influence: the 'sausage-seller' is asked his credentials for becoming 'leader of the people' and protests his low level of education – he knows his letters, 'but not very well'.[93] What is being parodied here (unfairly) is the lower educational level of the new leaders after Pericles in the late fifth century. So, if we accept that more Athenians had learnt to read and write than the citizens of other cities, they would have

---

[92] Lang 1976, for graffiti; cf. Stoddart and Whitley 1988 for *archaic* Crete.
[93] Lines 188–90: ἀλλ' ὦγαθ' οὐδὲ μουσικὴν / πλὴν γραμμάτων, καὶ ταῦτα μέντοι κακὰ κακῶς.

been encouraged by the associations of writing in Athens with democracy, public inscriptions, and the laws. These gave writing a prominence and political role and gradually ensured that it gained public trust for the secure transaction of public and private affairs.

It therefore seems impossible to pursue the question of how far an individual was disadvantaged by poor or non-existent literate skills without taking into account the precise local context, what writing was needed for, and what had to be written by yourself. I have taken the case of Graeco-Roman Egypt – where we have reasonable data on 'illiterates' – to illustrate the complexities and configurations involved here: the extent of bureaucratic control and of state demands for written records, and the cushioning effect of the scribal system which also enabled the state to supervise most effectively a population which was not only often non-Greek speaking but also illiterate in any language. It is not enough here to think simply in terms of subjects who are literate or illiterate. In some respect all inhabitants, illiterate (in Greek or Egyptian) or not, were at the mercy of the state bureaucracy – and yet, equally, could use the scribal system. But many people who were literate in one respect were illiterate in another, and had to go to the scribes for the specialized matter of writing (or writing certain types of documents). There probably are social distinctions discernible between those who were illiterate or literate in Greek (not to mention between Greeks and Egyptians). In that case, if Youtie is right to insist that there is little social cachet in being literate amongst the groups of people signing the documents, literate skills of some sort were subordinate to the greater advantages of social and economic status.

We have seen how little use was made of the written word for any kind of administrative record or bureaucracy by the Greek city-state. If we look for the characteristic written records of the *polis*, they seem to be the public, visible ones, inscriptions rather than archival documents – and that this is not simply an erroneous impression given by the surviving evidence, is suggested by the treatment given to inscriptions by ancient writers, and by the very hopes and anxieties about the survival of the stones expressed on the inscriptions themselves. But we need to go beyond the easy identifications of public writing with the democratic *polis*, and non-inscribed (therefore secret) writing with tyranny, for this strict division seems to break down on closer examination. Public inscribed texts were used by many cities for display, authority, intimidation, example – and this includes Athens, though not Sparta and Corinth – as well as to promote democratic accountability, as in classical Athens. The association of exclusively written law with democracy was the product of a gradual development in Athens. The place of the individual citizen and his need or ability to write should be seen accordingly, in the context of his particular city-state, or, as is clear in Graeco-Roman Egypt, within the wider social system as well. This throws us back to wider questions: how far, for instance, is the level of written record related to the system of taxation, or how did the city-state manage without so many of the written records we would take for granted? But one of the themes of this book has been that the study of ancient literacy and orality encompasses, as the study of various different forms of communication, far more than the question of whether men and women could read and write.

Epilogue: the Roman world

By comparison with Greece, the world of Roman history has remained unruffled by the controversies surrounding orality or the effects of literacy. On the whole, Rome has seemed safely distant from the beginnings of alphabetic writing and any related problems – though there are areas where such preoccupations are not irrelevant.[1] Certainly Roman society in the late Republic and Empire is far more dominated by books and documents than classical Greece. Latin literature inherited the learned weight of Hellenistic scholarship, and everyone would agree that there was plenty of reading matter (at least in the cities), a flourishing book-trade, and a fairly wide reading public, certainly by the second century A D.[2] It would be quite misguided to deny that the written word was important in administration, in the records of taxation, trials and the citizen-body, in the circulation of literature, and in everyday life. Writing in various forms was surely much more deeply integrated into the life of at least the cities by the first century B C than it had been in classical Greece. But how deeply? To deny a similarity between classical Greece and Rome does not reach the limit of possible enquiry. As current discussions about the nature of Roman administration show, for instance, much is unclear even about the precise place of the written document in Rome. Harris' recent book (1989) has performed an invaluable task in collecting much of the evidence for the Roman uses of writing: but Harris also emphasizes the areas of Roman life where writing might have been unknown or unimportant, and is primarily concerned to show how *rare* literacy was. If he is right, this raises the question of how much these low

---

[1] E.g. in the role of oral tradition: see Wiseman 1989; cf. Cornell 1991.
[2] Perry 1967; W. V. Harris 1989: 222–9, and ch. 7 generally. For a possible result, see Most 1990 on the formation of a literary canon. Richards 1991 provides much useful material on secretaries.

literacy rates mattered, and what the precise role of writing actually was.

Given that literacy is a culturally determined variable, and its manifestations are often a function of the society that uses it, there is still much room to examine the characteristically Roman approaches to writing. Why is the burning of books, for instance, a specifically Roman activity? One profitable approach could be along the lines of more recent detailed studies of writing in later periods that avoid any one-dimensional or determinist vision of writing. The comparative neglect of orality and literacy in the Roman sphere at least leaves the field uncluttered by old and perhaps superseded controversies. I do not need to reiterate the now familiar observation that performance, oratory, and oral presentation remained crucial, despite the presence of written documents and literature. But there do remain extremely interesting opportunities to examine the relation between oral and written communication and the characteristically Roman experience of literacy and orality.

Inevitably I can offer only a selective and superficial picture here. Quite apart from the vastness of the topic, the Roman world comprises a huge area, a range of different cultures (including Greek), and a wide variety of people, including urban and rural inhabitants as well as the sophisticated elite of Roman politics and literature.[3] I shall concentrate on areas where interesting issues and questions deserve to be raised, even if they cannot yet be answered, or where stimulating work has been done on the meaning of writing in Rome. Newly discovered evidence and a few recent studies are beginning to bring the Roman material into the debate about the uses of writing on a quite sophisticated level.

First, consider the position of written literary texts. It would, for instance, be extremely valuable to chart the undeniable Roman stress on the value of oral performance alongside the greater role of written literary texts. Perhaps Rome should be considered, to borrow Brian Stock's formulation (1983) for the early Middle Ages, as a society in which the spoken word, though important, was increasingly dominated and influenced by written texts. Eloquent speech remained the most characteristic feature of Graeco-Roman civilization, even in its most learned manifestations. In the late first and

[3] Clearly set out by W. V. Harris 1989: 175–90.

second centuries AD, the period of the Second Sophistic, this cultural 'renaissance' of the Greek world was centred on the production of archaizing speeches and highly theatrical 'declamations' to huge audiences, often on totally fictional subjects. However alien such expositions might seem to us, they attracted large gatherings, both at festivals like the one at Olympia, and in the Greek cities. The audiences may have consisted largely of orators, Sophists and their pupils, in other words the educated and wealthy elite (as the Sophists themselves preferred to think), but there are indications of a wider appeal.[4]

In earlier Roman oratory, the appearance of improvisation was carefully cultivated and the orator either memorized his text or actually improvised. Cicero and Quintilian devoted considerable attention to the art of memorization, and Quintilian disapproved of the extensive use of note-books, believing that you should never write out anything which was not intended to be memorized.[5] Even in the show declamations of the Second Sophistic in the second century AD, the most highly prized skills were those which enabled orators to improvise on the spur of the moment upon some topic suggested by the audience – and in the Attic Greek of an earlier era. Giving the same speech twice was frowned upon, so repetition in these circumstances was at least not an openly avowed aim.

At the same time, though, this was a world in which written texts were now used extensively for teaching purposes (students would form much of the audience), and many official or unofficial texts of a speech were in circulation, once it had been delivered. Though pagan teachers, unlike Christians, avoided the use of shorthand,[6] members of the audience pooled their notes or shorthand versions. The result was that a Sophist who attempted to use the same speech again might be in the embarrassing position of having his words chanted back at him by his audience.[7] There is obviously a complicated relationship between the oral nature of the performance and the use of writing. One incidental but important result of

---

[4] Philostratus, *Lives of the Sophists* 2.8, and Russell 1983: esp. 79ff; also Kennedy 1972 and 1983.

[5] Cicero, *De Oratore* 2.351ff; Quint. 10.7.30–2; 11.

[6] Norman 1960: 123.

[7] cf. Lucian, *Herodotus or Aëtion* 7–8; *Apologia* 3; cf. Russell 1983: 74–86 for some of the evidence.

the primacy of the oral version is that there might be no single written text which could be regarded as the author's own 'authorized' version. It remains an open question, however, and one usually unasked, what the precise significance of memorization really is in such a literary context: whether or how far these orators' ability to memorize was altered by the fact that they could use a written text to memorize from; and how far the skill of extemporization is helped by written texts which can serve as templates or models. One would think that these oral performances were very much part of the written literary tradition, even if the conventions against taking notes meant that the speeches themselves were transmitted inaccurately by the written word.

Interesting points also arise in the non-rhetorical sphere. Most assume that in the scholarly milieu of the learned philosophical and medical schools of the Roman Empire the place of books would be unproblematic, and probably easily recognizable to scholars today. But there was considerable debate about the value of books, even by such scholarly writers as Galen, not renowned for his restraint in publishing written works. But that of course puts it too baldly. As a recent article by Lovejoy Alexander has shown,[8] what was questioned was the value of books by themselves for teaching purposes. You must not 'try to navigate out of a book' as a contemporary proverb went; that is, you needed first-hand experience to learn a craft. This sounds like simple common sense. But there were elaborate ramifications to the discussion, in which the relation between written and oral could be seen in many different ways' (the debate was also pursued in Christian and Jewish writers[9]). Galen and his contemporaries were primarily concerned about the utility of the book for teaching. It might be grossly inadequate unless backed up by the help of the teacher himself: 'I order that these notes should be shared only with those who would read the book with a teacher', he says.[10] So a text might be regarded more as an aid to memorization of what had been passed on orally by a teacher, as a reminder to those who know: this is strongly reminiscent of Plato's strictures

[8] Alexander 1990, to which I am much indebted. She starts from Christian and Rabbinical attitudes.
[9] See Roberts 1979, for early Christian Egypt; Gerhardsson 1961, for Rabbinic Judaism and early Christianity; Graham 1987, on oral aspects of scripture; Vermes 1986, on written and oral Torah.
[10] *De libris propriis* 11, Kühn xix 42 = Galen, *Scripta Minora* ii 118.22–4.

in the *Phaedrus* (274b–279b) on the slight value of a written text for real knowledge.

So while written texts were certainly not forbidden in the philosophical schools, they might be seen as subordinate to the oral methods of teaching. One interesting corollary of this attitude is that the true teachings of a founder of a philosophical school (like that of Epicurus) might be thought to reside in the traditions continued by the school rather than in the original written texts left by the founder,[11] and this might even entail the interpolation of the texts. What is particularly striking here is that this is only one response, among several that one might expect, to the existence of a revered founder whose teachings had been at least partly preserved in writing. We do not find here a 'religion of the book' as Christianity has often been described, with the stress on exegesis of the original written text – though this did also develop later, to some extent – nor an equally predictable emphasis on exact memorization. But there is an apparently much more fluid process of interpretation and tradition in the schools, even interpolation of the philosophical texts, which eschews a strict regard for verbatim accuracy or individual intellectual copyright. Plato, incidentally, may have moved in yet another direction again, as he developed his idea of the 'unwritten doctrines' expressed in the *Seventh Letter*, believing that his deepest thoughts should never be written down at all lest they fall into the hands of the ignorant multitude.[12] There is a recurrent tendency amongst the devotees of 'higher education' in the ancient world to limit the number of texts available, rather than welcome their increase.

There are also rich possibilities for examination of the roles of the written word in other areas which involve non-literary texts. Take the role of the inscription, for instance. The practice of erecting inscribed texts, obviously in part inherited from the Greeks, is constant in neither period nor area, and the reasons deserve investigation. A provocative article by MacMullen (1982) has emphasized the extreme oddity of the stone inscription – and thus of the 'epigraphic habit' – as a response to the coming of writing. Comparing the distribution of papyri, he draws attention more forcefully than others to the very uneven distribution of inscriptions

---

[11] Alexander 1990: 233–6, citing J. M. Dillon, *The Middle Platonists* (London 1977), 338.
[12] 341c–e; Edelstein 1966.

found from the period of the Roman Empire, and to the way they rise dramatically in number towards the end of the second century AD during the Severan period. He thus questions any easy correlation between the frequency of inscriptions in any given area and the kind of conclusions about behaviour and social change that are often drawn from it. The increase in inscriptions (mainly epitaphs, in fact) must reflect some change in the very habit of erecting inscriptions, perhaps partly Romanization in areas of the empire such as North Africa, perhaps (he suggests) a 'sense of audience'; their decline must be explained by some kind of 'psychological shift'. But one can go rather further. A more precise social context has been suggested for epitaphs, at least, which confirms that their erection constituted a deliberate statement of Romanization or an upwardly-mobile quest for Roman status, and that they were closely connected to the 'rise and fall of inscriptional self-aggrandisement'. Those epitaphs in particular which mentioned both deceased and commemorator were specifically meant to proclaim that the deceased was a Roman citizen and that his heir had fulfilled his duty of erecting the epitaph.[13]

The gulf in content and meaning between these epitaphs and those, say, in archaic Greece could hardly underline more clearly that we are dealing with a culturally determined habit which (*pace* Harris 1989) is only marginally related to the extent of literate skills. It can scarcely be overemphasized that our epigraphic sources not only have had to survive the destructive effects of time, but are also the result of a selection process in which individual Romans (and non-Romans) decided whether to set up a stone and what would be suitable to put on it. Inscriptions might be intended for information, propaganda, memorial, or ostentation, but they all comprised a public use of writing which was related to wider social and political factors.[14] It is no coincidence that a very large proportion of inscriptions from the Roman Empire are honorific in some way, whereas epitaphs of classical Athens bore little but the name of the deceased. The use made of inscriptions may tell one a great deal about mentality.

A more symbolic purpose can be perceived behind certain kinds

---

[13] Meyer 1990: 95.

[14] See esp. Corbier 1987; F. Millar's chapter, in M. Crawford, ed., *Sources for Ancient History* (Cambridge 1983) provides an excellent introduction to the problems and possibilities in studying inscriptions.

of inscriptions, and this moves us rapidly closer to the picture I have traced for Greece. The surroundings of an inscription, for instance, were important. Documents could thus gain appropriate authority, or, if they were inscribed in temples, divine supervision.[15] In the first century A D there were at least 3,000 bronze tablets on the Capitoline Hill in Rome, all burned in the fire towards the end of Nero's reign (Nero committed suicide in A D 68): 'This was the most beautiful and most ancient record of empire (*instrumentum imperii*), comprising senatorial decrees, decisions made by the Roman people concerning alliance, treaty, and privilege granted to individuals, dating back almost to the foundation of Rome', as Suetonius put it (Suet. *Vespasian* 8.5).

The use of inscriptions for power and display stands out dramatically: the name of the man who financed the erection or restoration of a building would be displayed prominently. The emperor Augustus boasted on a public inscription that he restored the Temple of Capitoline Juppiter and the Theatre of Pompey 'without inscribing my name on either', a feat of considerable political restraint.[16]

One may ponder the function of the impressive bronze tablets of laws set up during Republic and Empire. Some at least were erected in such a way that the whole inscription could not have been legible without great difficulty, not to mention the use of a step-ladder. Yet, as Williamson has suggested recently (1987), they seem to have been created not so much for public legibility as to be eternal monuments of the laws passed, which were rendered sacred and inviolable by the fact that they were on bronze. To engrave a statute was an attempt to attain permanence. The formula specifying that a document be placed 'where it can be read from ground level' seems to have been applied only to the more temporary whitened boards (*alba*). A rather different symbolic purpose has been convincingly extracted by Mary Beard (1985) from the records of the priestly rituals of the Arval Brethren, which were elaborately inscribed every year at ever greater length in the sacred grove until even the stone furniture was covered with writing. The production of the written record was part of the ritual, and that, or some related aim, seems to have been its purpose, not the utilitarian creation of a record of the rituals that would be consulted later.

But once the spectre of 'symbolic function' has been raised, we

[15] Corbier 1987: 43–6; Culham 1989: esp. 109–12.
[16] *Res Gestae* 20.1: see Corbier 1987: 46 for other examples.

are faced with the problem encountered earlier for Greece: does a symbolic element corroborate or undermine other uses and intentions in the creation of written texts? This question was perhaps left open by Mary Beard, but to attribute a purely symbolic purpose to certain records does not seem to do justice either to the complexity of Roman society or to the implications of the written word within it. Besides, records might have been made, quite consciously, for purposes of reference, but were not used because they were not really needed, or because they were inadequately composed. And while the mere existence of documents does not entitle us to assume there was easy access to them, lack of access might be accounted for by other factors. This is an extremely difficult area which has received little investigation.

In the case of Roman laws, for instance, symbolic value coexists with their evident importance as records of legal documents. But some of their more surprising features may be related to differing attitudes to documents as such. Whatever their symbolic role, the inscribed bronze texts do seem to have been consulted.[17] The inscribed, public copy is clearly regarded as having legal force, and this holds true for all documents posted publicly. Indeed, it had more than legal force, for the removal of a bronze tablet seems to have been tantamount to a repeal of its written contents. When Caesar took down a tablet from the Capitoline Hill, he is said by Cicero to have cancelled several grants of Roman citizenship (*Ad familiares* 13.36). Cicero himself tried in 56 B C to remove certain statutes, probably inscribed on bronze, of his arch-enemy Clodius.[18]

It is admittedly true that the laws were fairly widely known and available in some form to senators and members of the elite who needed to consult them, and legal experts may have made their own copies from the versions deposited in the *Aerarium* (Treasury) or from private collections.[19] Wider knowledge of the laws would come from their being read aloud at the time of promulgation in any case.[20] But attested knowledge of the laws is a rather different matter from the question of the role of public inscriptions. It does

---

[17] Crawford 1988: 133; cf. Josephus, *Antiquitates Judaicae* 14.10 (consulting public texts on bronze). Other important works: Williamson 1987; Schwind 1973; Frederiksen 1965.

[18] Williamson 1987: 177–8 on tablet-breakers.

[19] See Crawford 1988: 132, 133 for some private copies (of Cato and Cicero); cf. Culham 1989: 104–5 on private copies of other kinds of records.

[20] W. V. Harris 1989: 161 (for oral and written promulgation).

not necessarily imply that the inscriptions did not also have symbolic, as well as functional, meaning.

But this still leaves open the problem of how easy access actually was to the written records (and it is not enough to blame any inadequacies on the disruption of the end of the Republic, without more explicit scrutiny). It is far from certain, for example, that all statutes were erected in permanent public form on bronze, rather than temporary whitened boards.[21] This would mean that there was no permanent, easily accessible copy of every statute. In many cases the only copy would have been in the *Aerarium* – but that does not seem to have been easy to consult either (see p. 167). One case is recorded where a mistake was corrected *after* a statute had been passed, inscribed, and a copy deposited in the *Aerarium*.[22] This is usually cited as proof that all laws went into the *Aerarium*, but it also betrays a surprising unconcern with legal and documentary punctiliousness of the kind which is taken for granted by modern scholars. Some degree of inaccessibility or confusion in the records is implied by Cicero's complaints (in effect) about extreme laxity towards the written records of the laws – reminding us of all the social and political barriers to the efficacy of written law noted in the case of Greece. In a much discussed passage, he complains (tendentiously) that the Greeks were much more careful about their laws than the Romans:

We have no guardianship of the laws; thus the laws are whatever our clerks want them to be; we get them from the scribes and have no public record officially established in public letters ('legum custodiam nullam habemus; itaque leges sunt, quas apparitores nostri volunt; a librariis petimus, publicis litteris consignatam memoriam publicam nullam habemus'). The Greeks were more careful about this, for they elected *nomophylakes* (guardians of the laws), who not only kept watch over the text of the laws ... but in addition observed men's acts. (*De legibus* 3.20.46)[23]

This brings us to the wider question of archives and the keeping of records generally. Here too, as for Greece, the modernizing assumptions that the Romans kept and reused their records as we might, and that archives were self-evidently intended mainly for consultation, are only occasionally questioned. However, a recent article by Culham (1989) has sought to undermine the idea that the

---

[21] Crawford 1988: 133; Williamson 1987: 172–4; Frederiksen 1965: 184.
[22] Suetonius, *Divus Julius* 28.2.
[23] See also *De Legibus* 3.20.48 where the gist is repeated; on the interpretation of this passage, Rawson 1973, esp. 352–4; W. V. Harris 1989: 165; Williamson 1987: 169.

Aerarium was a central state archive in the Republic, for records were widely diffused amongst different buildings and even private individuals. Access to the *Aerarium*, or any other store of records, was difficult and does not seem to have been an ideal much mentioned. Culham may be going too far in saying that records were left in the *Aerarium* primarily as a sacred place of storage, but certainly whitened boards posted up in public were the records to be routinely consulted. Moreover, the senate was notoriously secretive about publicizing its business, and in fact it was only in 59 B C that Julius Caesar proposed the future publication of their records.[24] They were kept in the *Aerarium* on waxed tablets, which were very easy to tamper with. One could interpret this as evidence of an extreme fragmentation and diffusion of public records in which there was only a blurred distinction between public records and private, and in which, accordingly, access to and reuse of the records were highly dependent on individual whim and personal contacts with the leading families.

On the other hand, there are conflicting indications in some fairly recently discovered evidence of extreme care and exactitude in keeping records. But the precise significance of this is still hard to gauge. An inscription found at the Greek city of Aphrodisias in south-west Turkey recording a *senatus consultum* (senatorial decree) of 39 B C actually gives the 'tablet numbers' of the records, presumably referring to senatorial or quaestorial records in Rome itself. This is rather impressive, though it should be said that the tablets or *deltoi*, translated in bureaucratic language by the editors as 'file numbers', would actually be waxed wooden tablets, and rather more vulnerable as records than the public bronze or stone copies put up in Rome and Aphrodisias.[25] Such exactitude may represent a special attempt to stress authenticity in a troubled period of civil war. The detailed character of the *commentarii* recording grants of Roman citizenship under the empire is fortunately revealed by extracts written out in the *Tabula Banasitana* (from Morocco) in the late second century A D. Marcus Aurelius and Commodus even request the procurator or local financial administrator to 'find out

---

[24] Culham 1989; cf. Posner 1972; Frederiksen 1965; cf. Talbert 1984: 303–37 on senatorial records.
[25] See J. Reynolds 1982: Doc. 8, lines 1–3, pp. 64–6 and bibliography there; cf. Doc. 6 = R. K. Sherk, *Rome and the Greek East to the death of Augustus* (Cambridge 1984) no. 87; cf. Culham 1989: 108, and Gabba 1961: 95 for the frequency of forgery.

the age of each [of the recipients], and write to us, in order that it
may be recorded in our *commentarii*'.[26] However, these *commentarii*
(of new citizens) were established only by the emperor Augustus –
perhaps because there had been no need for them earlier; and other
commentarii recorded trials and perhaps imperial letters (Pliny,
Epistles 10.65,66). They seem to be the immediate private records of
the emperor, completely under his control and probably essentially
the records of his own acts. As Fergus Millar has pointed out, it is
not clear what happened to them when the emperor travelled
around (and therefore how far his decisions were governed by his
carefully kept records), or what relation they bore to the other
public records in Rome.[27]

There are occasional hints that records even of important
decisions by emperor or governor might be hard to find. At least,
when Pliny as imperial legate of Bithynia needed certain information, he wrote straight to the emperor Trajan as the most direct
way of obtaining accurate records. There were some imperial
letters in Bithynia relevant to the problem he was trying to solve,
but he explains that he will not send them as they are inaccurately
copied and in any case Trajan will have versions in his records
(*scrinia*) which are 'accurate and carefully checked' (*vera et emendata*,
10.65.3). The exchange underlines a curiosity of Roman imperial
administration, that the 'onus of keeping and furnishing the documentary proof of important decisions and privileges lay with the
communities and individuals concerned and not with the Roman
authorities'. Provincial governors had minimal records of their own
and most of those they made returned with them to Rome.[28] Moreover, in a system so reliant on various localized copies of any
relevant decisions (especially imperial letters), it might well be
found, as Pliny feared, that the copies were inaccurate; in which
case, you could only resort to the emperor himself.[29]

[26] Conveniently translated in Millar's chapter in Crawford (ed.) 1983: 105; see also Millar
1977: 261–2, with further references there.
[27] Millar 1977: 259–68.
[28] Burton 1975: 104, and 103–4 for evidence on provinces generally; Sherwin-White (ed.)
1966: 604.
[29] The casual approach to verbal accuracy noted for Greece may persist in the Roman
Empire: e.g. Meritt 'Greek Inscriptions', *Hesperia* 32 (1963): 1–56: no. 27, inexactly copied
'duplicate' texts from third-century Athens. cf. Claudius' pronouncement on interpolation
of public documents in Lycia and Pamphylia: R. K. Sherk (ed.) *The Roman Empire:
Augustus to Hadrian* (Cambridge 1988) no. 48; Bean, *Anz. Österr. Akad. Wiss.* 99 (1962), 4–9,
no. 2; cf. *Anatolian Studies* 10 (1960), 71 no. 124 = *Archaiologike Ephemeris* 1961, 24, for
second-century A D case.

One can define still more closely the specifically Roman ways of using writing, beyond the possible lack of regularity and documentary correctness – and it was evidently these mannerisms which some of their non-Roman subjects took up.[30] Most characteristic, perhaps, are the persistent and ubiquitous use of short written messages for purposes of display and propaganda on coins, walls, inscriptions, and buildings; the love of elaborate abbreviations to a degree unparalleled in Greece and not yet adequately explained; the penchant for longer, detailed inscriptions, funerary or honorary, which further the acquisition of honour, status, and self-advancement; the detailed written records facilitating the organization of the army. Alongside these, one must surely set the characteristically Roman literature of opposition, the *libelli* (or pamphlets), and most striking of all, that Roman peculiarity, the burning of books. This is only reliably attested for the Roman period, though it was such a familiar feature that later, imperial writers, more used to this method of suppressing opposition, even attributed it to fifth-century Athens.[31] Nothing could illustrate better the changed place of the written work of literature – and perhaps the propagandist slant of Latin literature.

New epigraphic finds and increasingly sophisticated archaeological techniques of preservation are helping to produce evidence that should enable us to broaden the picture of writing in the Roman world considerably. It was at one time only in Egypt, a very dry environment, that there was a chance of discovering the kinds of document written on papyrus. But important military archives on papyri have now been found in Dura-Europus in Syria (mostly lists) and in Cyrenaica,[32] not to mention the rather earlier papyri found in tombs in mainland Greece, which can only be read through sophisticated new techniques. Even an archive of waxed

---

[30] See. W. V. Harris 1989: 175–90 for the evidence.

[31] Cramer 1945 for book-burning; Momigliano 1978: 70–1; cf. Tacitus *Annals* 4.35; Suet. *Tiberius* 61.3; Dio Cassius 57.24. See Dover 1975, on the evidence for fifth-century Greece. Burning of archives (but unofficially) is also attested in Dyme in Achaea in *c.* 115 BC (in a Roman context): *Syll.*³: 684 = R. K. Sherk, *Roman documents from the Greek East: senatus consulta and epistulae to the Age of Augustus* (Baltimore 1969) no. 43, lines 18–22; cf. W. V. Harris 1989: 128.

[32] For other military papyri, most can be found in Fink 1971 along with *Chartae Latinae Antiquiores*, ed. A. Bruchner and R. Marichal, vols IX–XI; the Dura-Europus documents were originally published by Welles, Fink, Gilliam 1959. cf. third-century AD *ostraka* produced by soldiers at Bu Ngem, Tripolitania: prelim. report, Marichal, in *CRAI* 1979, 436.

tablets with legible writing exists, admittedly preserved in the exceptional circumstances of Pompeii. A common writing material in northern Europe turns out to have been thin wooden leaves, now found in large quantities at Vindolanda on Hadrian's Wall. These were evidently a locally produced substitute for papyrus, with (happily for us) a better chance of survival in the damp British soil. They preserve documents of a kind no one hoped to find at the far western end of the empire. It is increasingly possible to get away from a view of writing drawn entirely from epigraphic, literary, and Egyptian papyrological texts. What seems to be emerging is how extremely varied the implications of writing are even in the Roman Empire. The Vindolanda tablets, still in the process of being published, consist of large numbers of military records, accounts, lists, and personal letters, written in ink during the late first and early second centuries A D. As the editors stress, they are important not merely for the immediate information of who wrote what, but for palaeography and its wider cultural implications. Analysis of individual handwriting and the immense variety of writing styles should help in reconstructing a picture of schooling and transmission of writing skills, and may underline the role of the army in fostering what seem so far to be surprisingly homogeneous writing habits.[33] This is a good example of the opportunities made possible by new kinds of evidence.

A superficial survey can only begin to indicate some of the new approaches being taken – or which could be taken – to the roles of writing and orality in the Roman world. Now that Harris (1989) has shown – to my mind conclusively – how little in the way of literate skills existed in certain parts of the empire and certain sectors of the population at various periods, the obvious next question to ask is how much significance this might have had, and to examine more closely the precise role played by the written word in such a society. Even where some kind of literacy exists, it still remains to ask what it was used for, by whom, and what the implications of being literate or semi-literate were. The most recent studies of the role of writing in other societies show the rich possibilities available.

---

[33] Vindolanda tablets: Bowman and Thomas 1983, for the first tablets, now considerably augmented by a new deposit dating to A D 85–125 (for which, see for the time being, Bowman and Thomas 1987).

Bibliographical essay

INTRODUCTION

The aim of this section is to suggest works which the reader may refer to for further discussion of topics treated in this book, or for a different perspective from the one offered here. Journals devoted specifically to literacy and orality (none primarily on the ancient world) include *Word and Image*, *Visible Language*, *Scrittura e Civiltà*, and a new one is to start in 1993, edited by M. Clanchy and D. Olson, entitled *Literacy* (Cambridge).

Work on literacy in the ancient world has been concerned mainly with deciding how many people were literate. William Harris' book, *Ancient Literacy* (1989), now provides the most comprehensive treatment of both Greek and Roman literacy: it manages to include a great deal of ancient evidence and an extensive bibliography, though the discussion is better for the Roman world than the Greek, and it can be schematic. The articles by Harvey (*REG* 79 (1966), 585–635) and Woodbury (*TAPA* 106 (1976), 349–57), both on Athenian literacy, and Cartledge on Spartan (*JHS* 98 (1978), 25–37) provide the most sensitive and detailed discussions for the Greeks. Turner, *Athenian Books in the Fifth and Fourth Centuries* (1952) and Kenyon, *Books and Readers in Ancient Greece and Rome* (1951) are also interesting, though they occasionally treat the Greeks as if they were modern classicists. Youtie's various articles on literacy, semi-literacy, and illiteracy (*HSCP* 75 (1971), *GRBS* 12 (1971), *ZPE* 17 (1975)) deal with papyrological material from Graeco-Roman Egypt which by definition provides detail unavailable elsewhere. A whole issue of the *Journal of Roman Archaeology*, published as a book, *Literacy in the Roman World*, by Mary Beard *et al.*, 1991, is now devoted to partial responses to William Harris, *Ancient Literacy*. Appearing as this book was in press, it promises to be important.

For the functions and manifestations of writing in Greece, the collection of articles edited by M. Detienne, *Les Savoirs de l'écriture. En Grèce ancienne* (1988), contains interesting and stimulating studies. It manages on the whole to avoid the more anachronistic approach of older works, or following the lines argued in the 1960s by Goody and Watt and Havelock about the effects of literacy on mentality. Andersen's brief article in *Literacy and*

Society edited by Schousboe and Larsen (1989) is a clear discussion and critique of some of the problems of Greek literacy. My own *Oral Tradition and Written Record in Classical Athens* (1989), especially chapter 1, is the most extensive reinterpretation of the place of writing in Greek culture and its relation to oral communication. Svenbro's *Phrasikleia* (1988) is entertaining and very imaginative, and gives an entirely new look to several aspects of writing in archaic Greece (note that it includes some essays published earlier or simultaneously elsewhere).

The wider debate about the meaning and significance of literacy – in which the Greek case has been examined primarily by non-classicists – can be best pursued through the various studies by Jack Goody. The article by Goody and Watt on 'The consequences of literacy', published most conveniently in Goody (ed.) *Literacy in Traditional Societies* (1968), is a classic. *The Domestication of the Savage Mind* (1977) modifies and improves considerably on the initial theory. *The Logic of Writing and the Organization of Society* (1986) is also important. For a critique of this and the kind of approach to literacy which Goody exemplifies (as does Havelock, *Preface to Plato*) the best discussion is still *Literacy in Theory and Practice* (1984) by Brian Street. This deals, from a sociological viewpoint, with general conceptions about literacy, but also with the arguments drawn from ancient Greece. Pattison, *On Literacy. The Politics of the Word from Homer to the Age of Rock* (1982) may put off the philologically-minded by the initial redefinition of literacy as 'ability to use language', but makes some similar points, is full of insights, and highly readable. For a critique more specifically and narrowly geared to the ancient world, see Andersen's article in *Literacy and Society*, edited by Schousboe and Larsen (1989), G. E. R. Lloyd, *Magic, Reason and Experience* (1979), for the development of Greek science and philosophy, and R. Thomas, *Oral Tradition and Written Record* (1989), chapter 1.

For further possibilities open to any study of writing, I would especially recommend the collection of articles in *Literacy and Society*, edited by Schousboe and Larsen (1989), and *Literacy in Traditional Societies* edited by Goody (1968), for a predominantly anthropological viewpoint. On the more historical side, I have found most stimulating M. Clanchy, *From Memory to Written Record* (1979), M. Carruthers, *The Book of Memory* (1990), a fascinating study of the role of memory and memorization in the Middle Ages, Brian Stock, *The Implications of Literacy* (1983), and P. Saenger, 'Books of Hours and the reading habits of the later Middle Ages', in R. Chartier (ed.), *The Culture of Print* (1989).

ORAL POETRY

The number of books and articles devoted to Homer and the Homeric question is vast. I note only the most essential here: further references can be found in the notes to chapter 3, which are slightly fuller than usual because both debate and bibliography are particularly complex.

For the character of oral poetry itself, the best place to start, apart, of course, from the Homeric poems themselves, is with Lord's *Singer of Tales* (1960), which is the most general introduction to Homeric and Yugoslav poetry as orally-composed epic; Adam Parry's discussion and critique of Milman Parry's original theory, in the Introduction to *The Making of Homeric Verse. The Collected Papers of Milman Parry*, edited by A. Parry (1971); and the classic article also by Adam Parry, 'Have we Homer's Iliad?', *YCS* 20 (1966). These last two studies are still among the best argued and most direct attempts to confront the literary subtlety of Homer and its implications for the theory that the epics are oral poetry. More recent appreciation of Homer has tended to set aside completely the question of orality or has continued along the original Parryesque lines. The argument about formulaic style and oral composition was particularly lively in the 1960s and early 1970s, with a series of closely interlocking and answering articles (often reprinted). *YCS* 20 (1966) was devoted to Homeric studies and has an important article by Kirk – who should be followed up for historical background but whose idea of accurate oral transmission over centuries is now generally disbelieved. Kirk (ed.), *The Language and Background of Homer* (1964), and Kirk, *Homer and the Oral Tradition* (1976) are important collections of articles by Kirk and others. Of the highly technical studies of formulaic technique, Hainsworth, *The Flexibility of the Homeric Formula* (1968) is extremely helpful, as is his article, 'Criteri di oralità nella poesia arcaica non omerica', in C. Brillante *et al.*, *I poemi epici rapsodici* (1981). Shive, *Naming Achilles* (1987) has now attacked Milman Parry's initial analysis of the epithet.

In order to glean some understanding of what such an oral society might have been like, comparative studies are sometimes more illuminating than the often highly technical Homeric discussions. Much can be learnt from the transcriptions of interviews with the Yugoslav singers and their poems – to be found in M. Parry and A. Lord, *Serbocroation Heroic Songs*, especially vols. I (1954) and III (1974). To get beyond the Yugoslav analogy, I recommend David Young's lively article in *Arion* 6 (1967), 279–324, which adduces much comparative material (in fact to attack the Parry–Lord view), Bowra's *Heroic Poetry* (1966), Hatto (ed.), *Traditions of Heroic and Epic Poetry* (1980), and above all, Finnegan's *Oral Poetry* (1977) which has done most to widen our conception both of oral poetry and of oral society. Jensen, *The Homeric Question* (1980) is full of intelligent insights into the nature of oral poetry, though her view that the Homeric poems were not written down until the sixth century has not won much support.

POST-HOMERIC ORALITY

The most sustained work on orality continues to focus on the Homeric question, and for a general understanding of post-Homeric orality, studies are scattered and somewhat fragmented. Gentili, *Poetry and its Public in Ancient Greece* (1988, translated from the original Italian edition of 1985) is a collection of somewhat disparate studies, but provides a background to performance and genre in archaic Greece, and has a lengthy bibliography (see also the bibliography by Fantuzzi (1980)). Andersen's article, 'Mündlichkeit und Schriftlichkeit im frühen Griechentum', *Antike und Abendland* 33 (1987) provides a detailed discussion of the relation of writing and orality in Greece. Herington, *Poetry into Drama. Early Tragedy and the Greek Poetic Tradition* (1985) is a brilliant study of poetry as performance and the antecedents of Greek drama, and has a valuable collection of the fragmentary ancient evidence for the performance of this poetry. For rhetoric, the reader may start with G. A. Kennedy, *The Art of Persuasion in Greece* (1963) and *The Art of Rhetoric in the Roman World* (1972). The role of the symposium is particularly well treated in O. Murray (ed.), *Sympotica. A Symposium on the Symposion* (1990). H. I. Marrou, *A History of Education in Antiquity* (1956 and 6th French edn. 1965) remains the standard work on ancient education.

Herodotus is presented as an oral story-teller by O. Murray, in 'Herodotus and oral history', in *Achaemenid History* II, edited by Sancisi-Weerdenburg and A. Kuhrt (1987), and as a reciter and performer by Evans, *Herodotus. Explorer of the Past* (1991). *Herodotus and the Invention of History*, *Arethusa* vol. 20 (1987), edited by D. Boedeker, has much tentative discussion of Herodotus as part of an oral culture.

For the character and workings of oral tradition in the Greek world, Finley's 'Myth, memory and history' (1965, reprinted most conveniently in *Use and Abuse of History* (1986)) is a classic and provocative article. J. K. Davies, 'The reliability of the oral tradition', in *The Trojan War*, edited by L. Foxhall and J. K. Davies (1981) is one of the most thorough discussions of the traditions concerning the Trojan War. R. Thomas, *Oral Tradition and Written Record* (1989) analyses in depth the mechanisms, changeability and reliability of oral traditions in classical Greece. An alternative view may be found in O. Murray's article cited above (1987). Vansina, *Oral Tradition as History* (1985), adding to and improving upon his earlier *Oral Tradition* (1973), is a fundamental anthropological study; Henige, *Oral Historiography* (1982), very compressed, and J. C. Miller (ed.), *The African Past Speaks* (1980) also provide general interpretations of oral tradition. The new edition of *The Voice of the Past* (1988) by P. Thompson has a fascinating discussion of the workings of memory in recollection; note also M. N. Bourget, L. Valensi and N. Wachtel (eds.), *Between Memory and History*, in *History and Anthropology*, 2 (1986), and R. Samuel and P. Thompson (eds.), *The Myths We Live By* (1990).

General interpretations of the character of orality are offered by W. Ong, *Orality and Literacy* (1982) and Havelock, *Preface to Plato* and *The Literate Revolution in Greece and its Cultural Consequences* (1982, a collection of

articles). R. Finnegan's articles on orality, which attack these approaches, are now more accessible in *Literacy and Orality* (1988).

THE USES OF WRITING: FURTHER BIBLIOGRAPHY

The works cited above (under Introduction) all contribute in some way to a study of the use of writing, even if indirectly. Harris, *Ancient Literacy* (1989) usefully catalogues the functions of writing that are indicated by the evidence. For wider, or less straightforward topics, such as the role of writing in magic, or the use of writing in the service of the city-state, it is mainly a matter of going to the primary evidence, or else sifting through secondary works which are not particularly concerned with the role of documents or writing as such.

The primary material for the use of writing in the form of graffiti and inscriptions, rather than for literary works, is of course vast: it can be found in the various corpora of inscriptions and in isolated publications of new inscriptions in articles scattered around the journals (and listed year by year in *Supplementum Epigraphicum Graecum (SEG)*). For isolated documents I have given the full reference, along with the editor, in the notes, in order to avoid cluttering the bibliography. The monumental *Inscriptiones Graecae (IG)* is primary – the archaic and fifth-century inscriptions of Athens are being re-edited in *IG* I³ by David Lewis. The archaic inscriptions and graffiti are more conveniently served by L. H. Jeffery's *Local Scripts of Archaic Greece* (1961) (*LSAG*): a further Supplement with finds since then and reference to further discussion has now been added by A. Johnston (1990). One of the most helpful features of *LSAG* is its lavish illustrations of the material. Note also the graffiti from the Athenian agora, published by M. Lang in *Athenian Agora*, vol. xxi *Graffiti and Dipinti* (1976).

The main general work on archives is by Posner, *Archives in the Ancient World* (1972). This drew on very much older works (mainly in German) which tended to approach ancient archives anachronistically. Klaffenbach, *Bemerkungen zum griechischen Urkundenwesen* (1960) is an important study, with a great quantity of epigraphic evidence. S. Georgoudi, 'Manières d'archivage et archives de cités', in Detienne (ed.), *Les Savoirs de l'écriture* (1988) is one of the few recent attempts to look at the character of ancient archives at all probingly.

Turner, *Greek Papyri. An Introduction* (1968: the new edition is a reprint with some subtractions), *Greek Manuscripts of the Ancient World* (second edition by P. Parsons, 1987), and L. D. Reynolds and N. G. Wilson, *Scribes and Scholars* (3rd edn. 1991) offer an introduction to the world of papyri and the survival of literary texts.

Bibliography

ALEXANDER, L. (1990) 'The Living Voice: scepticism towards the written word in early Christian and in Graeco-Roman texts', in D. J. A. Clines, S. E. Fowl and S. E. Porter (eds.), *The Bible in Three Dimensions*, Journal for the Study of the Old Testament, Suppl. series 87 (Sheffield), 221–47

ALEXIOU, M. (1974) *The Ritual Lament in Greek Tradition* (Cambridge)

ALY, W. (1921) *Volksmärchen, Sage und Novelle bei Herodot und seinen Zeitgenossen* (Göttingen)

ANDERSEN, O. (1987) 'Mündlichkeit und Schriftlichkeit im frühen Griechentum', *Antike und Abendland* 33: 29–44

(1989) 'The significance of writing in early Greece – a critical appraisal', in K. Schousboe and M. T. Larsen (eds.), *Literacy and Society*, 73–90

ANDREAU, J. (1974) *Les Affaires de Monsieur Iucundus* (Rome)

ATKINSON, K.M.T. (1939) 'Athenian legislative procedure and the revision of laws', *Bull. of J. Rylands Library* 23: 107–50

AUDOLLENT, A. (1904) *Defixionum Tabellae* (Frankfurt am Main)

AUSTIN, M.M. and P. VIDAL-NAQUET (1977) *Economic and Social History of Ancient Greece. An Introduction* (London)

AUSTIN, R.P. (1938) *The Stoichedon Style in Greek Inscriptions* (Oxford)

BADDELEY, A.D. (1976) *The Psychology of Memory* (New York)

(1983) *Your Memory: A User's Guide* (Penguin)

BAIN, D. (1977) *Actors and Audience* (Oxford)

BAINES, J. (1983) 'Literacy and ancient Egyptian society', *Man* 18: 572–97

BARKER, N. (1981) 'Typography and the meaning of words: the revolution in the layout of books in the eighteenth century', in G. Barber and B. Fabian (eds.), *Buch und Buchhandel in Europa in achtzehnten Jahrhundert. Fünftes Wolfenbütteler Symposium 1977* (Hamburg), 127–65

BARTLETT, F.C. (1932) *Remembering* (Cambridge)

BAUMANN, G. (ed.) (1986) *The Written Word. Literacy in Transition* (Oxford)

BEARD, M. (1985) 'Writing and ritual. A study of diversity and expansion in the Arval Acta', *PBSR* 53: 114–62

(1991) *et al. Literacy in the Roman World* (Ann Arbor)

BECK, F.A.G. (1975) *An Album of Greek Education* (Sydney)

BENSON, L.D. (1966) 'The literary character of Anglo-Saxon formulaic poetry', *Publications of Modern Language Association* 81: 148–68

BERNAL, M. (1987a) 'On the transmission of the Alphabet to the Aegean before 1400 BC', *Bulletin of the American Schools of Oriental Research in Jerusalem and Baghdad* 267: 1–19

(1987b) *Black Athena. The Afroasiatic Roots of Classical Civilization*, vol. 1 (London)

BIRT, T. (1907) *Die Buchrolle in der Kunst* (Leipzig)

BLOCH, M. (1989) 'Literacy and enlightenment', in K. Schousboe and M. T. Larsen, *Literacy and Society*, 15–38

BOAK, A.E.R. (1923) 'The Anagraphai of the Grapheion of Tebtynis and Kerkeosouchon Oros. Pap. Michigan 622', *Journal of Egyptian Archaeology* 9: 164–7

BOEDEKER, D. (ed.) (1987) *Herodotus and the Invention of History. Arethusa*, vol. 20 (Buffalo, New York)

BOEGEHOLD, A.L. (1972) 'The establishment of a central archive at Athens', *AJA* 76: 23–30

(1990) 'Andocides and the decree of Patrokleides', *Historia* 39 (1990): 149–62

BOGAERT, R. (1968) *Banques et banquiers dans les cités grecques* (Leiden)

BOHANNAN, L.A. (1952) 'A genealogical charter', *Africa* 22: 301–15

BONNER, R.J. (1905) *Evidence in Athenian Courts* (Chicago)

(1908) 'The use and effect of Attic seals', *CPh*. 3: 399–407

BONNER, R.J. and G. SMITH (1930, 1938) *The Administration of Justice from Homer to Aristotle* 2 vols. (Chicago)

BORING, T.A. (1979) *Literacy in Ancient Sparta* (Leiden)

BOURGET, M.N., L. VALENSI, and N. WACHTEL (eds.) (1986) *Between Memory and History*, in *History and Anthropology*, 2 (London, Paris, New York)

BOWIE, E.L. (1986) 'Early Greek elegy, symposium and public festival', *JHS* 106: 13–35

(1990) 'Miles ludens? The problem of martial exhortation in early Greek lyric', in O. Murray (ed.), *Sympotica. A Symposium on the Symposion* (Oxford), 221–9

BOWMAN, A.K. and J.D. THOMAS (1983) *Vindolanda: the Latin Writing-Tablets* (*Britannia* monograph 4)

(1987) 'New texts from Vindolanda', *Britannia* 18: 125–42

BOWRA, M. (1961) *Greek Lyric Poetry from Alcman to Simonides* (2nd edn) (Oxford)

(1966) *Heroic Poetry* (Oxford)

BRAUN, K. (1970) 'Der Dipylon-Brunnen B1: die Funde', *Ath. Mitt.* 85: 114–269

BRAVO, B. (1974) 'Une lettre sur plomb de Berezan: colonisation et modes de contact dans le Pont', *Dialogues d'histoire ancienne* 1: 111–87

BREMER, J.M., I.J.F. DE JONG and J. KALFF (eds.) (1987) *Homer: Beyond Oral Poetry. Recent Trends in Homeric Interpretation* (Amsterdam)

BREMMER, J. (1982) 'Literacy and the origins and limits of Greek atheism', in *ACTUS*, Studies in honour of H. L. W. Nelson, eds. J. den Boeft and A. H. M. Kessels (Utrecht), 43–55

BRILLANTE, C., M. CANTILENA, and C.O. PAVESE (eds.) (1981) *I poemi epici rapsodici non omerici e la tradizione orale. Atti del convegno di Venezia 1977* (Padova)

BURFORD, A. (1971) 'The purpose of inscribed building accounts', in *Acta of the Vth Internat. Congress of Greek and Latin Epigraphy* (Cambridge 1967) (Oxford), 71–6

BURKE, P. (1987) 'The uses of literacy in early modern Italy', in P. Burke and R. Porter (eds.), *The Social History of Language* (Cambridge), 21–42

BURKERT, W. (1984) *Die Orientalisierende Epoche in der griechischen Religion und Literatur* (Heidelberg)
(1985) *Greek Religion* (Oxford) (German original, 1977)

BURKHALTER, F. (1990) 'Archives locales et archives centrales en Egypte romaine', *Chiron* 20: 191–216

BURNS, A. (1981) 'Athenian literacy in the fifth century BC', *Journal of History of Ideas* 42: 371–87

BURTON, G.P. (1975) 'Proconsuls, assizes and the administration of justice under the empire', *JRS* 65: 92–106

BURZACHECHI, M. (1962) 'Oggetti parlanti nelle epigrafi greche', *Epigraphica* 24: 3–54

CALAME, C. (1977) *Les choeurs de jeunes filles en Grèce archaïque*, 2 vols. (Rome)

CALDERINI, R. (1950) 'Gli ἀγράμματοι nell' Egitto greco-romano', *Aegyptus* 30: 14–41

CALHOUN, G.M. (1914) 'Documentary frauds in litigation in Athens', *CPh* 9: 134–44
(1919) 'Oral and written pleading in Athens', *TAPA* 50: 177–93

CALLIGAS, P. (1971) 'An inscribed lead plaque from Korkyra', *Annual of the British School of Athens* 66: 79–94

CAMASSA, G. (1988) 'Aux origines de la codification écrite des lois en Grèce', in Detienne (ed.) (1988), 130–55

CAMP, J.M. (1986) *The Athenian Agora* (London)

CAMPBELL, J.K. (1964) *Honour, Family, Patronage: A Study of Institutions and Moral Values in a Greek Mountain Community* (Oxford)

CARRUTHERS, M. (1990) *The Book of Memory. A Study of Memory in Medieval Culture* (Cambridge)

CARTLEDGE, P. (1976) 'A New fifth-century Spartan Treaty', *LCM* 1: 87–92
(1978) 'Literacy in the Spartan oligarchy', *JHS* 98: 25–37

(1979) *Sparta and Lakonia: A Regional History, 1300–362* BC (London and Boston)

(1987) *Agesilaos and the Crisis of Sparta* (London and Baltimore)

CASTELL, S. DE, A. LUKE, and K. EGAN (eds.) (1986) *Literacy, Society and Schooling. A Reader* (Cambridge)

CHADWICK, J. (1973) 'The Berezan lead letter', *Proceedings of the Cambridge Philological Society* 199: 35–7

CHARTIER, R. (ed.) (1989) *The Culture of Print* (Princeton) (first published as *Les usages de l'imprimé*, 1987)

CLANCHY, M.T. (1979) *From Memory to Written Record* (London)

(1983) 'Looking back from the invention of printing', in D. P. Resnick (ed.), *Literacy in Historical Perspective* (Washington), 7–22

(1989) 'Reading the signs at Durham Cathedral', in Schousboe and Larsen (eds.), *Literacy and Society*, 171–82

CLINTON, K. (1974) *The Sacred Officials of the Eleusinian Mysteries* (Philadelphia)

(1982) 'The late fifth-century revision of the Athenian law code', *Hesperia Suppl. XIX*: 27–37

COCKLE, W.E.H. (1984) 'State archives in Graeco-Roman Egypt from 30 BC to the reign of Septimius Severus', *Journal of Egyptian Archaeology* 70: 106–22

COLE, M. and S. SCRIBNER (1981) *The Psychology of Literacy* (Cambridge, Mass.)

COLE, S.G. (1980) 'New evidence for the Mysteries of Dionysos', *GRBS* 21: 223–38

COLE, T. (1983) 'Archaic truth', *Quaderni Urbinati* 13: 7–28

(1991) *The Origins of Rhetoric in Ancient Greece* (Baltimore)

COMOTTI, G. (1989) *Music in Greek and Roman Culture*, transl. R. Munson (Baltimore and London) (original Italian edition, 1979)

CORBIER, M. (1987) 'L'écriture dans l'espace public romain', in *L'Urbs. Espace urbain et histoire (Ier siècle av. J.-C. – III siècle ap. J.-C.)* (Rome), 27–60

CORMACK, R. (1985) *Writing in Gold. Byzantine Society and its Icons* (London)

CORNELL, T. (1991) 'The Tyranny of the evidence: a discussion of the possible uses of literacy in Etruria and Latium in the archaic age', in Beard *et al.*, *Literacy in the Roman World* (Ann Arbor), 7–34

CRAMER, F.H. (1945) 'Bookburning and censorship in ancient Rome', *Journal of History of Ideas* 6: 157–96

CRAWFORD, M. (1988) 'The laws of the Romans: knowledge and diffusion', in *Estudios sobre la Tabula Siarensis*, eds. J. González and J. Arce (Madrid), 127–40

CRESSY, D. (1980) *Literacy and the Social Order. Reading and Writing in Tudor and Stuart England* (Cambridge)

(1983) 'The environment for literacy: accomplishment and context in seventeenth-century England and New England', in D. P. Resnick, *Literacy in Historical Perspective* (Washington, D.C.), 23–42

(1986) 'Books as totems in seventeenth-century England and New England', *Journal of Library History* 21: 92–106

CULHAM, P. (1989) 'Archives and the alternatives in Republican Rome', *CPh* 84: 100–15

DALY, L.W. (1967) *Contributions to a History of Alphabetization* (Brussels)

DANIEL, R.W. (1980) 'Liberal education and semi-literacy in Petronius', *ZPE* 40: 153–9

DAVIES, A. MORPURGO (1986) 'Forms of writing in the ancient Mediterranean world', in Baumann (ed.), *The Written Word*, 51–77

DAVIES, J.K. (1978) *Democracy and Classical Greece* (Glasgow)

(1981) 'The reliability of the oral tradition', in *'The Trojan War. Its Historicity and Context'. Papers of the First Greenbank Colloquium*, Liverpool 1981, eds. Lin Foxhall and J. K. Davies (Bristol), 87–110

DAVIES, M. (1988) 'Monody, choral lyric and the tyranny of the handbook', *CQ* 38: 52–64

DAVISON, J.A. (1962) 'Literature and literacy in Ancient Greece', *Phoenix* 16: 141–56 and 219–33

DENNISTON, J.D. (1927) 'Technical terms in Aristophanes', *CQ* 21: 113–21

DETIENNE, M. (1967) *Les Maîtres de vérité dans la Grèce archaïque* (Paris)

(1986) *The Creation of Mythology* (Chicago), transl. of *L'invention de la mythologie* (Paris 1981)

(ed.) (1988) *Les Savoirs de l'écriture. En Grèce ancienne* (Lille)

(1988a) 'L'espace de la publicité: ses opérateurs intellectuels dans la cité', in *Les Savoirs de l'écriture*, 29–81

(1988b) 'L'écriture et ses nouveaux objets intellectuels en Grèce', in *Les Savoirs de l'écriture*, 7–26

DIRLMEIER, F. (1971) *Das Serbokroatische Heldenlied und Homer* (Sitzungsberichte Heidelberg)

DORJAHN, A.P. (1947) 'On Demosthenes' ability to speak extemporaneously', *TAPA* 78: 69–76

DOVER, K.J. (1974) *Greek Popular Morality in the time of Plato and Aristotle* (Oxford)

(1975) 'The freedom of the intellectual in Greek society', *Talanta* 7 (1975): 24–54; repr. in *Collected Papers*. Vol. II *The Greeks and Their Legacy* (Oxford 1988), 135–58

(1978) *Greek Homosexuality* (London)

DOW, S. (1942) 'Corinthiaca', *HSCP* 53: 89–119

DREWS, R. (1973) *The Greek Accounts of Eastern History* (Cambridge, Mass.)

DU BOULAY, J. (1974) *Portrait of a Greek Mountain Village* (Oxford)

EASTERLING, P. (1985) 'Books and readers in the Greek world', *Cam-*

bridge History of Classical Literature, vol. I (Cambridge), ch. I.2 (pp. 16–41)

EDELSTEIN, L. (1966) *Plato's Seventh Letter* (Leiden)

EDER, W. (1986) 'The political significance of the codification of law in archaic societies: an unconventional hypothesis', in K. Raaflaub (ed.) *Social Struggles in Archaic Rome* (Berkeley, Los Angeles), 262–300

EDWARDS, A.T. (1988) 'ΚΛΕΟΣ 'ΑΦΘΙΤΟΝ and oral theory', *CQ* 38: 25–30

EDWARDS, G.P. (1971) *The Language of Hesiod in its Traditional Context* (Oxford)

EVANS, J.A.S. (1991) *Herodotus, Explorer of the Past* (Princeton)

EYRE, C. and J. BAINES (1989) 'Interactions between orality and literacy', in K. Schousboe and M. Larsen (eds.), *Literacy and Orality*, 91–119

FANTUZZI, M. (1980) 'Oralità, scrittura, auralità. Gli studi sulle techniche della communicazione nella Grecia antica (1960–1980)', *Lingua e Stilo* (Milano), 15: 593–612

FARAONE, C.A. (1985) 'Aeschylus' ὕμνος δέσμιος (*Eum.* 306) and Attic judicial curse tablets', *JHS* 105: 150–4

FENIK, B.C. (1978) *Homer: Tradition and Invention* (Leiden)

FERGUSON, W.S. (1898) *The Athenian Secretaries* (Ithaca, N.Y.)

FINE, JOHN V.A. (1951) '*Horoi. Studies in Mortgage, Real Security and Land Tenure in ancient Athens*', *Hesperia* Suppl. IX (Baltimore)

FINGARETTE, A. (1971) 'A new look at the Wall of Nikomachos', *Hesperia* 40: 330–5

FINK, R.O. (1971) *Roman Military Records on Papyrus* (Philological monographs of the APA, no. 26)

FINKELBERG, M. (1986) 'Is ΚΛΕΟΣ 'ΑΦΘΙΤΟΝ a Homeric formula?', *CQ* 36: 1–5

FINKELSTEIN, J.J. (1961) 'Ammisaduqa's Edict and the Babylonian "Law Codes"', *Journal of Cuneiform Studies* 15: 91–104

FINLEY, M.I. (1952) *Studies in Land and Credit in Ancient Athens 500–200 BC. The Horos Inscriptions* (New Brunswick) (repr. 1985)

(1965) 'Myth, Memory and History', *History and Theory* 4: 281–302 (repr. 1986, 11–33)

(1982) 'Le document et l'histoire économique de l'antiquité', *Annales (Economies, Sociétés, Civilisations)* 37: 697–713 (repr. in English in Finley 1985)

(1983a) 'The ancient historian and his sources' in *Tria Corda: Scritti in onore di Arnaldo Momigliano*, ed. E. Gabba (Como), 201–214 (expanded version in Finley 1985)

(1983b) *Politics in the Ancient World* (Cambridge)

(1985) *Ancient History. Evidence and Models* (London)

(1986) *The Use and Abuse of History* (London) (corrected reprint; first publ. 1975)

FINNEGAN, R. (1970a) *Oral Literature in Africa* (Oxford)

(1970b) 'A note on oral tradition and historical evidence', *History and Theory* 9: 195–201

(1975) *Communication and Technology* (Milton Keynes)

(1977) *Oral Poetry. Its Nature, Significance and Social Content* (Cambridge)

(ed.) (1982) *The Penguin Book of Oral Poetry* (Harmondsworth)

(1985) 'Oral composition and oral literature in the Pacific', in B. Gentili and G. Paioni (eds.), *Oralità. Cultura, letteratura, discorso* (conference 1980) (Urbino), 125–60

(1988) *Literacy and Orality* (Oxford)

FLORY, S. (1980) 'Who Read Herodotus' Histories?' *AJP* 101: 12–28

(1987) *The Archaic Smile of Herodotus* (Detroit)

FOLEY, J.M. (1981) 'Tradition-dependent and -independent features in oral literature: a comparative view of the formula', in *Oral Traditional Literature. Festschrift for Albert Bates Lord*, ed. Foley (Columbus, Ohio), 262–81

(1988) *The Theory of Oral Composition. History and Methodology* (Bloomington and Indianapolis)

FORNARA, C.W. (1983) *The Nature of History in Ancient Greece and Rome* (Berkeley)

FRANCISCIS, ALFONSO DE (1972) *Stato e Società in Locri Epizefiri (L'archivio dell' Olympieion Locrese)* (Naples)

FRÄNKEL, H. (1975) *Early Greek Poetry and Philosophy* (Oxford)

FRANKLIN, S. (1985) 'Literacy and documentation in early medieval Russia', *Speculum* 60: 1–38

FREDERIKSEN, M.W. (1965) 'The Republican Municipal Laws: errors and drafts', *JRS* 55: 183–98

FRIEDLÄNDER, P. (1948) *Epigrammata. Greek Inscriptions in Verse from the Beginnings to the Persian Wars* (Berkeley)

FURET, F. and J. OZOUF (1982) *Reading and Writing: Literacy in France from Calvin to Jules Ferry* (Cambridge)

GABBA, E. (1961) 'Cicerone e la falsificazione dei senatoconsulti', *Studi Classici e Orientali* 10: 89–96

GAGARIN, M. (1982) 'The organization of the Gortyn law-code', *GRBS* 23: 129–46

GAUR, A. (1984) *A History of Writing* (London) (1987 edn with corrections)

GELLNER, E. (1983) *Nations and Nationalism* (Oxford)

GENTILI, B. (1988) *Poetry and its Public in Ancient Greece from Homer to the fifth century* (Baltimore): transl. of *Poesia e pubblico nella Grecia antica da Omero al V secolo* (Bari, 1985)

GEORGOUDI, S. (1988) 'Manières d'archivage et archives de cités', in Detienne (ed.) *Les Savoirs de l'écriture*, 221–47

GERHARDSSON, B. (1961) *Memory and Manuscript: Oral Tradition and Written Transmission in Rabbinic Judaism and Early Christianity*, transl. E. J. Sharpe (Lund)

GERNET, L. (1938) 'Sur les actions commerciales en droit athénien', *REG* 51: 1–44 (repr. 1955, 173–200)

(1955) *Droit et société dans la Grèce ancienne* (Paris)

(1968) *Anthropologie de la Grèce antique* (Paris)

GLEDHILL, J., B. BENDER and M.T. LARSEN (eds.) (1988) *State and Society: the Emergence and Development of Social Hierarchy and Political Centralization* (London)

GOLDHILL, S. (1986) *Reading Greek Tragedy* (Cambridge)

(1991) *The Poet's Voice. Essays on Poetics and Greek Literature* (Cambridge)

GOODY, J. (ed.) (1968) *Literacy in Traditional Societies* (Cambridge)

(1977) *The Domestication of the Savage Mind* (Cambridge)

(1985) 'Oral composition and oral transmission: the case of the Vedas', in B. Gentili and G. Paioni (eds.), *Oralità: cultura, letteratura, discorso*: 7–17; repr. in Goody 1987, ch. 4

(1986) *The Logic of Writing and the Organization of Society* (Cambridge)

(1987) *The Interface between the Written and the Oral* (Cambridge)

GOODY, J. and I. WATT (1968) 'The consequences of literacy', in Goody (ed.), *Literacy in Traditional Societies* (Cambridge), 27–68 (first published 1962–3)

GOUGH, K. (1968) 'Implications of literacy in traditional China and India', in J. Goody (ed.) (1968); 69–84

GRAFF, H. (1979) *The Literacy Myth: Literacy and Social Structure in the Nineteenth-Century City* (New York)

(ed.) (1981) *Literacy and Social Development in the West* (Cambridge)

(1986) 'The legacies of literacy: continuities and contradictions in Western society and culture', in S. de Castell, A. Luke, and K. Egan, *Literacy, Society and Schooling. A Reader* (Cambridge), 61–86

(1987) *The Legacies of Literacy* (Bloomington, Indiana)

GRAHAM, W.A. (1987) *Beyond the Written Word. Oral Aspects of Scripture in the History of Religion* (Cambridge)

GREENE, W.C. (1951) 'The spoken and the written word', *HSCP* 60: 23–59

GRIFFIN, J. (1986) 'Homeric words and speakers', *JHS* 106: 36–57

GRIFFITH, M. (1983) 'Personality in Hesiod', *Classical Antiquity* 2: 37–65

GRIFFITHS, A. (1972) 'Alcman's Partheneion: the morning after the night before', *Quaderni Urbinati* 14: 7–30

GUARDUCCI, M. (1967) *Epigrafia Greca* vol. I (Rome)

HAINSWORTH, J.B. (1968) *The Flexibility of the Homeric Formula* (Oxford)

(1970) 'The criticism of an oral Homer', *JHS* 90: 90–8

(1981) 'Criteri di oralità nella poesia arcaica non omerica', in C. Brillante, M. Cantilena, and C. O. Pavese (eds.), *I poemi epici rapsodici*: 3–19

HALBWACHS, M. (1950) *La mémoire collective* (Paris). Transl. (1980), *The Collective Memory* (New York)

HANSEN, M.H. (1978) 'Nomos and psephisma in fourth-century Athens', *GRBS* 19: 315–30

(1986) *Demography and Democracy: The Number of Athenian Citizens in the Fourth Century BC* (Herning, Denmark)

HANSEN, P.A. (1975) *A List of Greek Verse Inscriptions down to 400 BC. An Analytical Survey* (Copenhagen)

(1976) 'Pithecusan humour. The interpretation of "Nestor's cup" reconsidered' *Glotta* 54: 25–43

(1985) *A List of Greek Verse Inscriptions c. 400–300 BC* (Copenhagen)

HARBSMEIER, M. (1988) 'Inventions of writing', in Gledhill *et al.* (eds.), *State and Society*, 253–76.

(1989) 'Writing and the other: travellers' literacy, or towards an archaeology of orality', in Schousboe and Larsen (eds.), *Literacy and Society*, 197–228

HARRIS, R. (1986) *The Origin of Writing* (London)

HARRIS, W.V. (1983) 'Literacy and epigraphy', *ZPE* 53: 87–111

(1989) *Ancient Literacy* (Cambridge, Mass.)

HARRISON, A.R.W. (1955) 'Law-making at Athens at the end of the fifth century BC', *JHS* 75: 26–35

(1968) *Law of Athens I. Family and Property* (Oxford)

(1971) *Law of Athens II. Procedure* (Oxford)

HARTOG, F. (1988) *The Mirror of Herodotus. The representation of the Other in the writing of History* (first published as *Le Miroir d'Hérodote*, 1980) (Berkeley, Los Angeles)

HARVEY, A.E. (1955) 'The classification of Greek Lyric Poetry', *CQ* 5: 157–75

HARVEY, F.D. (1966) 'Literacy in the Athenian democracy', *REG* 79: 585–635

HATTO, A.T. (ed.) (1980) *Traditions of Heroic and Epic Poetry. I. The Traditions* (London)

HAVELOCK, E.A. (1963) *Preface to Plato* (Oxford)

(1982) *The Literate Revolution in Greece and its Cultural Consequences* (Princeton)

(1986) *The Muse Learns to Write: Reflections on Orality and Literacy from Antiquity to the Present* (New Haven and London)

HAVELOCK, E.A. and J.P. HERSHBELL (eds.) (1978) *Communication Arts in the Ancient World* (New York)

HEATH, S.B. (1986) 'The functions and uses of literacy', in S. de Castell *et al.* (eds.) *Literacy, Society and Schooling* (Cambridge), 15–26

HENDRICHSON, G.L. (1929) 'Ancient reading', *CJ* 25: 182–96

HENIGE, D.P. (1974) *The Chronology of Oral Tradition. Quest for a Chimera* (Oxford)

(1980) 'The disease of writing: Ganda and Nyoro Kinglists in a newly

literate world', in J. C. Miller (ed.) *The African Past Speaks* (1980, Folkstone), 240–61
(1982) *Oral Historiography* (London, New York, Lagos)
HENRY, A.S. (1977) *The Prescripts of Athenian Decrees, Mnemos.* Suppl. 49 (Leiden)
(1979) 'Archon-dating in fifth century Attic decrees: the 421 rule', *Chiron* 9: 23–30
HERINGTON, J. (1985) *Poetry into Drama. Early Tragedy and the Greek Poetic Tradition* (Berkley, Los Angeles)
HERRMANN, P. (1981) 'Teos und Abdera im 5. Jahrhundert v. Chr.', *Chiron* 11: 1–30
HERZFELD, M. (1987) *Anthropology through the Looking-Glass* (Cambridge)
HEUBECK, A. (1978) 'Homeric studies today: results and prospects', in B. Fenik (ed.), *Homer, Tradition and Invention* (Leiden), 1–17
(1979) *Schrift*, (Archaeologia Homerica 3.X) (Göttingen)
HEUSS, A. (1934) 'Abschluss und Beurkundung des griechischen und römischen Staatsvertrages', *Klio* 27: 14–53, and 218–57
HOBSBAWM, E. and T. RANGER (eds.) (1983) *The Invention of Tradition* (Cambridge)
HODKINSON, S. (1983) 'Social order and the conflict of values in classical Sparta', *Chiron* 13: 239–81
HOEKSTRA, A. (1957) 'Hésiode et la tradition orale: contribution à l'étude du style formulaire', *Mnemos.* 10: 193–225
(1964) *Homeric Modifications of Formulaic Prototypes* (Amsterdam and London)
HOLBEK, B. (1989) 'What the illiterate think of writing', in Schousboe and Larsen (eds.) *Literacy and Society*, 183–96
HOPKINS, K. (1991) 'Conquest by book', in Beard *et al.*, *Literacy in the Roman World* (Ann Arbor), 133–58
HOUSTON, R.A. (1985) *Scottish Literacy and the Scottish Identity* (Cambridge)
(1988) *Literacy in Early Modern Europe. Culture and Education, 1500–1800* (London)
HUDSON-WILLIAMS, H.LL. (1951) 'Political speeches in Athens', *CQ* 1: 68–73
HUMPHREYS, S.C. (1978) *Anthropology and the Greeks* (London)
(1985) 'Social relations on stage: witnesses in Classical Athens', *History and Anthropology* 1: 313–69
(1988) 'The discourse of law in Archaic and Classical Greece', *Law and History Review* 6: 465–93
HUSSELMAN, E. (1970) 'Procedure of the Record Office of Tebtynis in the first century AD', *Proc. XII Internat. Congr. Pap.* Ann Arbor, Michigan 1968, 223–8
IMMERWAHR, H.R. (1964) 'Book rolls on Attic vases', *Classical, Medieval and Renaissance Studies in Honour of B. L. Ullman*, vol. 1, 17–48
(1990) *Attic Script* (Oxford)

ISSERLIN, B.S.J. (1982) 'The earliest alphabetic writing', *Cambridge Ancient History*, 2nd edn, vol. III, 1: 794–818

JACOBY, F. (1923–58) *Die Fragmente der griechischen Historiker* (Berlin and Leiden) (=*FGH*)

JANKO, R. (1982) *Homer, Hesiod and the Hymns* (Cambridge)
 (1984) 'Forgetfulness in the golden tablets of memory', *CQ* 34: 89–100

JEFFERY, L.H. (1961) *The Local Scripts of Archaic Greece* (Oxford); revised edition with supplement by A. W. Johnston, 1990
 (1967) '᾽Αρχαῖα γράμματα: some ancient Greek views', *Europa: Festschrift ... E. Grumach* (Berlin), 152–66
 (1976) *Archaic Greece. The City States c. 700–500 B C* (London)

JEFFERY, L.H. and A. MORPURGO-DAVIES (1970) 'ΠΟΙΝΙΚΑΣΤΑΣ and ΠΟΙΝΙΚΑΖΕΙΝ: A new archaic inscription from Crete', *Kadmos* 9: 118–54

JENSEN, M.S. (1966) 'Tradition and individuality in Hesiod's *Works and Days*', *CM* 27: 1–27
 (1980) *The Homeric Question* (Copenhagen)

JOHNSTON, A. (1983) 'The extent and use of literacy; the archaeological evidence', in *The Greek Renaissance of the Eighth Century B C: Tradition and Innovation*, ed. R. Hägg (Stockholm), 63–8

JORDAN, D.R. (1980) 'Two inscribed lead tablets from a well in the Athenian Kerameikos', *Ath. Mitt.* 95: 225–39
 (1985) 'A survey of Greek defixiones not included in the special corpora', *GRBS* 26: 151–97

KAHRSTEDT, U. (1938) 'Untersuchungen zu athenischen Behörden', with appendix, 'Das athenische Staatsarchiv', *Klio* 31: 25–32

KENNEDY, G.A. (1959) 'The earliest rhetorical handbooks', *AJP* 80: 169–78
 (1963) *The Art of Persuasion in Greece* (Princeton)
 (1972) *The Art of Rhetoric in the Roman World* (Princeton)
 (1983) *Greek Rhetoric under Christian Emperors* (Princeton)

KENYON, F.G. (1951) *Books and Readers in Ancient Greece and Rome* (Oxford)

KIPARSKY, P. (1976) 'Oral poetry: some linguistic and typological considerations', in B. A. Stolz and R. S. Shannon (eds.), *Oral Literature and the Formula*, 73–106

KIRK, G.S. (1962) *Songs of Homer* (Cambridge)
 (ed.) (1964) *The Language and Background of Homer* (Cambridge)
 (1966) 'Formular language and oral quality', *YCS* 20: 153–74, repr. in *Homer and the Oral Tradition* (1976), ch. 8
 (1972) 'Aetiology, ritual, charter: three equivocal terms in the study of myths', *YCS* 22: 83–102
 (1976) *Homer and the Oral Tradition* (Cambridge)

KLAFFENBACH, G. (1960) *Bemerkungen zum griechischen Urkundenwesen*, (Sitzungsberichte Berlin)

KNOEPFLER, D. (ed.) (1988) *Comptes et Inventaires dans la cité grecque. Actes du colloq. int. d'épigraphie, Neuchâtel 1986* (Neuchâtel and Geneva)

KNOX, B.M.W. (1968) 'Silent reading in Antiquity', *GRBS* 9: 421–35
(1985) 'Books and readers in the Greek world', in *Cambridge Hist. of Classical Literature*, vol. I, ed. P. E. Easterling and B. M. W. Knox (Cambridge), ch. 1.1

KROLL, J.H. (1977) 'An archive of the Athenian cavalry', *Hesperia* 46: 83–140

KULLMANN, W. and M. REICHEL (eds.) (1990) *Der Übergang von der Mündlichkeit zur Literatur bei den Griechen* (Tübingen)

LAMBRINUDAKIS, W. and M. WÖRRLE (1983) 'Ein hellenistisches Reformgesetz über das öffentliche Urkundenwesen von Paros', *Chiron* 13: 283–368

LANG, M.L. (1976) *Athenian Agora* vol. XXI *Graffiti and Dipinti* (Princeton)
(1982) 'Writing and spelling on ostraka', *Hesperia* Suppl. XIX, *Studies ... E. Vanderpool*, 75–87
(1984) *Herodotean Narrative and Discourse* (Cambridge, Mass.)

LANGDON, M.K. (1976) *A Sanctuary of Zeus on Mount Hymettus, Hesperia* Supplement 16

LARSEN, M.T. (1988) 'Introduction: literacy and social complexity', in Gledhill, Bender and Larsen (eds.), *State and Society*, 173–91
(1989) 'What they wrote on clay', in Schousboe and Larsen, *Literacy and Society*, 121–48

LATTE, K. (1920) *Heiliges Recht* (Tübingen)

LEFKOWITZ, M. (1988) 'Who sang Pindar's Odes?', *AJP* 109: 1–11

LEHMANN, L. (1960) *Samothrace* vol. 2, II (New York)

LESKY, A. (1966) 'Mündlichkeit und Schriftlichkeit im homerischen Epos', in *Gesammelte Schriften* (Bern), 63–71 (also in J. Latacz (ed.), *Homer. Tradition und Neuerung* (1979))

LÉVI-STRAUSS, C. (1976) *Tristes Tropiques*, English transl. (Penguin); first published, 1955 (Harmondsworth)

LEWIS, D.M. (1966) 'After the profanation of the Mysteries', *Ancient Society and Institutions: Studies ... V. Ehrenberg* (Oxford), 177–91
(1973) 'The Athenian rationes centesimarum', in M. I. Finley (ed.), *Problèmes de la terre en Grèce ancienne* (Paris), 187–212
(1984) 'Democratic institutions and their diffusion', in *ΠΡΑΚΤΙΚΑ. ΤΟΥ Η' ΔΙΕΘΝΟΥΣ ΣΥΝΕΔΡΙΟΥ ΕΛΛΕΝΙΚΗΣ ΚΑΙ ΛΑΤΙΝΙΚΗΣ ΕΠΙΓΡΑΦΙΚΗΣ* (Fifth International Epigraphical Congress, Athens, October 1982) (Athens), 55–61

LEWIS, I.M. (1968) 'Literacy in a nomadic society: the Somali Case', in Goody (ed.), *Literacy in Traditional Societies*, 265–76
(1986) 'Literacy and cultural identity in the Horn of Africa: the Somali case', in G. Baumann (ed.) *The Written Word* (Oxford), 133–49

LEWIS, N. (1974) *Papyrus in Classical Antiquity* (Oxford)
(1986) *Greeks in Ptolemaic Egypt* (Oxford and New York)

(1989) *Papyrus in Classical Antiquity. A Supplement* (Brussels)

LLOYD, G.E.R. (1979) *Magic, Reason and Experience: Studies in the Origin and Development of Greek Science* (Cambridge)

(1987) *Revolutions of Wisdom* (Berkeley, Los Angeles)

LOHMANN, D. (1970) *Die Kompositionen der Reden in der Ilias* (Berlin)

LONGO, O. (1981) *Tecniche della communicazione nella Grecia antica* (Naples)

LORAUX, N. (1986) *The Invention of Athens. The Funeral Oration in the Classical City* (Cambridge, Mass.); transl. of *L'invention d'Athènes* (Paris, 1981)

LORD, A. (1953) 'Homer's originality: oral dictated texts', *TAPA* 84: 124–34

(1960) *The Singer of Tales* (New York)

(1967) 'Homer as an oral poet', *HSCP* 72: 1–46

(1981) 'Memory, fixity and genre in oral traditional poetries', in J. M. Foley (ed.), *Oral Traditional Literature. Festschrift for Albert Bates Lord* (Columbus, Ohio), 451–61

(1986) 'Perspectives on recent work on the oral traditional formula', *Oral Tradition* 1: 467–503

(1991) *Epic Singers and Oral Tradition* (Ithaca, N.Y.) (=Collected essays)

LURIA, A.R. (1976) *Cognitive Development: its Cultural and Social Foundations* (ed. M. Cole) (Cambridge, Mass.)

MCKENZIE, D.F. (1986) *Bibliography and the Sociology of Texts* (London)

MCKITTERICK, R. (1989) *The Carolingians and the Written Word* (Cambridge)

MACMULLEN, R. (1982) 'The Epigraphic Habit in the Roman Empire', *AJP* 103: 233–46

MACVE, R.H. (1985) 'Some glosses on "Greek and Roman Accounting"', in *CRUX. Essays ... de Ste. Croix* (Exeter and London), 233–64

MAFFI, A. (1988) 'Écriture et pratique dans la Grèce classique', in Detienne (ed.) *Les Savoirs de l'écriture*, 188–210

MARROU, H.I. (1956) *A History of Education in Antiquity* (London) (6th French edn, Paris 1965)

MARTIN, H-J. (and B. Delmas) (1988) *Histoire et pouvoirs de l'écrit* (Paris)

MAJER-LEONHARD, E. (1913) Ἀγράμματοι (Diss. Frankfurt)

MEIGGS, R. (1972) *The Athenian Empire* (Oxford)

MEIGGS, R. and D.M. LEWIS (1969) *Greek Historical Inscriptions to the end of the Fifth Century BC* (Oxford); repr. with Addenda, 1988 (= ML)

MERITT, B.D. (1967) 'Greek Historical Studies', *Univ. of Cincinnati Classical Studies* vol 1 = *Semple Lectures* 1961–5, 118–32

MEYER, E.A. (1990) 'Explaining the epigraphic habit in the Roman Empire: the evidence of epitaphs', *JRS* 80: 74–96

MICKWITZ, G. (1937) 'Economic rationalism in Graeco-Roman agriculture', *English Historical Review* 208: 577–89

MILLAR, F. (1977) *The Emperor in the Roman World* (London)

(1983) 'Epigraphy' in M. Crawford (ed.) *Sources for Ancient History*: ch. 2 (Cambridge)

MILLER, J.C. (ed.) (1980) *The African Past Speaks: Essays on Oral Tradition and History* (Folkstone)

MILLETT, P. (1982) 'The Attic horoi reconsidered in the light of recent discoveries', *Opus* 1: 219–30

MOMIGLIANO, A. (1966a) 'Historiography on written and oral tradition', in *Studies in Historiography*: 211–20 (London) (first publ. 1961)

(1966b) *Studies in Historiography* (London)

(1972) 'Tradition and the Classical historian', *History and Theory* 11: 279–93; repr. *Essays*, 1977

(1977) *Essays in Ancient and Modern Historiography* (Oxford)

(1978) 'The historians of the classical world and their audiences; some suggestions', *Ann. d. scuola norm. di Pisa* 8: 59–75

MONTEVECCHI, O. (1988) *La Papirologia*, rev. edn (Milan)

MOST, G. (1982) 'Greek Lyric Poets', in T. J. Luce (ed.) *Ancient Writers: Greece and Rome* (New York), 75–98

(1990) 'Canon fathers: literacy, mortality, power', *Arion* 3rd series 1: 35–60

MUELLER, M. (1984) *The Iliad* (London)

MULLEN, W. (1982) *Choreia: Pindar and Dance* (Princeton)

MURRAY, O. (1980) *Early Greece* (Brighton)

(1983a) 'The Greek symposium in history', in *Tria Corda, Scritti ... A. Momigliano* (Como), 257–72

(1983b) 'The symposium as social organization', in *The Greek Renaissance of the 8th c. BC: Tradition and Innovation*, ed. R. Hägg (Stockholm), 195–9

(1987) 'Herodotus and oral history', in *Achaemenid History II: the Greek Sources*, ed. H. W. Am. Sancisi-Weerdenburg and A. Kuhrt (Leiden), 93–115

(1988) 'The Ionian Revolt', *Cambridge Ancient History*, vol. IV, 2nd edn (Cambridge), 461–90

(ed.) (1990) *Sympotica. A Symposium on the Symposion* (Oxford)

NAGLER, M.N. (1974) *Spontaneity and Tradition. A Study in the Oral Art of Homer* (Berkeley and Los Angeles)

NAGY, G. (1987) 'Herodotus the Logios', in D. Boedeker (ed.), *Herodotus and the Invention of History*, *Arethusa* vol. 20: 175–84

(1989) 'Early Greek views of poets and poetry', in *Cambridge History of Literary Criticism*, ch. 1

(1990a) *Pindar's Homer. The Lyric Possession of an Epic Poet* (Baltimore and London)

(1990b) *Greek Mythology and Poetics* (Ithaca and London)

NAVEH, J. (1973) 'Some Semitic considerations on the antiquity of the Greek alphabet', *AJA* 77: 1–8

NIEDDU, G.F. (1982) 'Alfabetismo e diffusione sociale della scrittura nella Grecia arcaica e classica; pregiudizi recenti e realtà documentaria', *Scrittura e Civiltà* 6: 233–61

(1984) 'Testo, Scrittura, libro nella Grecia arcaica e classica: note e osservazioni sulla prosa scientifico-filosofica', *Scrittura e Civiltà* 8: 213–62

NORA, P. (1988) *Les lieux de mémoire* (Paris)

NORMAN, A.F. (1960) 'The book-trade in fourth-century Antioch', *JHS* 80: 122–6

NOTOPOULOS, J.A. (1938) 'Mnemosyne in oral literature', *TAPA* 69: 465–93

(1964) 'Studies in early Greek poetry', *HSCP* 68: 1–77

OBER, J. (1989) *Mass and Elite in Democratic Athens. Rhetoric, Ideology, and the Power of the People* (Princeton)

OLSON, D., N. TORRENCE, A. HILDYARD (eds.) (1985) *Literacy, Language and Learning: the Nature and Consequences of Reading and Writing* (Cambridge)

ONG, W. (1982) *Orality and Literacy* (London)

(1986) 'Writing is a technology that restructures thought', in Baumann (ed.) *The Written Word* (Oxford), 23–50

OSBORNE, M.J. (1973) 'The stoichedon style in theory and practice', *ZPE* 10: 249–70

OSBORNE, R. (1985) *Demos: the Discovery of Classical Attika* (Cambridge)

OSTWALD, M. (1969) *Nomos and the Beginnings of the Athenian Democracy* (Oxford)

(1973) 'Was there a concept ἄγραφος νόμος in classical Greece?' in *Exegesis and Argument: Studies in Greek Philosophy Presented to G. Vlastos* ed. E. N. Lee, A. P. D. Mourelatos and R. M. Rorty (*Phronesis* suppl. vol. 1), 70–104

(1986) *From Popular Sovereignty to the Sovereignty of Law. Law, Society and Politics in Fifth-Century Athens* (Berkeley)

PACKARD, D.W. (1974) 'Sound patterns in Homer', *TAPA* 104: 239–60

PAGE, D. (1951) *Alcman: the Partheneion* (Oxford)

(1963) 'Archilochus and the oral tradition', *Entretiens Hardt* 10, *Archiloche* (Vandoeuvres), 117–79

(1981) *Further Greek Epigrams* (Cambridge)

PARASSOGLOU, G.M. (1979) 'Some thoughts on the postures of the ancient Greeks and Romans when writing on a papyrus roll', *Scrittura e Civiltà* 3: 7–31

PARKE, H.W. (1946) 'Citation and recitation: a convention in early Greek historians', *Hermathena* 67: 80–92

PARKER, R. (1983) *Miasma. Pollution and Purification in Early Greek Religion* (Oxford)

PARRY, A. (1956) 'The language of Achilles', *TAPA* 87: 1–7 (repr. in Kirk, ed., *Language and Background of Homer* (1964), and in A. Parry (1990))

PARRY, A. (1966) 'Have we Homer's Iliad?, *YCS* 20: 177–216

PARRY, A. (1990) *The Language of Achilles and Other Papers* (Oxford)

PARRY, J.P. (1989) 'The Brahmanical tradition and the technology of the intellect', in Schousboe and Larsen, *Literacy and Society*, 39–71

PARRY, M. (1971) *The Making of Homeric Verse. The Collected Papers of Milman Parry*, ed. A. Parry (Oxford)

PARRY, M. and A. LORD (1954) *Serbocroatian Heroic Songs*, vol. I *Novi Pazar* (Cambridge, Mass. and Belgrade)

PARRY, M. and A. LORD (1974) *Serbocroatian Heroic Songs*, vol. III *The Wedding of Smailagić Meho*. [By] Avdo Med̄edović. ed. and transl. by A. Lord (Cambridge and Belgrade)

PATTISON, R. (1982) *On Literacy. The Politics of the Word from Homer to the Age of Rock* (Oxford)

PAULOS, J.A. (1989) *Innumeracy* (London)

PEEK, W. (1955) *Griechische Vers-Inschriften*, I. *Grab-Epigramme* (Berlin; repr. Chicago 1988)

PERRY, B.E. (1967) *The Ancient Romances* (California)

PFEIFFER, R. (1968) *History of Classical Scholarship*, vol. I (Oxford)

PFOHL, G. (1967) *Greek Poems on Stones*, vol. I *Epitaphs from the Seventh to Fifth Centuries B C* (Brill)

PHILIPPSON, P. (1944) *Genealogie als mythische Form* (Basel)

PIERCE, R.H. (1968) 'Grapheion, catalogue and library in Roman Egypt', *Symbolae Osloenses* 43: 68–83

PÖHLMANN, E. (1990) 'Zur Überlieferung griechischer Literatur vom 8. bis zum 4. Jh.', in W. Kullmann and M. Reichel (eds.) *Der Übergang von der Mündlichkeit zur Literatur bei den Griechen* (Tübingen); 11–30

POMEROY, S. (1984) *Women in Hellenistic Egypt from Alexander to Cleopatra* (London)

POPE, M. (1985) 'A nonce-word in the *Iliad*', *CQ* 35: 1–8 .

POST, L.A. (1932) 'Ancient memory systems', *CW* 25: 105–9

POSNER, E. (1972) *Archives in the Ancient World* (Cambridge, Mass.)

POWELL, BARRY B. (1988) 'The Dipylon Oinochoe and the spread of literacy in eighth-century Athens', *Kadmos* 27: 65–86

(1989) 'Why was the Greek alphabet invented? The epigraphical evidence', *Classical Antiquity* 8: 321–50

(1991) *Homer and the Origin of the Greek Alphabet* (Cambridge)

PREISENDANZ, K. (1972) 'Fluchtafel (*Defixio*)', *Rivista di Archeologia Cristiana*, 8: 1–24

PRINGSHEIM, F. (1950) *Greek Law of Sale* (Weimar)

(1955) 'The transition from witnesses to written transactions in Athens', in *Gesammelte Abhandlungen*, vol. II, 401–9 (=*Festschrift Simonius* (1955), 287–97)

(1961) *Gesammelte Abhandlungen*, 2 vols. (Heidelberg)

PUCCI, P. (1988) 'Inscriptions archaïques sur les statues des dieux', in Detienne (ed.), *Les Savoirs de l'écriture*, 480–97

RASCH, G. (1910) *De Anthologiae Graecae epigrammatis quae colloquii formam habent* (Diss. Münster)

RASCHKE, M.G. (1974) 'The office of the agoranomos in Ptolemaic and Roman Egypt', in *Akten des XIII Int. Pap.-Kongr. Marburg. 1971*, eds. E. Kiessling and M. A. Rupprecht (Munich), 349–56

RATHBONE, D. (1989) 'The ancient economy and Graeco-Roman Egypt', in *Egitto e Storia antica dall' ellenismo all' età araba*, Atti del colloquio internazionale, Bologna 1987, eds. L. Criscuolo and G. Geraci (Bologna), 159–76

RATHBONE, D. (1991) *Economic Rationalism and Rural Society in 3rd century AD Egypt. The Heroninos Archive and the Appianus Estate* (Cambridge)

RAWSON, E. (1973) 'The interpretation of Cicero's *De Legibus*', *Aufstieg und Niedergang der römischen Welt* 1.4: 334–56

REDFIELD, J.M. (1975) *Nature and Culture in the Iliad: the Tragedy of Hector* (Chicago and London)

RESNICK, D.P. (ed.) (1983) *Literacy in Historical Perspective* (Washington, D.C.)

REYNOLDS, J. (1982) *Aphrodisias and Rome* (London)

REYNOLDS, L.D. and N.G. WILSON (1991) *Scribes and Scholars*, 3rd edn (Oxford)

RHODES, P.J. (1981) *A Commentary on the Aristotelian Athenaion Politeia* (Oxford)

RICHARDS, E.R. (1991) *The Secretary in the Letters of Paul* (Tübingen)

RICHARDSON, N.J. (1987) 'The individuality of Homer's language', in Bremer *et al.* (eds.) *Homer: Beyond Oral Poetry*, 165–84

RICHTER, G. (1961) *The Archaic Gravestones of Attica* (London)

RIEPL, W. (1913) *Das Nachrichtenwesen des Altertums, mit besonderer Rücksicht auf die Römer* (Leipzig, Berlin)

ROBB, K. (1978) 'The poetic sources of the Greek alphabet: rhythm and abecedarium from Phoenician to Greek', in E. A. Havelock and J. P. Hershbell, eds., *Communication Arts in the Ancient World*, 23–36

ROBERT, L. (1938) *Études épigraphiques et philologiques* (Paris)
  (1961) 'Epigraphie', in *L'Histoire et ses méthodes*, ed. Ch. Samaran (Encyclopédie de la Pléiade), 453–97

ROBERTS, C.H. (1979) *Manuscript, Society and Belief in Early Christian Egypt* (Oxford)

ROBERTSON, N. (1990) 'The laws of Athens, 410–399 BC: the evidence for review and publication', *JHS* 110: 43–75

ROSENMEYER, T.G. (1965) 'The formula in early Greek poetry', *Arion* 4: 295–311

RÖSLER, W. (1990) 'Mnemosyne in the symposium' in O. Murray (ed.) *Sympotica. A Symposium on the Symposion* (Oxford), 230–37

ROUX, G. (1979) *L'Amphictionie. Delphes et le temple d'Apollon au IVème siècle* (Paris)

RUSCHENBUSCH, E. (1966) *Solonos Nomoi, Historia Einzelschriften* (Wiesbaden) 9

RUSSELL, D. (1983) *Greek Declamation* (Cambridge)

RUSSO, J. (1966) 'The structural formula in Homeric verse', *YCS* 20: 219–40

(1968) 'Homer against his tradition', *Arion* 7: 275–95

RUZÉ, F. (1988) 'Aux débuts de l'écriture politique: le pouvoir de l'écrit dans la cité', in Detienne (ed.), *Les Savoirs de l'écriture*, 82–94

SAENGER, P. (1982) 'Silent reading: its impact on late Medieval script and society', *Viator* 13: 367–414

(1989) 'Books of Hours and the reading habits of the later Middle Ages', in R. Chartier (ed.), *The Culture of Print* (Princeton), 141–73 (first published as *L'Usage de l'imprimé*, 1987)

STE. CROIX, G.E.M. DE (1956) 'Greek and Roman accounting', in *Studies in the History of Accounting*, ed. A. C. Littleton and B. S. Yamey (London): 14–74

SAMPSON, GEOFFREY (1985) *Writing Systems. A Linguistic Introduction* (London)

SAMUEL, R. and P. THOMPSON (eds.) (1990) *The Myths We Live By* (London)

SANMARTI, E. and R.A. SANTIAGO (1987) 'Une lettre grecque sur plomb trouvée à Emporion', *ZPE* 68: 119–27

(1988) 'Notes additionelles sur la lettre sur plomb d'Emporion', *ZPE* 72: 100–102

SCHMITT-PANTEL, P. (1990) 'Sacrificial meal and symposium: two models of civic institutions in the archaic city', in O. Murray (ed.), *Sympotica* (Oxford), 14–36

SCHOFIELD, R.S. (1968) 'The measurement of literacy in pre-industrial England', in *Literacy in Traditional Societies*, ed. J. Goody (Cambridge), 311–25

SCHOUSBOE, K. and M.T. LARSEN (eds.) (1989) *Literacy and Society* (Copenhagen)

SCHWIND, F. (1973) *Zur Frage der Publikation im römischen Recht*, 2nd edn (Munich)

SCOBIE, A. (1983) *Apuleius and Folklore* (Folklore Society, London)

SCRIBNER, R.W. (1984) 'Oral culture and the diffusion of Reformation ideas', *Hist. of European Ideas* 5: 237–56

SEGAL, C.P. (1962) 'Gorgias and the psychology of the logos', *HSCP* 66: 99–155

SEIDL, E. (1962) *Ptolemäische Rechtsgeschichte*, 2nd edn (Glückstadt)

SHERWIN-WHITE, A.N. (ed.) (1966) *The Letters of Pliny* (Oxford)

SHERWIN-WHITE, S.M. (1985) 'Ancient archives: the Edict of Alexander to Priene, a reappraisal', *JHS* 105: 69–89

SHILS, E. (1981) *Tradition* (London and Boston)

SHIVE, D. (1987) *Naming Achilles* (Oxford and New York)

SIJPESTEIJN, P.J. (1965) 'Die χωρίς κυρίου χρηματίζουσαι δικαίῳ τέκνων in den Papyri', *Aegyptus* 45: 171–89

SILK, M. (1987) *The Iliad* (Cambridge)

SIMONDON, M. (1982) *La Mémoire et l'oubli dans la pensée grecque jusqu'à la fin du Ve siècle avant J.-C.* (Paris)

SKEAT, T.C. (1956) 'The use of dictation in ancient book production', *Proc. Brit. Acad.* 42: 179–208

SMITH, J.D. (1977) 'The singer or the song. A reassessment of Lord's oral theory', *Man* 12: 141–53

SNELL, B. (1953) *The Discovery of the Mind: the Greek Origins of European Thought*, transl. T. G. Rosenmeyer (Oxford; orig. German edn 1948)

STOCK, B. (1983) *The Implications of Literacy. Written Language and Models of Interpretation in the Eleventh and Twelfth Centuries* (Princeton)

STODDART, S. and J. WHITLEY (1988) 'The social context of literacy in Archaic Greece and Etruria', *Antiquity* 62 (1988): 761–72

STOLZ, B.A. and R.S. SHANNON (eds.) (1976) *Oral Literature and the Formula* (Ann Arbor)

STONE, L. (1969) 'Literacy and education in England, 1640–1900', *Past and Present* 42: 69–139

STRAUSS, G. and R. GAWTHROP (1984) 'Protestantism and literacy in early modern Germany', *Past and Present* 104: 31–55

STREET, B. (1984) *Literacy in Theory and Practice* (Cambridge)
  (1987) 'Orality and literacy as ideological constructions: some problems in cross-cultural studies', *Culture and History* 2: 7–30

STROUD, R.S. (1978a) 'State Documents in Archaic Athens', in *'Athens comes of Age. From Solon to Salamis'*, *Papers of Symposium of Archaeological Institute of America* (Princeton), 20–42
  (1978b) *'The Axones and Kyrbeis of Drakon and Solon'*, Univ. of Calif. Publ. in Classical Studies 19

STUPPERICH, R. (1977) *Staatsbegräbnis und Privatgrabmal im klassischen Athen* (Diss. Münster)

SVENBRO, J. (1987) 'The voice of letters. On silent reading and the representation of speech', *Culture and History* 2: 31–47
  (1988a) *Phrasikleia* (Paris)
  (1988b) 'J'écris, donc je m'efface. L'énonciation dans les premières inscriptions grecques', in Detienne (ed.), *Les Savoirs de l'écriture*, 459–79; repr. in *Phrasikleia*: ch. 2
  (1989) 'Phrasikleia – an archaic theory of writing', in Schousboe and Larsen, *Literacy and Society*, 229–45 (=ch. 1 of *Phrasikleia*)

TALBERT, R. (1984) *The Senate of Imperial Rome* (Princeton)

TAMBIAH, S.J. (1973) 'Form and meaning of magical acts: a point of view', in R. Horton and R. Finnegan (eds.), *Modes of Thought* (London), 199–229

TAPLIN, O. (1977) *The Stagecraft of Aeschylus* (Oxford)
(1978) *Greek Tragedy in Action* (London)

TAUBENSCHLAG, R. (1955) *The Law of Greco-Roman Egypt in the Light of the Papyri, 332 BC–AD 640* (2nd edn Warsaw)

TAYLOR, M.W. (1981) *The Tyrant Slayers: the Heroic Image in Fifth Century BC Athenian Art and Politics* (New York)

THOMAS, C. (1977) 'Literacy and the codification of law', *Studia et Documenta Historiae et Juris* 43: 455–8

THOMAS, K. (1986) 'The meaning of literacy in early modern England', in G. Baumann (ed.), *The Written Word* (Oxford), 97–131

THOMAS, R. (1989) *Oral Tradition and Written Record in Classical Athens* (Cambridge)

THOMPSON, P. (1988) *The Voice of the Past. Oral History.* 2nd edn (Oxford)

THOMPSON, W.E. (1981) 'Athenian attitudes towards wills', *Prudentia* 13: 13–23

THREATTE, L. (1980) *The Grammar of Attic Inscriptions, vol. I Phonology* (Berlin and New York)

TOD, M.N. (1946–8) *Greek Historical Inscriptions* 2nd edn (2 vols) (Oxford)

TODD, S. (1990) 'The purpose of evidence in Athenian courts', in P. Cartledge, P. Millett and S. Todd (eds.), *NOMOS. Essays in Athenian Law, Politics and Society* (Cambridge), 19–39

TOWNEND, G.B. (1969) 'Some problems of punctuation in the Latin hexameter', *CQ* 19 (1969): 330–3

TRENKNER, S. (1958) *The Greek Novella in the Classical Period* (Cambridge)

TURNER, E.G. (1952) *Athenian Books in the Fifth and Fourth Centuries* (London); 2nd edn (1977) with addenda
(1968) *Greek Papyri. An Introduction* (Oxford) (repr. with slight changes, 1980)
(1987) *Greek Manuscripts of the Ancient World*, 2nd edn, edited by P. Parsons (orig. edn 1971) (London)

VALLOIS, R. (1914) 'ΑΡΑΙ', *BCH* 38: 250–71

VAN GRONINGEN, B.A. (1953) *In the Grip of the Past: an Essay on an Aspect of Greek Thought* (Leiden)

VANSINA, J. (1973) *Oral Tradition. A Study in Historical Methodology* (Penguin, Harmondsworth). (Originally publ. in French, 1961; 1st English edn 1965)
(1974) 'Comment: traditions of Genesis', *Journal of African History* 15: 317–22
(1980) 'Memory and oral tradition', in *The African Past Speaks*, ed. J. C. Miller: 262–76
(1985) *Oral Tradition as History* (London and Nairobi)

VERMES, G. (1986) 'Scripture and oral tradition in Judaism: written and oral Torah', in Baumann (ed.), *The Written Word*, 79–95

VEYNE, P. (1983) *Les Grecs ont-ils cru à leurs mythes?* (Paris) (English transl. 1988)

WACHTEL, N. (1986) Introduction to *Between Memory and History*, eds. M. N. Bourget, L. Valensi, N. Wachtel, in *History and Anthropology* 2: 207–24

WADE-GERY, H.T. (1952) *The Poet of the Iliad* (Cambridge)

WAGNER, D. (ed.) (1987) *The Future of Literacy in a Changing World* (Oxford)

WEBSTER, T.B.L. (1970) *The Greek Chorus* (London)

WEISS, E. (1923) *Griechisches Privatrecht auf rechtsvergleichender Grundlage* I (Leipzig)

WELLES, C. BRADFORD (1949) 'The Ptolemaic administration of Egypt', *Journal of Juristic Papyrology* 3: 21–47

WELLES, C.B., R.O. FINK, and J.F. GILLIAM (1959) *The Excavations at Dura-Europos, Final Report* (New Haven) V, part I

WEST, M.L. (1974) *Studies in Greek Elegy and Iambus* (Berlin)
  (1981) 'Is the *Works and Days* an oral poem?' in C. Brillante, M. Cantilena, C. O. Pavese (eds.), *I poemi epici rapsodici non omerici e la tradizione orale* (Padova), 53–67
  (1985) *The Hesiodic Catalogue of Women* (Oxford)
  (1988) 'The rise of the Greek epic', *JHS* 108: 151–72
  (1990) 'Archaische Heldendichtung: Singen und Schreiben', in W. Kullmann and M. Reichel, *Der Übergang von der Mündlichkeit zur Literatur bei den Griechen* (Tübingen), 33–50

WEST, S. (1985) 'Herodotus' epigraphical interests', *CQ* 35: 278–305

WEST, W.C. (1989) 'The public archives in fourth-century Athens', *GRBS* 30: 529–43

WHITEHEAD, D. (1977) *The Ideology of the Athenian Metic. PCPS* suppl. (Cambridge)
  (1986) *The Demes of Attica, 508/7–ca. 250 BC* (Princeton)

WILHELM, A. (1909a) *Beiträge zur griechischen Inschriftenkunde* (Vienna)
  (1909b) 'Über die öffentliche Aufzeichung von Urkunden', suppl. to *Beiträge zur griechischen Inschriftenkunde* (Vienna), 229–99

WILLIAMSON, C. (1987) 'Monuments of bronze: Roman legal documents on bronze tablets', *Classical Antiquity*: 160–83

WINGO, E.O. (1972) *Latin Punctuation in the Classical Age* (Hague)

WINKLER, J.J. (1990) *The Constraints of Desire. The Anthropology of Sex and Gender in Ancient Greece* (New York, London)

WINTEROWD, W.R. (1989) *The Culture and Politics of Literacy* (Oxford)

WISEMAN, T.P. (1974) 'Legendary genealogies', *GR* 21: 153–64
  (1989) 'Roman legend and oral tradition'. *JRS* 79: 129–37

WOODBURY, L. (1976) 'Aristophanes' *Frogs* and Athenian literacy: *Ran.* 52–3, 1114,' *TAPA* 106: 349–57

WUENSCH, R. (1897) *Defixionum Tabellae Atticae: IG* III³ Appendix

WYCHERLEY, R.E. (1957) *The Athenian Agora III, Literacy and Epigraphical Testimonia* (Princeton)

YATES, F. (1966) *The Art of Memory* (London)

YOUNG, D. (1967) 'Never blotted a line? Formula and premeditation in Homer and Hesiod', *Arion* 6: 279–324

YOUTIE, H.C. (1971a) ''ΑΓΡΑΜΜΑΤΟΣ: an aspect of Greek society in Egypt', *HSCP* 75: 161–76

(1971b) 'βραδέως γράφων: between literacy and illiteracy', *GRBS* 12: 239–61

(1975) 'ὑπογραφεύς: the social impact of illiteracy in Graeco-Roman Egypt', *ZPE* 17: 201–21

ZIEBARTH, E. (1895) 'Der Fluch im griechischen Recht', *Hermes* 30: 57–70

Index

DATE DUE